# Conflict and Christianity in Northern Ireland

Brian Mawhinney and Ronald Wells

Lion Publishing

**LION PUBLISHING**
**P.O. Box 50, Berkhamsted, Herts**

Text copyright © 1975 Wm B Eerdmans Publishing Co, USA
This illustrated edition © 1975 Lion Publishing

First UK edition 1975

ISBN 0 85648 042 8

**Acknowledgements**
The authors are indebted to all those who have helped in shaping
the ideas expressed in this book. In particular, Brian Mawhinney
would like to thank those Christians in Northern Ireland, and
especially his parents, who taught and demonstrated to him the
relevance of faith in Jesus Christ to every aspect of
life. Ronald Wells expresses thanks to The Institute of United
States Studies at the University of London, where his work
on British emigration began.

Camera Press pictures on pages 37 bottom, 41, 42, 44, 45, 46, 57,
58, 68, 71, 74, 75, 77, 79, 80, 81, 83, 84, 85, 86, 87, 88, 89, 92, 93,
96, 97, 100, 103, 105, 106, 107, 109, 110, 111, 112, 113 left, 114,
118, 119, 121.
London Corrymeela Venture pictures on pages 124, 125.
Mansell Collection pictures on pages 10, 11, 13, 16, 22, 25, 28, 29
middle, 32, 34, 36 bottom, 50, 53, 64.
Mary Evans Picture Library pictures on pages 21, 31.
Popperfotos on pages 23, 113 right.
Radio Times Hulton Picture Library pictures on pages 11, 12, 15,
17, 18, 19, 20, 26, 29 top and bottom, 30, 33, 35, 36 top, 37 top,
38, 39, 49, 54, 55, 78, 117.
The prayer on page 1 is from *Prayers for Today's Church*, edited by
R H L Williams and published by the Church Pastoral Aid Society.

Printed in Great Britain by William Clowes & Sons Ltd.,
London, Colchester and Beccles

# CONTENTS

# ILLUSTRATIONS

# AUTHORS' PREFACE

It makes me cry to see the things
some men do to one another.
It makes me cry to see the things
some men do.   *Rod McKuen*

THIS BOOK IS written out of a deep concern both for the
people of Northern Ireland in their sufferings, and for the
good name of Christianity which seems to be seriously
called in question by the events that have taken place in
that Province.

Many people in Ireland, in Britain and much further
afield are troubled and at a loss to understand what is
happening, and why. It is our conviction that this concern
can be most constructively channelled if it can be understood that a root cause of the problems of Northern Ireland is that there has been too much "religion" and too
little Christianity. While we will need to discuss politics,
economics, and diplomacy, we will nevertheless bring
those points to bear upon a basic question: how can the
people of Northern Ireland extricate themselves from an
historic situation of bitterness and hatred in which religious affiliations have become the emblems of the conflict?

Our aim here is to provide a brief, factual and historical background to and explanation of the current crisis,
since understanding is essential if there is to be any progress or improvement in the situation. We have obviously
had to be highly selective in our use of material; a great
deal has had to be omitted. But we have made every effort
to be both accurate and impartial in what we have written.

Perhaps we should give a word of explanation about
our partnership. Brian Mawhinney is a native of Ulster
now living in London. Ronald Wells is an American historian, born in Massachusetts of emigrant British stock,
now living in Michigan. We are both, by our backgrounds,
involved in the present "troubles." We are concerned
about the future of Ulster, concerned to find an answer to
the basic question. We are both Christians, considering the problems of Ulster from a Christian rather than
a political viewpoint, although realizing the need for political and social change. We are also Protestant Christians,
but we hope and believe that we have not given either a
doctrinaire "Protestant" or "Catholic" viewpoint here.
We do not view Irish history in sectarian terms, and we

hope to provide a critique of the important issues which all Christians can share. The essence of the gospel, after all, is that God's work in the world gave the potential for all men to be reconciled to each other and their Creator.

We have no easy solutions to offer. Like others who have studied Northern Ireland's history, we are struck by the sheer length of time during which the peoples there have been divided. It would surely be naive of us to think that we, at long last, could offer the talisman that would bring peace to a troubled land. This book will succeed in its purpose, however, if readers are helped to deepen their awareness of the particulars of the "troubles"— particulars that are essentially variations on the theme of the human condition for which Christianity has a remedy. It is difficult to tell now what social and political arrangements will obtain in Northern Ireland when its people have reached the end of the road of justice, toleration, and peace. Our hope is that this book might somehow aid the initial steps down that road.

--- Provincial boundaries

Areas included in Northern Ireland

# 1 A HISTORY OF "TROUBLES"

*SOME PEOPLE INSIST* that the beginnings of the "Irish problem" are traceable to 1916. Others would claim that 1690 is a more appropriate date. In fact, the arrival in Ireland of England's Henry II in 1171 first wove together two of the four strands that constitute the background of today's troubles. Henry brought his considerable army to Ireland as a precautionary measure because some of his barons had already settled in parts of that country and had become local rulers. Henry, fearful lest any of them should become too powerful and so threaten the throne, used his mighty visual aid to remind English and Irish alike that he was still the supreme power in the land. Since that day England has been involved in Ireland—as a civilizing or an oppressing force, depending on one's point of view.

Henry's excursion also introduced the religious connection. The Celtic Church at that time, while formally recognizing the authority of Rome, was both weak and independent. "Reform," if it was to take place, needed the backing of a strong secular government. The Pope therefore gave Henry's visit his official blessing in the hope that the king would set up a permanent, albeit foreign, administration. Thus, religion and its relationship to the state became a sensitive issue early in Irish history.

Having exerted rather than established his authority in Ireland, Henry turned his attention to other matters. Consequently, his influence and that of his successors began to wane until, by the middle of the fourteenth century, only about one-third of the country, mainly centered around Dublin, was ruled by the English crown. That is to say, most of Ulster, Munster, and Connaught had reverted to Irish control. The English finally determined to stop the erosion of their power, but their policy lacked both the imagination and the drive necessary to tame the Irish. Put simply, the English problem was this: wherever Irish and English intermingled, the Gaelic influence eventually predominated and the English were absorbed. Their "solution" to the problem was the age-old one of separation, which was formally proclaimed in 1366. In that year a parliament was held in Kilkenny under the direction of the Duke of Clarence, son of King Edward III. The statutes it enacted touched most aspects of the peoples' lives. They make interesting reading, for in them one can visualize

Evidence of Christian faith in Ireland goes back to very early times. A book-cover decoration found in Athlone from about the 8th century AD.

the difficulties the two communities had in living together. They included measures to improve the defenses of English-held territory, to prohibit private warfare, and to regulate trade. At the level of interpersonal relations, however, the restrictions imposed are even more revealing. Intermarriage between the communities and the fostering of each other's children were forbidden. (The number of interfaith marriages in Ireland today among the descendants of these two cultures is still very small.) The statutes also forbade the English, and those Irishmen who wanted to live with and as the English, to use the Irish language, names, laws, or dress. They even banned the Irish practice of bareback horse riding. Finally, they re-enacted existing laws that excluded the Irish from cathedral chapters and religious houses.

The picture that emerges is one of a beleaguered and insecure English community among an alien people—people not so much intent on driving them out as swallowing them up, identity and all. In the light of this, it is worth noting how routinely these statutes were ignored. In fact, the church apparently exerted a greater influence on the people to obey the laws than did the state. The bishops threatened to excommunicate any who broke the laws, whereas the state had to import civil servants from England to administer them, so widely were they flouted even by those whose job it was to enforce them. England's concern over her role in Ireland was obviously justified, but the separatist statutes of Kilkenny proved inadequate to safeguard English interests. One hundred years later, on Henry VII's accession, the area of English dominance in Ireland, "The Pale," had shrunk considerably.

## THE TUDOR PERIOD

The accession of the Tudors to the English throne made little immediate difference in Ireland. Effective power remained in the hands of the earls of Kildare during the

*Right*. Henry II, after landing in Ireland, presenting the Pope's Bull to the Archbishop of Cashel.

*Below*. Confirmation by Prince John of his father Henry II's grant of the City of Dublin to his men of Bristol (1185).

latter part of the fifteenth and early sixteenth centuries. This power was not democratic in nature but stemmed from ownership of large tracts of land and from political astuteness. The latter had caused them to enter into alliances with many neighboring Irish chieftains in an attempt to establish a durable peace. As a result, they were a natural choice to be the king's deputies in Ireland and to govern the country for him.

Periodically, and for various reasons, the earls forfeited the royal favor and were removed from their governing position. During one of these interludes an important political event took place. In 1494, Sir Edward Poynings, the temporary deputy, called a parliament in Drogheda. From it issued a law that was to govern Irish politics for the succeeding three hundred years. Poynings' Law, as it was called, prohibited the meeting of any Irish parliament without the prior consent of the king and council in England. Such consent, they made clear, would not be given unless they were first told why parliament was being called and what bills were to be presented. This law made the Irish legislature essentially subservient to the English, and it was bitterly resented by many people.

Lord Thomas Fitzgerald, 10th Earl of Kildare, renouncing his allegiances to Henry VIII.

Henry VIII pictured triumphing over Pope Clement and receiving the Bible in English from Thomas Cranmer.

Thus, in a new and lasting way politics, along with foreign intervention and religion, became the third strand that bound the two communities together in discord.

The English reconquest of Ireland started to gather momentum during the reign of Henry VIII. His coronation as King of Ireland in 1541 put Anglo-Irish relations on a totally new footing. It formally committed the king to Ireland in a way that had not bound his predecessors. At the very least, he was now obliged to defend and protect his fellow countrymen in that land. How much wealth he could recoup from Ireland also became a matter of royal concern. In Ireland the coronation radically affected the heads of family clans, whose ancestors had always been supreme in their own land. It forced them to seek an accommodation between Henry's authority and their natural desire to remain in local control.

Henry chose the policy of "surrender and regrant" as the instrument by which he tried to implement his authority. Under it, the Irish chieftains surrendered their land to Henry, thereby acknowledging his leadership. He immediately regranted it to them to administer on his behalf, thereby protecting the chiefs' positions in their own communities. In an effort to guard against any undue independence by the Irish, a few restrictions were written into the regrants. The chieftains were not allowed to maintain private armies without the king's permission. In this way their potential ability to make trouble for Henry was greatly reduced. Secondly, they were forced to follow and obey English customs and laws. By these means Henry attempted to persuade them to "think English" and to accept England's claim to rule them.

Yet in the long run Henry's policy was as ineffective in subduing and integrating Ireland as were the statutes of Kilkenny, and for much the same reason. They were both English policies that took no account of Irish tradition. Henry's problem was that the idea of primogeniture—the understanding that when a leader dies he is succeeded by his son—which was at the heart of his policy, was foreign to the Irish. He had hoped, by including it, to ensure that the act of surrender would be honored through each succeeding generation. Irish chieftains, however, were traditionally men who had enforced their supremacy over all other claimants. Their rights to the land they ruled "went with the job" and were certainly not hereditary. When they tried to make them hereditary, it was not long before the rank and file Irish rose up in opposition. They saw in the alliance between king and chieftains a move to deprive them of their land. And in their view, any policy that cost them land, their only source of wealth, was a bad one—one to be resisted.

On the religious front, Henry's policy of "Catholicism without a pope" caused little stir in Ireland. The Irish chiefs felt no particular obligation to a pope, and the Anglo-Irish were prepared to follow the lead of their English brethren. Thus, both were content to support Henry's desire to be royally supreme over the church. In fact, the effect of Henry's edicts on the grass-roots level of Irish

A friar preaching in the open air from a moveable pulpit.

religious life was minimal. The Irish Church was weak because of internal dissension and poor because its ecclesiastical dues were often difficult to collect in a war-torn land. Many of its churches were in ruins or in poor repair, and the religious teaching and ministering to the peoples' needs were undertaken mainly by itinerant friars. These clerics remained unaffected by Henry, since he produced no one to take their place. Even "his" English Bible and later Edward's English prayer book were in a language the Celtic people did not understand. So religious life continued largely unaffected by the major theological issues of the day.

When Elizabeth I came to the throne, she caused the Irish to accept her Protestantism by having it adopted by a parliament that met in Dublin in January 1560. The political consequences of this establishment of a Reformed church were soon apparent. First, the papacy, which had been England's ally in Ireland for the four hundred years since Henry II, became her enemy. Secondly, the new church attracted few supporters, and as a result Elizabeth's authority was decreased. To most of the natives and the Anglo-Irish its organization and form of worship were foreign, and they preferred to continue to practice their own religion under the guidance of Jesuit priests who had come over from the continent. These priests developed strong personal ties with their parishioners and

Elizabeth I, Queen of England
and Ireland.

exercised great influence at the local level. (This ability to
identify with and influence people locally still character-
izes Irish Catholic priests today.) The net result of the
Reformation in Ireland, therefore, was more political than
religious and very enduring. For the first time it caused
the native and Anglo-Irish populations to work together to
such an extent that, outside the Pale, national sentiment
became associated with Catholicism. Today, four hundred
years later, the association is still strong.

Elizabeth launched the third attempt by English mon-
archs to come to grips with governing Ireland. After the
failures of the two Henrys, Elizabeth tried the policy of
plantation. This involved taking land out of Irish ownership and giving it to English and Scottish settlers—those
loyal to the crown—who were "planted" in it. The policy

was first enforced in 1567 when, after the queen's armies had quelled a rebellion by local chiefs in Munster, large tracts of their land were confiscated and assigned to Englishmen. Elizabeth expected to apply her policy even more rigorously in Ulster after The O'Neill, Ulster's premier chieftain, rebelled because of his increasing distaste for English laws, the Reformed Church, and the erosion of Gaelic traditions. Following O'Neill's victory over Sir Henry Bagenal at the battle of the Yellow Ford, Elizabeth sent the Earl of Essex to Ireland with twenty thousand men to reassert her authority. This he failed to do through negotiations, but his successor, Lord Mountjoy, proved successful through a long war of attrition, which ended six days after Elizabeth's death in 1603. Thus, the accession of James I to the English throne marked not only the end of the Tudors but also the end of the reconquest of Ireland.

The Earl of Tyrone, who contacted both the Pope and Spain in his search for allies against England during the 1594–1603 rebellion, is seen here parleying with Robert Devreux, Earl of Essex, the Queen's Lieutenant in Ireland.

### 1603-1800

Although Hugh O'Neill was defeated in 1603, the plantation of Ulster did not start until 1607. It was made possible by what has since become known as "the flight of the earls." The earls of Tyrone and Tyrconnell, two of Ulster's

*lose agunt filij iniquitatis*

Tyrone *desired a parley with the* Lord Lieutenant.

most important earls, decided that their postwar position had become impossible. While they had been allowed to retain their vast estates, they nevertheless felt that their power and independence were gone. In September 1607, they embarked for Europe, perhaps to seek military aid, taking many of their allies with them. Immediately their flight was interpreted as evidence of treason, and their estates—covering the counties of Armagh, Fermanagh, Londonderry, Tyrone, Cavan, and Donegal—were seized by the crown. Into these counties were shipped both English and lowland Scots settlers. The latter brought with them their own brand of Protestantism—Presbyterianism. The counties of Antrim and Down, on Ulster's east coast, were not included in the plantation; they had already been settled by people from the "mainland." Finally, in 1609-10, the city of Derry was "planted" by City of London companies, who changed its name to Londonderry. As a result, city companies enjoyed extensive privileges in that area, including effective influence within the Church of Ireland.

It is not hard to understand why the native Irish resented having their lands, and thus their wealth, confiscated and given to English intruders with a foreign culture and religion. Perhaps it was at this point historically that the whole question of wealth, and subsequently economics, became the fourth strand in the web of issues that together form the basis of the present difficulties.

Sir Thomas Wentworth, James I's deputy in Ireland.

Sir Thomas Wentworth, who was the king's deputy in Ireland from 1632-40, increased the alienation between the counties still further. He harried the Ulster Protestants because of their sympathy for British Puritans, and he provoked the Catholic natives by continually seeking ways to deprive them of their land. However, his main contribution to the growing discord between the Irish and English was in the field of trade. He actively discouraged the Irish wool industry, one of her few thriving industries, for no apparent reason other than to protect its English counterpart. This in turn increased Irish economic dependence on England, a dependence that still lies at the heart of the Irish problem.

During the decade 1640-50, two significant events took place in Ireland, the first of which left a continuing legacy of bitterness. This was the advent of Cromwell. He landed with twelve thousand men in Dublin in August 1649, as Lord Lieutenant of Ireland, to reconquer the country after the insurrection of 1641. In this bloody uprising, which started in Ulster, thousands of colonists were massacred by the natives and the exaggerated horror stories of

*Above.* Owen Roe O'Neill, Irish patriot and general (1590–1649).

*Right.* Workers in the wool industry.

the atrocities provoked stern retaliatory measures from London. Although Cromwell remained for only nine months, the cruelty and brutality of his methods, especially his sacking of Drogheda and Wexford after the garrisons in those towns had refused to accept his terms, have not been forgotten. These events still form part of the anti-British bias within Irish Catholic folk history. The reason is threefold. First, it was primarily they who suffered under Cromwell; Protestants had rallied to his cause. He was further disliked by Irish Catholics because the "liberties" for which he fought excluded the liberty of saying mass—on penalty of death! Finally, he saw himself as the instrument of God's wrath and judgment against them, even while he was putting two thousand of "those barbarous wretches" to the sword in Drogheda.

The second significant event of the 1640s was the

establishment of a permanent Scottish Presbyterian ecclesiastical system in Ireland. For the first time the Protestant faith was formally divided. Thus, by 1660, Ireland had three main religious groups: Anglicans, Catholics, and Protestant Dissenters, each characteristic of an historically different group of people and each viewing the other two groups with suspicion and distrust.

The economic realities of life were made abundantly clear to the Irish during the latter part of the seventeenth century. The English parliament passed self-protective laws that excluded Irish cattle from the English market, restricted Irish trade with the American colonies, and further restricted their wool industry. Because the deprivation of market outlets was so serious, some people claimed that these acts, plus the flow of money to absentee English landlords from their poor Irish tenants, was a deliberate attempt to keep Ireland poor and subservient. Whatever the English motivation, Irish resentment continued to grow.

James II fled to France in December 1688. Four months

Oliver Cromwell, as Lord Lieutenant of Ireland, taking Drogheda by storm.

The Siege of Londonderry.

later, William and Mary were pronounced king and queen. These two events formed the prelude to one of the most famous milestones in Irish history. On his accession, James had made the brother of the Catholic Archbishop of Dublin Earl of Tyrconnell, and had sent him to Ireland as his representative. By this act early in his reign, James had made clear his attitude toward the Irish. He needed their support for political reasons and devised his policy accordingly, despite the desire of a majority of Englishmen to maintain a Protestant ascendancy in Ireland. Within a short time Protestants were removed from the army, and Catholics were appointed judges and given control of restyled municipal corporations. Thousands of Protestants, apprehensive of the new policy, flocked to England to help in moves to dethrone James. Thus, it was not surprising that James, when he had collected an army with which to attempt to regain the throne he had lost during the English revolution, should start his campaign in Ireland. It was equally natural that the country's Protestants should unite to oppose him. Since most of the Protestants were in the north, the main opposition was centered in Ulster—most famously behind the walls of Londonderry and Enniskillen.

English troops arrived in August 1689 to raise the siege of Londonderry, and they, along with the Protestants, held off James's troops until William landed the following June.

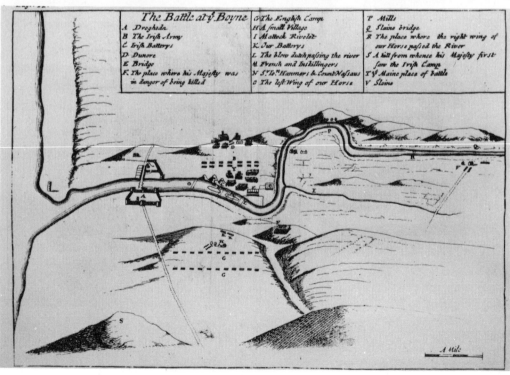

The Battle at ye Boyne

| A Drogheda | G The English Camp | P Mills |
| B The Irish Army | H A small Village | Q Slaine bridge |
| C Irish Batterys | I Mattock Rivelet | R The place where the right wing of |
| D Dunore | K Our Batterys | our Horse passed the River |
| E Bridge | L The blew dutch passing the river | S A hill from whence his Majesty first |
| F The place where his Majesty was | M French and Inskillingers | saw the Irish Camp |
| in danger of being killed | N Sr. Jo. Hanmers & Count Nassaus | T ye Maine place of battle |
| | O The left Wing of our Horse | V Slaine |

William III and the English army ranged against James I at the Battle of the Boyne.

A plan of the battle showing the main deployment of the two armies.

On July 1, 1690, William and James, the latter's army supplemented by an additional seven thousand troops from France, met and fought on the banks of the River Boyne near Drogheda (now celebrated on July 12th each year, due to a calendar change). James's army was beaten, and subsequently it was decisively defeated at Limerick in October 1691. Because of the strength of religious feeling at the time, and because the politics of both William and James were intimately bound up with religious principles, William's victory was quickly credited with having rendered Catholics inferior in Ireland. The Protestant ascendancy was vindicated and assured for many years, and mythology and history combined to form the basis of today's religious intolerance.

This Protestant (Anglican) domination, bolstered by

The Battle of the Boyne is still alive in Ireland today. This portrait of William III at the battle is painted on a wall in a loyalist area of Londonderry.

discriminatory legislation, was not undermined until the nineteenth century. Acts were passed that effectively excluded Catholics from the Irish Parliament and curtailed their right to acquire or lease land. Their inferior position was further underscored by the requirement that they pay tithes to the Church of Ireland. Nor were they the only unhappy citizens, for sacramental tests imposed during Anne's reign debarred Dissenters along with Catholics from public service. Thus the ascendancy, Anglican in character and socially divisive by nature, flourished in discontent and in increasing poverty that was made worse by further trade restrictions around the turn of the century. The very success of these discriminatory laws caused another significant change in Ireland. The numbers and influence of the Catholic gentry were so reduced that their role as political leaders and spokesmen was assumed by the clergy. Ironically, the laws thus tended to establish the powerful influence of the church they were designed to stop.

Jonathan Swift, writing in 1727, gave a graphic description of conditions in Ireland:

> It is manifest that whatever stranger took such a journey (through Ireland) would be apt to think himself travelling in Lapland or Iceland, rather than in a country so favoured by nature as ours, both in fruitfulness of soil and temperature of climate. The miserable dress, and diet, and dwelling of the people; the general desolation in most parts of the kingdom; the old seats of nobility and gentry all in ruins and no new ones in their stead; the families of farmers who pay great rents living in filth and nastiness upon buttermilk and potatoes, without a shoe or stocking to their feet, or a house so convenient as an English hogsty to receive them— these may, indeed, be comfortable sights to an English spectator who comes for a short time to learn the language, and returns back to his own country, whither he finds all our wealth transmitted.

England, by right of conquest, exercised authority in Ireland. Yet by her extortionist policies, her harsh laws against the native Catholics and their religion, and her promotion of a Protestant ruling class, whose major qualification was its compliance with English views, she forfeited any right to be considered equitable, progressive, or humane. The bitterness engendered by the Reformation, the plantations, Cromwell, and the Battle of the

A highly symbolic portrait of William III, with the crowns of England, Scotland and Ireland on his left and the symbols of Rome and error beneath his feet.

Boyne grew during this period of relative calm in Irish affairs to form an indestructible and enduring core of resentment. This resentment was rooted in ethnic, political, religious, and economic bigotry—but a bigotry attributable in large part to those who never were Irish.

Parliament was the natural focus for the discontent of the Protestant ascendancy. It had been trying for some years to establish two claims, its own sole right to legislate for Ireland and the principle that supply bills should not be drawn up in England. These issues had precipitated the public outcry 1723-5 over the authority which the British government gave to William Wood of Wolverhampton to coin halfpence, due to a copper shortage in Ireland. Later, in the 1750s, further public feeling was aroused over the dispute between the Irish Parliament and the British government over who should have the

A scene from the rebellion of 1798. The mob plunders the palace of the Bishop of Ferns.

right to dispose of Irish surplus revenue.

Interestingly the war with the American colonists helped to bring matters to a head. As Beckett wrote in *A Short History of Ireland:*

> Irishmen were naturally interested in a country with whose population they had such close family ties, and they could not help recognizing that the Constitutional question was directly relevant to their own situation. As a Dublin newspaper expressed it: By the same authority which the British parliament assumes to tax America, it may also and with equal justice presume to tax Ireland without the consent or concurrence of the Irish parliament.

The dislocation of trade, rise in prices and unemployment produced by the war caused bitter resentment against England. The subsequent entry of France into the war required the withdrawal of English troops from Ireland and led to the formation of a national volunteer and exclusively Protestant army. As they were not required to fight (for the French did not invade Ireland), the volunteers turned to politics. Their political pressure and determination led first to relaxations in the restrictions governing Irish trade, and eventually to political change. In

1782, the Irish Parliament met and an address to the king, which was virtually a declaration of independence, was moved in the House of Commons by Grattan and carried unanimously. The newly elected Whig government in England yielded and a new constitutional relationship between the two kingdoms was agreed. The parliamentary acts embodying it drastically modified but did not entirely revoke Poynings' Law and the rights granted to the Irish Parliament were great, in theory. However, in practice they solved neither the problem of Roman Catholic involvement in political power nor the unsatisfactory basis of Anglo-Irish relations.

In the last decade of the century trouble started to brew again in Ireland. In 1791, the United Irishmen organization was established in Belfast and Dublin by Wolfe Tone. This group, comprised of Catholics and Presbyterians, supported the twin causes of religious equality and radical political reform. They enjoyed some initial success when restrictions on Catholic education and voting rights were removed in 1793. The economic depression caused by the French Revolution stimulated agrarian unrest in Ireland. This became sectarian in character. Aggressively Protestant Orange Societies sprang up by about 1795 composed almost exclusively of churchmen and by 1797 Ulster was in the grip of civil war between sectarian groups. The United Irishmen grew increasingly extreme in their demands, and in 1798 they joined the French in open rebellion against England. It has been said that their decision to make this alliance with France was prompted by the hope that, if victorious, Ireland would be granted her independence, as the French propagandists had promised. Yet it was this very alliance that doomed the rebellion to ultimate failure. For Ulster Presbyterians, no matter how strongly they disliked the English government, could not finally bring themselves to side with the French in an effort to create an independent Catholic, Celtic Ireland. The rebellion centered mainly in Antrim, Down and Wexford. It was ruthlessly put down and led to severe political consequences. The Irish Parliament was abolished, and an appropriate number of members of parliament were integrated into Westminster by the Act of Union (1800).

The union was reluctantly accepted in Ireland. Protestants could see no other way to maintain their dominant position in light of the events that had so strikingly shown their dependence on English aid. Catholics accepted these closer ties with the old enemy, at least in part, because

English Prime Minister Pitt promised them a Catholic emancipation bill as part of the union package. To Pitt, union seemed the only way to restore order and justice in Ireland. In the former he succeeded; in the latter he failed. His attempt to have Catholic emancipation added to the Union Act was defeated, for it gained little support in England at the time. Another twenty-eight years were to pass before Catholics were allowed to enter parliament, and the disenchantment and political agitation that occurred during this period contributed to the eventual failure of the union.

## 1800-1920

As the population of Ireland climbed to about eight million by 1840, their standard of living, dependent on the land, fell. Along with this increasing poverty there was an upsurge in sectarian violence. Members of the Orange Order

A political cartoon showing general rejoicing as William Pitt celebrates the Union with England (left) and Ireland (right).

Catholic emancipation is fatal to the English constitution. John Bull, seated, is forced to take food offered by Wellington and Peel.

An ATTEMPT to CHOKE JOHN BULL with IRISH-MADE DISHES.

William Pitt the Younger.

The Church of Ireland in danger. Peel and Wellington try to pull it down while the Catholic Church seeks to blow it up.

became more intolerant, especially after passage of the Catholic Emancipation Act of 1829, and Protestant-Catholic animosity was encouraged on both sides by clerical and lay fanatics. One of the first modern religious riots, a forerunner of today's troubles, took place in Belfast in 1835. Two people were shot dead and others injured when soldiers clashed with people celebrating the anniversary of the Battle of the Boyne in Sandy Row—then, as now, a Protestant stronghold. At about the same time, Catholics were wrecking the Protestant area of Smithfield. Serious sectarian riots are also reported to

have occurred in 1843, 1849, 1857, 1864, 1872, 1880, 1884, 1886, and 1898.

Andrew Boyd, in his book *Holy War in Belfast*, describes in detail eyewitness accounts of the 1857 riots, which like many others took place during the "marching" season. The following descriptive statements have been taken from his account to show how discouragingly little progress toward community accommodation has been made in 117 years and that, as the Bible indicates, there is nothing new under the sun. All these statements have appeared repeatedly, and in substantially the same form, in our newspapers over the past five years.

- There were emblems and flags (and) sectarian music.
- The mob from Sandy Row were taunting the Catholics and screaming insults about the Pope. The Catholics were equally abusive.
- The aspect of those localities was that of the camp of two armies, waiting only for a convenient time of actual battle.
- Gunmen had barricaded themselves in a nearby house.
- The firing continued every day from these positions, yet the police were unable to capture the gunmen responsible.
- The terrorizing of innocent individuals continued.
- [They] packed their belongings on a handcart and left Stanley Street never to return.
- The council of war decided that . . . the youngest

and fittest constables would lay aside their heavy equipment and thus be able to pursue the mobs and make arrests. [These sound like the original snatch squads.]

- [They took] ammunition in the form of paving stones which they prised from the streets.
- The soldiers were hampered by army regulations.
- A special "Inquiry into the Conduct of the Constabulary" was set up.

To return to the general chronology: in 1823, Daniel O'Connell organized the Catholic Association, which sought and achieved Catholic emancipation through Peel and Wellington. Nevertheless, resistance to change was strong, and the implementation of the act was very slow. By 1886, for example, only twelve hundred justices of the peace of a total of five thousand were Catholics. The significance of O'Connell, though, is greater than this political achievement. By helping to change the upper-middle-class Catholic movement into a popular one, featuring clergy and peasantry, he finally and indissolubly cemented together the Catholic Church and Irish nationalism. Of equal significance, he helped to drive the Presbyterians, the former allies of the Catholics, into the arms of the Protestants (i.e. Anglicans), and so prepared the way for the emergence of the "bloc" in Ulster comprising English and Scots (i.e. Anglicans and Presbyterians) who were referred to as Protestants.

The years 1845-55 saw a profound change in the face of Ireland. During the first four years, about one million people died of disease and starvation; another two million

Violent reactions to Daniel O'Connell.

*Left.* Catholic jubilation in Dublin over O'Connell's release in 1844.

*Right.* A Protestant mob in the Belfast riots of 1864 carries his effigy through the streets.

Hungry peasants at the gates of a workhouse during the famine.

emigrated, most of them to the United States. These "lucky" ones took with them a hatred for Britain fanned to a fever pitch by the great famine of 1847, in which a quarter of a million Irish people died of starvation. The cause of the famine was the failure of the potato crop—their main food—and while Britain obviously could not be held responsible for the actual famine, many nevertheless felt that the magnitude of its consequences could have been considerably lessened if the British government had made more help available more quickly. One indirect effect of the famine was to further divide Ulster from the rest of Ireland. People to the north were much less dependent on agriculture than their southern countrymen. The linen trade, which did not compete with England, had not been crushed as the wool trade had. Ulster was therefore able to become industrialized and drawn into the English market, providing increased wealth in the community, while the South remained agricultural and stagnant. Thus, the impact of the famine was reduced, and Ulstermen did not share to the same degree the general Irish anger toward Britain.

The advent of William Gladstone as British Prime Minister in 1868, with his famous declaration, "My mission is to pacify Ireland," marks another milestone in Irish history. His conversion to the cause of Irish home rule is one of the more remarkable changes that has taken place in modern political history. Yet the actions he took (in his first ministry) indicate that he thought even then that the basis of the union was insecure. And insecure it has proved to be.

In 1869, Gladstone removed one of the major Irish Catholic grievances when he disestablished the Church of Ireland in the face of strong conservative opinion in Britain. His opponents claimed—and they were correct, as it turned out—that such a move would undermine both British and Protestant control in that country. Yet the move was logically defensible. The 1861 census showed that 78% of the population was Catholic, 12% Anglican, and 9% Presbyterian. And although 70% of the Anglicans were in Ulster, even there they constituted a minority. The other main item of Irish legislation in Gladstone's first ministry was the Land Act of 1870, which gave tenant farmers greater security and more clearly defined rights. These had been actively sought since the formation of tenant associations immediately after the famine. The real significance of this act, however, was that it indicated a willingness on the part of the British government to start assuming some of its social responsibilities in Ireland.

The creation of the Home Rule League in 1870 by Isaac Butt, the son of an Anglican minister, returned the whole question of constitutional reform to the forefront of political discussion. The league acted as a channel for nationalist sentiment, and in 1874, fifty-nine Home Rulers, who resolved to act as an independent group, were returned to Westminster. Gladstone attempted to lower the political temperature by introducing in 1881 a second land act designed to strengthen the tenant rights of the Irish peasantry; but this failed. In 1885, eighty-six home rule members were returned to office, and together they held the balance of British legislative power. In return for their parliamentary support, Gladstone introduced the first of the three home rule bills. In each of these bills the concept of Irish independence was strictly limited by the overall supremacy of the Westminster Parliament. What was envisioned by the concept of home rule was little more than glorified local government. Why then were passions so easily aroused? The answer is that everyone thought his particular vested interest was being threatened.

The reasons for English opposition were economic and nationalistic. Ireland was a prime market for English goods and an important source of food supplies, both of

Opposition to Gladstone's disestablishment of the Church of Ireland, presenting the Church as martyred by barbarians.

which might be threatened by home rule. Even more importantly, conservative England saw in the move a challenge to her territorial integrity. Greeks, Italians, Australians, and Canadians should be, and indeed were, encouraged to manage their own affairs. But no recalcitrant group at home could be allowed to call into question the dominance of England or upset the status quo. So when Lord Randolf Churchill told the people of Larne that "Ulster will fight [against home rule] and Ulster will be right," and when he told the people in Belfast's Ulster Hall that there were many in England who would stand with them regardless of the consequences, he was voicing the opposition of the majority at the time. In Ulster the opposition was political, religious, and economic. The people considered themselves British because of their heritage, and they were unwilling to surrender that privilege. Secondly, they saw in the organization and policy of the

Gladstone tackling the Irish land problem.

TAKING THE (IRISH) BULL BY THE HORNS.

Isaac Butt MP, founder of the Home Rule League in 1870.

home rule movement an identity between Catholicism and nationalism which to them justified the slogan "home rule is Rome rule." Finally, they felt—probably correctly— that any break with Britain would seriously undermine their industries, whose output was directed toward British not Irish markets.

Under the influence of Charles Stewart Parnell, who succeeded Butt and led the Irish M.P.'s at Westminster, the rest of Ireland was initially prepared to accept limited autonomy as a realistic step toward independence. Parnell's achievement of persuading the English Liberals to propose it on the one hand, and of convincing his nationalist colleagues that it was desirable on the other, was considerable. After his death in 1891, however, republican sentiment, fed by the injustices and hatreds of the past, again boiled to the surface, and Ireland was determined to be free.

The first home rule bill was defeated in the House of Commons by a split in the Liberal party's ranks. (The very fact that it was debated at all caused serious disquiet in Ulster and resulted in a great revival of the Orange Order.) The second bill, passed by the Commons but defeated in the Lords, stimulated 12,000 Orangemen from northern constituencies to affirm their total, and if necessary violent, opposition to home rule. By 1912 and the introduction of the third bill, James Craig, later Lord Craigavon, first Prime Minister of Northern Ireland, and Sir Edward Carson, the two leaders of Ulster unionism, were prepared for any eventuality. A provisional Ulster government was established, ready to come into operation on the day that a home rule bill became law. And gunrunning took place to the North and South, which the English seemed powerless to stop. On Ulster Day, Sunday, September 28, 1912, after morning religious services, 471,414 Ulster men and women signed a solemn covenant against home rule. Subsequently, an Ulster Volunteer Force (UVF), made up of covenant subscribers, began to drill and march openly in the North in preparation for the expected battle.

In the rest of Ireland two groups competed for public loyalty. The Irish Nationalist party in Westminster, now under the leadership of John Redmond, was still striving for home rule by constitutional means. The second group, started in 1906 and led by Arthur Griffith, was called Sinn Fein ("ourselves alone"). It owed much to the Irish Republican Brotherhood (founded 1858), which formed the core of the "fenian" movement and, though condemned by the

*Above.* Sir James Craig (Lord Craigavon) speaking to officers during a royal visit to Belfast.

*Below.* The Ulster Volunteer Force in possession of Larne Harbour unloading a cargo of rifles, bayonettes and cartridges from a gun-runner for distribution to Anti-Home-Rule Units (1914).

Roman Catholic Church, had support among Irish colonies especially in United States. It held that the union with England was illegal and that Irish M.P.'s should withdraw from Westminster and set up an Irish parliament in Dublin. While its influence was not immediately felt, it was certainly responsible, at least in part, for organizing the Irish Volunteers, who became the southern counterpart of the UVF. There was much support in England for the unionists, especially in the Conservative party, and even British statesmen made speeches with violent overtones. Bonar Law, for example, publicly supported the Ulster Volunteers; in 1912 he told a rally in England that he could imagine no lengths of resistance to which Ulster might go that he and, in his belief, an overwhelming majority of the British people would not be prepared to support.

The House of Lords delayed final passage of the bill from 1912 to 1914, during which time Prime Minister Asquith and the King considered excluding Ulster from the bill; but Redmond stoutly resisted. Due to the imminence of war, the act, once passed, was immediately suspended with the agreement of Redmond, Craig, and Carson, who all thought that the conflict with Germany was of more immediate concern. Republican elements in Ireland, however, viewed the war as an ideal opportunity to strike for independence while England was otherwise engaged. Thus, on Easter Monday, 1916, with little public support, Patrick Pearse, James Connolly, and Joseph

Arthur Griffith, Sinn Fein leader (1918).

Irish Volunteers march in Dublin during the 1916 uprising. Their leader is Eamon DeValera (marked with an X), later to become President of Ireland.

Plunkett led an uprising in Dublin, and from the captured General Post Office declared Ireland a republic. The rebellion failed, many were hurt in the ensuing skirmishes, and hundreds were arrested. Fifteen of the leaders were tried and executed, though one of them, Eamonn De-Valera, the now-retired Irish President, was merely imprisoned; he had influential American friends who exerted pressure on the British government in his behalf. To the British the uprising was simply an act of treason that had to be dealt with promptly and ruthlessly. To the Irish, not even its romantic absurdity could quench the spark of hope and anticipation that it briefly ignited. James Connolly said, "Never had man or woman a grander cause, never was a cause more grandly served." And despite its magnificent failure, many Irishmen began to agree with him.

In the two years following the Anglo-German war, attitudes in the North and South hardened still further. Those in the North contrasted their military service in the armed forces with the treasonable actions of Sinn Fein and renewed their anti-home rule vows. In the South, Griffith and Michael Collins trained and organized anti-British terrorists, while DeValera went on a propaganda and fund-raising trip to America. The pressure of violence finally led the British government to declare illegal both Sinn Fein and the "Irish government" meeting in the Dail in Dublin. The latter was formed by the seventy-three Sinn Fein candidates who were elected to Westminster in

The Black and Tans in action. A Sinn Feiner is held at revolver point and searched (1920).

Eamon DeValera with Roman Catholic Archbishop Hayes of New York during St Patrick's Day celebrations.

the 1918 election but refused to take their seats there.

The upshot of all this was "the troubles." The Irish Republican Army (IRA), the military wing of Sinn Fein, began a brutal campaign against the police. The force of the law was assisted by the Black and Tans, a special force of British ex-servicemen who owed their name to the black belts and khaki uniforms they wore. This savage guerilla war, which raged from 1920-22, was characterized by atrocities and reprisals on both sides. In Ulster alone, nearly three hundred people were killed, many of them in Belfast. At the same time, there was considerable pressure on both sides to find an acceptable end to the conflict. Foreign opinion, especially American opinion, was strongly against the British, who to them appeared to be coercing a people seeking self-determination. But the IRA also had its problems. Even after its policy was formally adopted by DeValera on behalf of the Dail in

1921, it still suffered from all the characteristic difficulties of insurgents: lack of money, ammunition, and manpower. Thus, the situation was a stalemate. Britain could win the war militarily, but to do so would mean abandoning political influence. The IRA could not win militarily but had the support of the people.

The compromise solution came in two parts. In 1920, the Government of Ireland Act provided for two Irish parliaments: the one in Belfast was to govern Antrim, Down, Tyrone, Fermanagh, Armagh, and Londonderry; the parliament in Dublin was to govern the rest of the country. The authority of the northern parliament, which was opened by George V, was initially rejected by Ulster's Catholic population. To suspicious unionist minds this indicated collusion with the terrorists of the South, and the new province got off to a bad start from which it has never recovered. In the South, all the elected Sinn Fein members boycotted the Dublin parliament, and eventually "independence" negotiations started between Lloyd George of England and Arthur Griffith and Michael Collins of Ireland. The resulting "treaty," signed on December 6, 1921,

One of the most momentous gatherings in Irish history: The Dail Eireann in session to consider a reply to the independence proposals from Lloyd George, with DeValera presiding.

gave Ireland independent dominion status within the British Commonwealth. In fact, it was similar to the 1914 Home Rule Act. The treaty included three provisions, however, which the Irish found distasteful and on which DeValera based his opposition to it. These were: an oath of allegiance to the British crown as befitted Commonwealth subjects, the freedom of Northern Ireland to withdraw from the newly created state and remain within the United Kingdom, and the retention by Britain of certain Irish naval bases. The treaty was finally approved by the Dail, and a provisional government under Michael Collins was set up in January 1922. Perhaps it is a commentary on the strength of nationalist feeling on both sides of the Irish Sea that within a year of the treaty signing, Lloyd George was out of office, Griffith had died, and Collins had been murdered.

**SINCE 1921**

The division of Ireland became the main bone of contention in both North and South once the two governments took office. Although the election in June 1922 produced in Dublin a pro-treaty majority, the country was deeply divided on the treaty, and a form of civil war broke out soon afterwards. The new government took over the anti-IRA role that had been relinquished by the British, while political opposition to the settlement was led by DeValera. However, the IRA commanded decreasing support among the people, and DeValera finally announced the end of resistance in 1923. Intermittent violence continued, but it became even more isolated when DeValera and his followers took the oath of allegiance and assumed their place in the Dail in 1927. By this time Collins had been succeeded by W.T. Cosgrave, whose administration laid the foundation of Ireland's political philosophy, one that remains substantially unaltered to this day. Politically, she has sought to emphasize her sovereign independence, including her desire to see a united Ireland. Successive governments have tried to support an attractive and diversified industrial policy so that the country might attain both greater wealth and a greater degree of economic independence from Britain. Culturally, Ireland has stressed her "Irishness."

DeValera, who was prime minister from 1932 to 1948, continued these general policies but did not feel bound by the provisions of the treaty he had opposed. Early in his administration he abolished the oath of allegiance and from 1936-38 produced a new constitution that made the

OBLACHT NA H EIREANN.

THE PROVISIONAL GOVERNMENT
OF THE
IRISH REPUBLIC
TO THE PEOPLE OF IRELAND.

MEN AND IRISHWOMEN: In the name of God and of the dead generations
ich she receives her old tradition of nationhood, Ireland, through us, summons
ren to her flag and strikes for her freedom.

Ing organised and trained has manhood through her secret revolutionary
tion, the Irish Republican Brotherhood, and through her open military
tions, the Irish Volunteers and the Irish Citizen Army, having patiently
her discipline, having resolutely waited for the right moment to reveal
now seizes that moment, and, supported by her exiled children in America
sillant allies in Europe, but relying in the first on her own strength, she
a full confidence of victory.

declare the right of the people of Ireland to the ownership of Ireland, and to
tered control of Irish destinies, to be sovereign and indefeasible. The long
on of that right by a foreign people and government has not extinguished the
can it ever be extinguished except by the destruction of the Irish people. In
neration the Irish people have asserted their right to national freedom and
nty; six times during the past three hundred years they have asserted it in
ending on that fundamental right and again asserting it in arms in the face
orld, we hereby proclaim the Irish Republic as a Sovereign Independent State,
dge our lives and the lives of our comrades-in-arms to the cause of its freedom,
fare, and of its exaltation among the nations.

Irish Republic is entitled to, and hereby claims, the allegiance of every
y and Irishwoman. The Republic guarantees religious and civil liberty, equal
and equal opportunities to all its citizens, and declares its resolve to pursue
piness and prosperity of the whole nation and of all its parts, cherishing all
ren of the nation equally, and oblivious of the differences carefully fostered
ion government, which have divided a minority from the majority in the past.
il our arms have brought the opportune moment for the establishment of a
nt National Government, representative of the whole people of Ireland and
y the suffrages of all her men and women, the Provisional Government, hereby
ed, will administer the civil and military affairs of the Republic in trust for
ple.

place the cause of the Irish Republic under the protection of the Most High God,
essing we invoke upon our arms, and we pray that no one who serves that
all dishonour it by cowardice, inhumanity, or rapine. In this supreme hour
nation must, by its valour and discipline and by the readiness of its children
ice themselves for the common good, prove itself worthy of the august destiny
h it is called.

Signed on behalf of the Provisional Government.
THOMAS J. CLARKE.
SEAN MAC DIARMADA.    THOMAS MacDONAGH.
P. H. PEARSE.    EAMONN CEANNT.
JAMES CONNOLLY.    JOSEPH PLUNKETT.

A call for unity and common
purpose, issued by the
Provisional Government of the
Republic of Ireland soon after
its appointment in 1922.

country a republic in everything but name. In fact, the degree of separation from Britain was underscored by the neutral stance that his government took during the Second World War. J.A. Costello, who followed him in 1948, completed the separation by proclaiming Ireland a republic on Easter Monday, 1949. In that same year Westminster passed the Ireland Act, which established two constitutional points of great importance. The first was that the constitutional position of Northern Ireland could not be changed without the consent of the Northern Ireland Parliament at Stormont. (Today this is usually expressed in the phrase "without the consent of the majority.") The second was that the imperial government could not intervene in Ulster's internal affairs unless a breakdown in law and order occurred. This was the basis of the Downing Street Declaration of August 1969, which dispatched British troops to quell the Belfast riots.

In Ulster, Craigavon quickly accepted partition as the salvation of Northern Ireland, and unionists pointed to the civil war in the South to illustrate their completely different attitudes toward Britain. Belfast's policy was to increase its British links and to maintain the Protestant ascendancy by whatever means necessary. Craigavon, who governed until 1940, said in 1934: "I have always said I am an Orangeman first and a politician and a member of this parliament afterwards . . . all I boast is that we are a Protestant parliament and a Protestant State." And Craigavon's successor, Sir Basil Brooke (later Lord Brookeborough), who was prime minister until 1963, urged: "There are a great number of Protestants and Orangemen who employ Roman Catholics. . . . I would appeal to loyalists, whenever possible, to employ good Protestant lads and lassies." Eight months later, referring to this statement, he said: "Thinking out the whole question carefully . . . I recommend those people who are loyalists not to employ Roman Catholics, ninety-nine per cent of whom are disloyal. . . ."

Terence O'Neill, though from a background similar to that of his predecessor, at least tried to establish a working relationship with the South. To this end he met with Sean Lemass, the Irish Prime Minister, in both Belfast and Dublin during 1965. These meetings took place at a time of reduced tension both between North and South—after the abortive IRA terror campaign of the fifties had ended —and between the two communities in Northern Ireland. Nevertheless, they immediately provoked protest. Right-wing unionists interpreted them as the beginning of a rap-

The Rev. Ian Paisley addresses a meeting in the streets of Belfast. On his sash is pinned the badge of the Ulster Constitution Defence Committee.

prochement that would eventually undermine their monopoly of power. Catholics, though always pleased to have increased good will, really wanted substantial reforms and saw in the talks a chance to achieve them.

Early opposition to the more liberal attitudes introduced by O'Neill was spearheaded by an evangelical minister, Rev. Ian R.K. Paisley. He construed the government's policies in religious terms as a move toward an accommodation with Roman Catholicism, and in political terms as a betrayal of the province's historical heritage; thus he acted as a vociferous spokesman for many Protestants. His threat to lead his followers into the Catholic Divis Street area of Belfast to remove a tricolor (the Irish flag, whose display is illegal in Northern Ireland) flying above the republicans' headquarters during the election campaign of 1964 forced the Home Affairs minister at Stormont to order the police to do the job instead. The republicans and their sympathizers reacted violently, and the ensuing riots had a significance far beyond the immediate threat to life and property. First, because they took place during an election campaign, they were given immense press and television coverage all over the world. People were thus forcibly reminded of the undercurrents of bitterness that are an integral part of Ulster society. Secondly, the violence redivided that society into two antagonistic camps with a rigidity that had been missing since the early days of the province. Thirdly, the riots

signaled the beginning of the end of uninterrupted Unionist dominance. After this, people started to make their
own voices heard through spokesmen for new political
and special interest groups. It was almost as if they were
claiming that all the major political parties were an irrel-
evance at the grass-roots level.

Two of these new groupings were the Ulster Volunteer
Force (UVF) and the Civil Rights Association (CRA). The
former was an extreme right-wing Protestant group,
which declared war on the IRA in the summer of 1966.
After four Catholics were shot by its members on Malvern
Street in 1968, O'Neill placed the UVF alongside the IRA
on the outlawed list. This, of course, further outraged
loyalist Protestant opinion. The Civil Rights Association
was organized in February 1967, with a five-fold objective. It sought:

(i)   to define the basic rights of all citizens;
(ii)  to protect the rights of the individual;
(iii) to highlight all possible abuses of power;
(iv)  to demand guarantees for freedom of speech, as-
      sembly and association;
(v)   to inform the public of their lawful rights.

Initially such lofty intentions drew support from both
Protestants and Catholics. But by 1968 these principles
had been translated into a much more practical form. The
civil rights movement was by then pursuing, more mili-
tantly: universal franchise at the local level; the redrawing of local election boundaries; legislation to outlaw discrimination in local government; a points system for the
allocation of council houses; and the repeal of the Special
Powers Act. The particular stigma of the latter was that
it included the right of the government to intern people
without trial.

To most Protestants these pursuits proved that the CRA
had abandoned its democratic ideals and had descended
to religio-political warfare. They felt that this program
was in effect challenging the very existence of the state
by trying to change the well-tried formulas of government.
Before long, the CRA had become largely Catholic, and its
associations with People's Democracy, a radical student
group based at Queens University that kept up a pressure
of demonstrations and demands on Stormont, further
alienated conservative unionists. The inevitable clashes
began between these conservative unionists, radical
Catholics, republicans, and the police. The two worst
took place in Derry in October 1968, when police clashed

*Above.* A rally of the People's Democracy in Northern Ireland is heckled by militant Protestants carrying Union Jacks.

Two militant groups stage a show of strength, in their para-military uniforms (officially illegal in Ireland).

*Left top.* IRA "Blackshirts" at the funeral of hunger-striker Michael Gaughan, in Dublin.

*Left bottom.* The Ulster Defence Association march through Belfast.

with CRA marchers, and at Burntollet in January 1969, when all four parties were involved. In fact, the violent behavior of the police in Derry was thought by some to be the incident that started the deterioration in law and order that finally led to the downfall of O'Neill's government. Also, at about that time Paisley was sent to jail for his part in an assault on news media personnel in Armagh during the previous November.

In April, Bernadette Devlin, a twenty-two-year-old radical student and leader of the CRA, won a parliamentary bye-election and, by making a pungent maiden speech on behalf of "the minority" only minutes after being sworn in at Westminster, acquired world-wide exposure for Catholic demands. One week later, O'Neill, having lost Unionist support, resigned and was succeeded by his distant cousin Chichester-Clark. The latter continued the policies of reform and on May 6th ordered all prosecutions against civil rights leaders and militant Protestants dropped in an attempt to improve community feeling.

The Orange celebrations on the 12th of July, 1969 were marked by passionate outbursts in both speech and action. At Castlereagh, Paisley told assembled Orangemen that they were engaged in "the great battle of Biblical

Bernadette Devlin MP being interviewed after her attack on Mr Maudling in the House of Commons.

A street in the Catholic Bogside area of Londonderry during the riots.

Protestantism against popery." The Prime Minister, at Moneymore, depicted some Irish republicans as murderers. Rioting occurred in the streets of Belfast, Lurgan, Derry, and Dungiven. By early August, Paisleyites, Catholics, and police were clashing with greater violence and an increasing disregard for life and property. Finally, the Apprentice Boys march and actions in Derry on August 12th so provoked that city's Catholics that they attacked the marchers and later the police. Two days of bloody warfare followed before the police were able to "retake" the Bogside area in which the Catholics had barricaded themselves. People everywhere in the province were terror-stricken, intimidated, and vulnerable to attack, and Northern Ireland was on the verge of civil war.

It can be said that civil war started in Belfast on the 14th. That night extremists of both sides and B-specials, an auxiliary—largely Protestant—police force, went on a spree of shooting and arson that claimed eight lives. The spectacle of Bombay Street, between the Protestant Shankill and Catholic Falls Roads, burning from end to end, signaled the total inability of Stormont to enforce law and order or to protect the citizenry. Consequently, the British government had to step in, and Prime Minister Wilson sent six thousand officers and men into West Belfast to restore order. Thus, Britain, after a physical absence of less than fifty years, was again directly involved in the affairs of Ireland.

# 2 THE BURDEN OF NORTHERN IRELAND AND ITS MEANING FOR AMERICA

*THE TRAGIC EVENTS* unfolding in Northern Ireland, reported so relentlessly by the news media in recent years, have become a burden on the consciences of thoughtful people everywhere. This is especially true in North America, where there are millions of persons of British and Irish descent. Accurate information is often difficult to obtain, and most people realize that it is not as simple as the partisan sloganeers would have it: the conflict is far more complex than "law and order versus criminal anarchy" or "liberation and justice versus the degradation of a subject people." To Christians the burden is all the greater because the principals in the conflict continue to echo the slogans of the Reformation—slogans that shame all of us when shouted over barricades amid the sounds of rifle fire, or when whispered by small groups of men and women alongside a lonely Irish road while waiting to commit the next act of sectarian violence against an approaching victim. The burden imposed by the events in Northern Ireland requires the understanding and sympathy of those of us who are vitally interested and involved because of ethnic heritage and/or religious conviction. If for no other reasons, we are all involved in Northern Ireland because we are human beings and because humanity is being violated as long as the violent and brutal struggle continues. The bells of both Protestant and Catholic churches toll nearly every day in Ulster for the ever-mounting number of victims of "the troubles." We should "ask not for whom the bell tolls," for we are all involved in Northern Ireland.

## I

There is in the United States a powerful lobby urging American participation in any solution of the Northern Ireland problems. People in Britain tend to regard this as unwarrantable outside interference. But this is less than just, in view of the historical factors underlying it. The United States and Canada are at the center of a North Atlantic community that was internationalized by the folk-migrations of the nineteenth century. Surely one of the most important themes of modern history is the migration of some 55 million people from Europe, approximately 37.5 million of whom came to the United States and Canada (33 million and 4.5 million respectively). Migrants to the New

World brought with them the talents and expectations that have helped to create the strength and vitality of North American culture; but, as part of their cultural baggage, they also brought with them the mentalities and ideologies of the nations and peoples from which they came. Although most migrants were assimilated, in varying degrees, in their adopted lands, it was understandable that they wished to maintain contacts with their homelands through various channels of kinship and friendship. The United States, and to a lesser extent Canada, assumed some of the problems of the Old World—political, religious, and ethnic—when it received "the huddled masses yearning to breathe free." The animosities of Europe were thus partially transferred to new shores, and continuing difficulties in Europe and elsewhere have been followed with great interest because of the contacts North Americans have maintained with those still "at home." In many cases this interest has taken the form of a fraternal association that sought to maintain cultural or linguistic links with the traditional heritage. Less frequently, but with potential explosiveness, this interest has become so intense as to demand recognition in American foreign policy.

The United States, precisely because it opened its doors to the restless and expectant peoples of the world, created within itself a forum in which its citizens sought not only to settle their own problems but also to settle, or at least become involved in, the problems of the rest of the world.

Historically, one of the most important connections between the United States and Europe has been the link with Ireland, since the Irish have been one of the most numerous and important immigrant groups. Because of agricultural disasters, overpopulation, an exploitative land-tenure system, and religious strife, the Irish went to the United States in millions. Due to a phenomenal natural increase, as well as continual accessions from the old country, Irish-Americans now comprise one of the largest numerical minority groups in the United States.

Irish immigration came in two waves. The first, mostly during the eighteenth and early nineteenth centuries, was overwhelmingly Protestant. They are known as Scots-Irish, but the inserted reference to a Scottish background has less to do with nationality than religion: "Scots-Irish" should be understood as Protestant Irish. Many of them were from Dissenter (Presbyterian) backgrounds; their ancestors had emigrated from Scotland to Ireland in the

Irish emigrants leaving home with the priest's blessing (1851).

previous century to escape religious oppression. The descendants, finding themselves under similar disabilities because of the ascendancy of the Church of Ireland (Anglican), continued the quest for a place to practice their religion freely by migrating to the United States. These Protestant Irish seldom remained in the eastern cities of America; they typically moved to farm areas along the then-western edge of the frontier. They usually had some capital or brought farm implements with them, and they were able to establish communities in what is today western Pennsylvania, West Virginia, western Maryland and Virginia, eastern Tennessee and Kentucky, and western North Carolina. They played an important part in the American Revolution, not only because they occupied the sensitive frontier settlements, but also because they hoped that the Revolution would result in the disestablishment of the Church of England in several colonies.

If the Protestant Irish migration was a wave, the Roman Catholic Irish migration was a tidal wave, and it reached truly gigantic proportions during the middle third of the nineteenth century. Because their Protestant countrymen were called "Scots-Irish" in America, the Roman Catholics were known simply as "the Irish"—a linkage that

Mealtime between decks on an Irish emigrant ship (1872).

acquired tragic dimensions, prefiguring a later development in Irish consciousness in which to be Catholic was to be Irish, but to be Protestant was to be British. The Protestants, mostly in the north of Ireland, chose to migrate to America because they wanted to live in an environment that afforded greater economic and religious freedom. The Catholics had no such luxury of choice. They did not choose America as such: migration was not an option freely exercised—it was the last resort in the efforts of a people to survive. Mostly from the south of Ireland, and especially from the still underdeveloped southwest, the Catholics had been driven to the wall, partly because of overpopulation, but mostly because of an exploitative land policy carried out in the name of absentee English landlords. Their impoverished diet had been reduced to a literal dependence on the potato. The blight on the potato crop during the 1840s and 1850s caused a famine, which left only two choices open to many Catholics—migration or starvation. For those who were still able to eke out a living at home, the political climate was also blighted by

the demise of the democratic movement led by the powerful but nonviolent Daniel O'Connell, and by his death
in 1847.

The transit to, and initial reception in, North America
was a continuation of the tragic history of the Irish emigrants. Possessing very little money, they typically booked
their passage on the ships charging the lowest fares, so
they had to content themselves with appalling conditions
aboard ship. Emigrant ships usually took both saloon (first-
class) passengers and steerage (ordinary) passengers.
The conditions in the steerage of emigrant ships varied
enormously. Many of the Irish who came during the flood
tide of migration endured the worst of these conditions.
The crowding and the lack of privacy or washing facilities
on some ships were rivaled only in the infamous "middle
passage" which slaves had endured when they were
being transported from Africa. As to food, the slaves may
well have fared better in some instances, if for no more
noble reason than the economic advantage of bringing
healthy slaves to New Orleans or Charleston. The ship
owners who brought the Irish to Boston, New York, or
Quebec had no such incentive: the passage had been paid
in advance. Deaths aboard ship were common, and if a
contagious disease broke out, the death toll often rose to
one-half the approximately 400 passengers, as was reported in several instances.

Those who survived the journey and arrived in good
health faced immediate problems of finding a means of
livelihood. Some were fortunate enough to have relatives
in North America, who may well have paid the passage for
the emigrant. But in most cases, even if a relative was
there to receive them, there was often little extra room or
food for the new arrivals. Many Irishmen could not afford
the passage all the way to the United States, even if that is
where they wanted to go. Thousands used all their money
to book passages as far as St. John's, Newfoundland,
Halifax, Nova Scotia, or St. John, New Brunswick. In some
cases they remained in their new homes, but many of
them eventually continued their journey to the United
States. The most popular Canadian destination for the
poor emigrants was Quebec, simply because it was the
furthest point in North America to which their money
could take them. Few remained in Quebec or Montreal,
despite Catholic predominance there; this was perhaps
due both to linguistic difficulties and an aversion to settle
in any domain still under British rule.

Unlike the Protestant Irish of the earlier migration,

the Catholics brought little money with them, which is understandable enough given the circumstances of their migration; but this simple fact had a great deal to do with their pattern of settlement and their adjustment to and acculturation in the United States. Despite Horace Greeley's injunction to go west, few young Irishmen did. Although land on the frontier was either cheap or free, one needed a certain amount of money to finance both the trip west and the beginnings of a settlement. Another deterrent to going west was the fluidity of the ecclesiastical situation on the frontier. The harsh truth is that the perception of Christianity by the Catholic Irish was severely circumscribed by their clergy, who, perhaps with good intentions, herded their followers together into parishes in the eastern cities. Preying upon the simplicity and ignorance of the common people, the priests often created the "state of siege" mentality within which the Irish were content to live in their miserable ghetto communities. The young, intent on trying their luck on the frontier, were dissuaded from doing so by the priest, who portrayed the horrors of being cut off from the church, which alone was the guardian of the means of grace. Many people did go west, of course, and they were soon followed, or preceded, by a dedicated and courageous clergy; but most Irish migrants stayed in or near the city in which they first landed. Their descendants often remained also, thus accounting for the large Irish proportion of the population in such cities as Boston, Providence, New York, Philadelphia, and Baltimore.

Because conditions in Ireland were so desperate, the highest priority for the newly arrived immigrant was usually saving enough money to pay for the passage of the next member or members of the family. The conditions at home required the dismembering of families and may well have contributed to the development of clannishness in Irish families in America; once together again, they would abide no more separations. A young man might have been selected to go first; he would hope to find a well-paying job while he kept his personal expenses low by taking his meals and a room with a cousin who had gone to Boston the year before. In the course of time the family could hope for prepaid tickets to America. Young girls often went alone to work as servants, but few of them entertained hopes of earning enough money to bring anyone else. Their main reason for going may have been that once gone they would no longer be a drain on the already overburdened resources of the family. In the middle nineteenth century the common assumption was that nearly every Catholic family in Ireland had a member in America. Whether or not that was statistically accurate, it suggests the fundamental wrenching of the Irish family because of emigration. To be Irish was to know the pain of being separated from loved ones, not always by choice, but often of necessity. The heartbreak of enforced estrangement was part of Irish life, both in Ireland and America; this was doubly poignant for a people predisposed to melancholy and sentiment. The Irish-American folk song "The Leaving of Liverpool" suggests the feeling. It begins with hope and self-confidence:

> Fare thee well, my own true love,
> When I return, united we will be,
> It's not the leaving of Liverpool that grieves me,
> But my darling when I think of thee.

But the last verse recognizes that in all probability this is not farewell but good-bye:

> The sun is on the harbour, love,
> And I wish I could remain,
> But I know it will be a long, long time
> Before I see you again.

The economic conditions that the Irish found in America were scarcely more promising than those they had left in Ireland. Economically viewed, the Irish were a "surplus labor pool" that enabled industry in New England to go through the initial stages of economic growth. For industry to grow at this stage, profits had to be plowed back

The emigrants take their problems with them. The effects of a musketry fusillade on Orange rioters in New York (1871).

into capital expansion. Profits, of course, can be attained by several means, including charging high prices for the products manufactured or paying low wages to the workers in the industry. In the initial stages of growth, New England industrialists, especially in textiles, were reluctant to raise prices unduly because this would have eroded their competitive advantage in the domestic American market in relation to English goods. However, the other option for maximizing profits could be employed because of the overabundance of unskilled Irish labor in eastern New England. In the days before the successful organization of labor unions, the surplus labor pool was tapped very cunningly by the manufacturers, and the profits rolled in.

The industrial exploitation of the Irish paralleled the plantation exploitation of the slaves. Both in providing a commodity for foreign exchange and in providing a raw material for domestic manufacturing, the "cotton kingdom," built on slavery, was the vital first step in the great economic growth of the United States. The second step in economic growth came in the Northeast. The unskilled workers, a majority of whom were Irish, were caught in an economic system that stopped short of slavery but left the Irish workers nonetheless in a vicious circle of poverty and dependence. Indeed, despite the "monstrous injustice" of the institution of slavery, the slave may have

Poor whites who settled in American cities often had to accept slum conditions little better than those they had left behind.

been better off in terms of daily subsistence. He seldom wanted for food and shelter, and his relatively good treatment was a necessity for his master, if for no other reason than to protect his investment (the value of prime field-hands rose threefold between 1830 and 1860). The personal welfare of the industrial worker was not the responsibility of his employer, and if one fell by the wayside, there was another to take his place.

The social climate that greeted the Irish in the United States was nearly as harsh as the economic conditions they encountered. Despite the fact that the Irish were welcomed as cheap labor by the employers, other segments of the "native" population, especially in New England, were opposed to Irish immigration. The economic threat of surplus labor gave tangible shape to the wild stories and fears that excited the Protestant population. Ethno-religious descrimination was so blatant in New England that job advertisements would frequently say, "No Irish Need Apply"; such discrimination was practiced openly until well into the twentieth century. The presence of large numbers of Catholics in America was a threat to the belief held by many Americans, particularly

City conditions forced many into petty crime to survive. Mulberry Street, called "Bandit's Roost" pictured with a very early flashlight camera (1887).

in New England, that the United States was a Protestant country. This country, the belief assumed, was "the world's last best hope," and one needed to pledge one hundred percent allegiance to it in order to be a full citizen. This immediately excluded all "Romanists" because of their subservience to the pope of Rome, who was the head of a foreign state. Protestant critics were fond of quoting Jesus' words, "You cannot serve two masters." The anti-Catholic sentiment found its most pointed political expression in the "Know-Nothing" party in the northeastern states during the time of heaviest Irish migration. This sentiment drove the Irish into the willing arms of the Democrats, who later would build their majority in many states on the basis of immigrant support. Until very recently, in most of New England the almost irrevocable rule of politics allied the Protestants and Republicans against the Catholics and Democrats. As late as 1928, the Democratic nominee for President, Alfred E. Smith, was opposed by Herbert C. Hoover, who ran victoriously, at least in part, on a sentiment that would unite Protestant America in opposition to a "Catholic in the White House."

In the decades following the Civil War, and especially in the twentieth century, the descendants of Irish immigrants grew in political strength and sophistication. Long before "Black Power" was suggested by militant blacks, "Irish Power" was being practiced successfully in many cities by leaders such as John "Honey-Fitz" Fitzgerald, the grandfather of John Fitzgerald Kennedy. As Irish political strength grew, politicians became more sensitive to Irishmen's needs. Not only did the Irish demand domestic redress of grievance, they also demanded that the United States do something either to help Ireland gain its independence from Britain, or to persuade Britain to act more beneficently toward Ireland—especially toward its Catholic population. In several foreign policy questions the United States appeared to reflect the anti-British Fenian attitude of Irish nationalists who had become expatriates in the United States. During the Civil War, when a group of Fenians invaded Canada in a vain attempt to link once again the slaves with the Irish in a common desire for emancipation, the general attitude of "twisting the British lion's tail" almost caused open hostilities.

Given the large number of Americans of Irish descent and their political acumen, as well as their belief that Ireland's tragic history has been largely a story of British-Protestant exploitation, it is understandable that Irish-Americans have remained concerned and involved

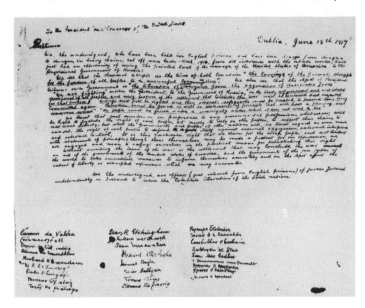

A letter written to the American Government by a group of "officers (just released from English prisons) of forces formed independently in Ireland to secure the complete liberation of the Irish nation". The letter applauds the principles of freedom propounded by the Americans and asks that the American Government keep vigilant in the cause of Irish freedom.

in the problems of Ireland. First it was independence, and more recently it has been the unification of the dismembered state. Those who migrated lost none of the dimension of feeling for the exploitation of the Irish. Because of their unhappy history in Ireland under British rule and their scarcely less unhappy history in America, Irish-Americans tend to link Protestantism with exploitation, both in Ireland and the United States. Now that Irish-Americans as a group have overcome through political power their economic and social disabilities in America, and in view of the independence of the Republic of Ireland, their most poignant concern is for the Catholic minority in Northern Ireland, who allegedly remain second-class citizens. The Irish-Americans who speak out against British policy in Ulster do not view themselves as foreign nationals interfering in the domestic affairs of a friendly state, but as participants in the final phase of the struggle of Celtic, Roman Catholic peoples to free themselves, at long last, from the domination of Anglo-Saxon, Protestant peoples.

## II

President John F. Kennedy was a personal link between the Irish of the new and old worlds. He has been viewed by Catholics in Ireland, both in the Republic and in Ulster, as "one of us who made it" in the Protestant-dominated, Anglo-Saxon, North Atlantic culture. Kennedy's constituency included more than Massachusetts or even the

The Kennedy family pictured in 1934. John is seated in the centre of the group and Edward on Joseph Kennedy's knee.

United States; it extended across the Atlantic to the "Emerald Isle" because of innumerable personal ties that Irish people have created and maintained over the centuries. Whereas Northern Ireland Protestants might have a picture of Queen Elizabeth and the Duke of Edinburgh in their homes, Catholics usually have pictures of either John Kennedy or the Kennedy brothers. Edward M. Kennedy is heir to the tradition that began with his brothers. He has inherited the Irish-American constituency and with it the responsibility of being one of its principal spokesmen. For that constituency the main issue remains the same: justice for Irish Catholics, especially in Northern Ireland, and justice can only obtain when Ireland is reunited.

Senator Edward Kennedy has made the most comprehensive statement by a leading American politician on the problem of Northern Ireland ("Ulster is an International Issue," *Foreign Policy*, Summer, 1973; reprinted in abridged form in *The London Times*, 31 May, 1973, as "Why Unity is the only Path to Peace in Ireland"). His ideas deserve careful attention because they may well represent the thinking of a majority of Irish-Americans. It is the view of the present writers that, while some of Senator Kennedy's ideas are both helpful and deserving of public acceptance in the United States, many others are neither helpful nor deserving of public acceptance with a view toward making them American public policy toward Ireland and Britain. If this review of the Senator's ideas is largely unfavorable, it is not because the authors have a particular axe to grind in favor of one side or the other in the current problems of Northern Ireland, nor between Republicans and Democrats in the United States; rather, it is because we respect the Senator enough to express publicly our doubts about his suggestions for a solution in Northern Ireland, and to question the wisdom of his insistence on American participation in the solution, however wise or just that solution may be.

No one can deny the substantial accuracy of Senator Kennedy's assertion that the Catholics of Northern Ireland have been historic victims of political, social, and economic discrimination. One must also concede the substantial accuracy of his allegation that a principal root of the recent troubles was the historic reluctance of British leaders at Westminster and Protestant leaders in the Northern Ireland Parliament at Stormont to act decisively in behalf of the legitimate demands of the Catholic minority; however, encouraging momentum in this direction from Westminster can now be seen.

Having correctly suggested that social injustice toward Catholics exists in Northern Ireland, Senator Kennedy goes on to suggest that social justice will not really obtain unless and until the six counties in Northern Ireland are reunited with the twenty-six counties in the Republic. Whether or not he is correct in this, there are many problems along the way to be considered before such a hope can be realized. The principal problem is that the constitutional position of Northern Ireland as a part of the United Kingdom is clearly established and that no constitutional changes can occur without the consent of the people of Northern Ireland. Since the Protestant majority wants to maintain the status quo, the advocates of change must necessarily discuss the constitutional issue in a larger context. What is at stake is the historic principle of self-determination—a cardinal tenet of Western democratic faith. But the concept of "the self-determination of all peoples," in defense of which the United States has gone to war several times, is a concept that is more difficult to apply in certain circumstances than at first it might appear.

In March 1973, a plebiscite was held on the constitutional issue, in which the voters of Northern Ireland were asked to respond to two questions: Should Northern Ireland remain a part of the United Kingdom? should Northern Ireland become a part of the Republic of Ireland? Given the electoral majority of the Protestants, it was predictable that the vote would result—as it did—in an overwhelming endorsement of the status quo. This is the nub of the constitutional issue: since partition in 1920 was a regional adjustment to the divisions in Ireland, and the people of Ulster were promised that their constitutional position would not be changed without their consent, it is extremely difficult to know how one can demand a change in the rules at so late a date. Kennedy comes to the attack frontally and questions the entire notion of how one understands the "self-determination of all peoples." To Kennedy, Northern Ireland is not "a state," and Ulstermen are not "a people" as such; to grant them self-determination "is a travesty of a noble principle." The Irish people, Kennedy apparently believes, are one people (which can be shown to be erroneous), and any political divisions between them must be regarded as temporary and illegitimate. Kennedy's words become venomous when discussing Ulster: Northern Ireland is neither a state nor a province but an "uncouth entity that Britain spawned in 1920"; Britain sought to perpetuate it by abusing the noble concept of self-determination because it knew that "the calculated and cynical gerrymander that produced Ulster 50 years ago" would always return Protestant (and British) majorities. Kennedy asks an important question: "If there is to be self-determination for Ulster, why not self-determination for Londonderry, or County Tyrone or any other predominantly Catholic area in Ulster?" The matter of how one can and should configure "a state" or "a people" so that they can determine their own future is a subject that deserves serious consideration.

The fact is that a state or a people is usually configured on the basis of what is likely to benefit the outcome which the determining nation desires. This was seen in Indo-

China: those who wanted "Vietnam for the Vietnamese" opposed American policy because they believed that the people of Vietnam were one, notwithstanding the temporary division of the nation in 1954; those who supported American policy suggested that the South Vietnamese were "a people" whose right to self-determination was being interfered with by the aggression of an "outside power," representing another "people." In short, no real debate on the constitutional aspects of self-determination ever really took place in the context of Indo-China because critics or supporters of various wartime administrations chose their positions more with an eye to political realities than constitutional scruples. Whether or not one would apply Kennedy's term for Ulster ("uncouth entity") to South Vietnam tells a great deal about one's thoughts regarding the events there during the past decade. The basic constitutional question is: must the larger entity always prevail over the smaller entity? This complements a basic sociological question: when and how does a group of persons become different enough to desire a future for their own community separated from the larger community?

North Americans need go no further than their own history to understand the difficulty of the problem. Canadians know well the uneasiness with which they viewed the United States, especially during the nineteenth century, when the jingoists were shouting manifest destiny slogans. The American expansionists believed that it was the destiny of the United States to bring the entire North American continent under its domain. What would have occurred if a North American plebiscite had been held? Is there any doubt that the North American "people" would have opted for continental unity? In the actual event, the "people" of Canada rejected American overtures for annexation; it was a case of the smaller prevailing over the larger. In another Canadian instance—the French-speaking population of Quebec—the reverse has been true, and the larger has prevailed over the smaller. Surely, if ever a case for separate identity existed, it is the case of the Quebecois, who were forced by conquest to unite with English-speaking British North America. In both of these Canadian cases one may argue that more justice has resulted because of the way events turned out; but one can easily imagine another set of definitions for "nation" and "people" that would result in different conclusions in both cases.

In the United States, the most traumatic episode in its

history—the Civil War—focused the questions of "nation" and "people"; but once again the questions were not settled constitutionally but militarily. Because the South lost the war, the constitutional issues raised by Confederate political philosophers have been lost sight of in American political debates during the ensuing years. For our present purposes, it may be worthwhile to review briefly the principles that moved the Confederate leaders to secede, because it may give us another perspective with which to view the constitutional problem of Northern Ireland.

The issue of states' rights versus federal authority has been debated throughout American history. It was present in the first constitutional document of the nation, the Articles of Confederation, which conceived of effective power residing with the state governments rather than with the national government. The conservatives who wrote the Constitution in 1787, however, vested far more power in the national government; but even they had to compromise with states' rights advocates on several important matters. Southerners have raised the issue many times because of their belief that the national government, while possibly reflecting the sentiments of a majority of Americans, did not reflect the sentiments of a majority of (white) people in their region. The immediate issues that have caused Southerners to protest what they have regarded as the abuse of power by the national government have varied in the past 180 years: Thomas Jefferson and James Madison led the states' rights cause with the Virginia and Kentucky Resolutions (1798), because they believed that the administration of John Adams had usurped and abused power in the matter of civil liberties when it passed the Alien and Sedition Laws; John C. Calhoun led the states' rights cause in 1828 against Andrew Jackson's administration because of his belief that the government's tariff policy was ruinous to the economy of the South; Jefferson Davis, Alexander Stephens, and others moved the states' rights position its next logical step in 1861, when the Southern Confederacy removed itself from the Union in opposition to what it saw as the Lincoln administration's position on slavery, the region's "peculiar institution"; in more recent history, Governors Faubus and Wallace have raised the standard of states' rights against the Eisenhower and Kennedy administrations, respectively, on the matter of federally directed school integration. In each of these examples, the issue was resolved, in varying degrees, by a victory for the advocates of federal authority. Indeed, the institutional history of American politics has been largely the story of a federal government that has continually expanded its powers at the expense of the states, and, within the federal government itself, of a presidency that has continually expanded its powers at the expense of the other branches. This process has done violence to the intentions of the founding fathers, who viewed good government as the result of a delicate balance between the various branches on local, state, and federal levels. If balanced government could be maintained, the fathers believed, their two goals would be realized: the will of the majority would prevail in most cases; but, of equal importance, the rights of a minority interest would be safeguarded.

The most important American political philosopher whose life and work was the defense of a minority interest was John C. Calhoun of South Carolina. While nearly all students of American politics would agree with Richard Hofstadter's view that Calhoun was "the last American statesman to do any primary political thinking," most give little attention to Calhoun because his views are associated with the political heresy of secession and the moral outrage of slavery. Calhoun's biographer, Charles M. Wiltse, sees him as "the supreme champion of minority rights" (however, it should perhaps be noted that another eminent southern historian, Clement Eaton, offers a contrary viewpoint in *Freedom of Thought in the Old South*). Calhoun, therefore, is controversial because the original political thinking he did during the first half of the nineteenth century was associated either with causes that were defeated or were thought to offend the essence of the American democratic faith. He deserves to be heard, however, not because he was correct on race relations (he was not), nor because he defended minority rights out of a love of liberty for all men (he did not); he deserves to be heard because he is virtually the only American statesman (other than perhaps Herbert Hoover) who saw what many Americans have only lately begun to see: that —as Alexis de Tocqueville warned—the worst tyranny to be feared in the American political system is the tyranny of the majority. This is an important matter, because it is the tyranny of the majority in the present state of Northern Ireland that Catholics protest; and similarly, Protestants in Northern Ireland fear unity with the Irish Republic precisely because they believe that they would be tyrannized by the Catholic majority.

Calhoun, it is interesting to observe, was born in 1782 in South Carolina into a Scots-Irish family whose members

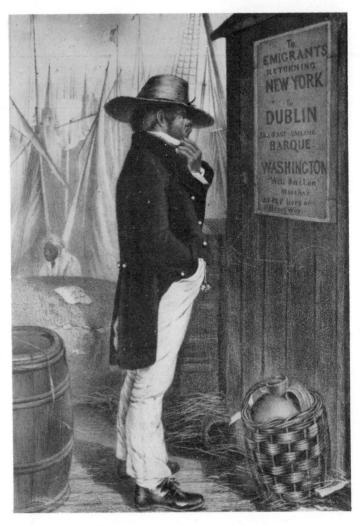

An emigrant to America
dreams of home.

had emigrated from the north of Ireland in the middle of
the eighteenth century. They had originally gone to Pennsylvania, but later moved to the southern "back country."
After an education at Yale, he returned to practice law in
South Carolina. He soon entered politics and was sent to
Congress in 1810. During the next four decades he was a
major force in American politics, serving as a congress-
man, senator, secretary of war, secretary of state, and
Vice-President. At the beginning of his career he was an
ardent supporter of federal authority and national unity.
However, as the South became more and more dependent
on the cotton economy (and therefore on slavery) Calhoun
realized that the South was evolving into a region that
was becoming very different from the rest of the United

States. That divergence of his region, and the fear that that region would not be treated fairly by a national government controlled by the interests of other regions, caused the movement of Calhoun's political philosophy in the direction that would result in the Civil War.

It was the tariff, not cotton and slavery, that began the process in Calhoun's mind. The passage of the exorbitant "tariff of abominations" in 1828 was so discriminatory to the South that Calhoun joined the issue with his now famous *South Carolina Exposition and Protest*. In the 1850s, in the full flush of the debate over the institution of slavery, Calhoun wrote *Discourse on the Constitution and Government of the United States* and *A Disquisition on Government*. The three essays form a piece if one sees in them Calhoun's basic thrust: that some restraint on the unchecked control of government by the majority must be found in order to allow a minority some constitutional remedy for retaining freedom of action. Rather than one majority, Calhoun believed, there ought to be a "concurrent majority," a system that would prevent one or several interests from tyrannizing another. In *A Disquisition on Government*, he wrote:

> To do this each division or sector of the political organism should have either the right to a concurrent voice in legislative and policy formulation or, if not this, a decisive veto power over the majority. The different orders, classes or sectors of political society must end their conflict and struggles by concurring or agreeing as to aims before any meaningful action of the body politic can be undertaken.

The American political system, of course, was never required to give a constitutional answer to Calhoun's philosophy. Rather, the constitutional issue was settled militarily at Fort Sumter, Gettysburg, and Appomattox; it is possible that that was the only way in which it could have been settled. But no other way was ever seriously attempted, and once settled in that way, such ideas were forever regarded as illegitimate. While we may concede that Calhoun's defense of a minority section of the country was conceived in a circumstance and for a reason that has little positive relevance to our own time, the pamphlets written more than a century ago speak clearly to the contemporary world situation, which witnesses the desire of minorities to be freed from the tyranny of the majority (e.g., Nigeria, Pakistan, Viet Nam, South Africa, and Northern Ireland, to name only a few). But the difficulty in these cases, and in Calhoun's case, consists in defining a "state" or a "people," and then in knowing what consequences ought to follow once the definitions are agreed upon.

In the case of Northern Ireland, Senator Kennedy believes that the historic principle of self-determination is being abused by the British because the people of the six counties are not "a people" in "a state." The only "people" to which Kennedy will agree is a unified Irish people. Since Ulster is, in the Senator's view, "an uncouth entity," he will not hear of granting it self-determination; rather, he asks, "Why not self-determination for Londonderry, or County Tyrone, or any other Catholic area in Ulster?" Such a question is rather carping, because, as the Senator must realize, it can evoke the following response: "Why not self-determination for Belfast, or County Antrim, or any other Protestant area in Ulster?" The answers to the questions are not easy, and, as noted above, the resolution of them depends on how the interpreter will view presuppositional definitions of "people" and "state," and how the rights of minorities can be safeguarded. One must concede to Senator Kennedy that the Protestants of Northern Ireland are less convincing in worrying about safeguarding their rights as a minority in a future all-Ireland republic while they show little concern for the rights of the minority in Ulster (just as Calhoun's defense of the South's rights seems hollow when one recalls the institution of slavery). By the same token, however, it would seem ill-advised to force the Protestants of Ulster into a minority status without due consideration of minority rights (just as it did not really solve the constitutional problem in the United States to bludgeon the South into a minority and an historically inferior position vis-à-vis the other regions of the nation).

The simple truth, perhaps unpalatable to Irish nationalists, is that there has been and is an historic Protestant presence in Ireland, which, because of its minority status, views its identity in terms of unity with the other parts of the United Kingdom. Senator Kennedy and others who dream of Irish unity tell the Protestants of the North that they *ought* to feel kinship with their Irish brothers to the South; the plain fact is that they do not. In the impenetrable past the Protestants were implanted in Ireland, a movement fraught with tragic consequences for Irish history; but it is now too late to ask them to "go back where they came from." Senator Kennedy and his Irish constituency in America must surely be sensitive to this: there

were Protestants in Ireland long before the great migration brought the Catholic Irish to New England, but there
is no legitimacy to the suggestion that Irish-Americans go
back to Ireland. All Americans are faced with current
circumstances that are the result of an historic process of
the mingling of migratory peoples. Perhaps, because the
situation in Ireland is part of a larger story of human
tragedy, it may be impossible to resolve. But if the situation is to be brought to some acceptable conclusion, it will
be neither on the basis of the naked abuse of power by
Ulster Protestants, nor on the basis of the shouting of
nationalistic and democratic slogans by Irish Catholics on
both sides of the Atlantic.

Even less acceptable than Senator Kennedy's constitu-
tional arguments, in our view, are his suggestions of
American involvement in the resolution of the problems of
Ulster. He writes:

> There are those who say that America should
> stand silent in the face of the daily tragedy taking
> place in Northern Ireland. I do not agree. . . . Our
> heritage as citizens in a nation that has been a
> spokesman for peace and human liberty in the
> world for two centuries requires us to speak out
> and find a helpful role to play in contributing to
> a permanent peace in Ulster. A larger issue is the
> question of what kind of foreign policy we want for
> America as we enter the final quarter of this cen-
> tury. I believe we want a policy that places far
> more emphasis on the billions of ordinary people
> throughout the world who seek a decent life. . . .
> In my view, it is time to let America's voice be
> heard. We should establish a continuing public
> tone in the foreign policy of the Administration,
> a tone that reflects the legitimate concerns of mil-
> lions of American citizens for an end to the vio-
> lence in Northern Ireland and a recognition that
> the minority in Ulster is entitled to participate
> fully in the government of their province. . . . In
> the long run we should leave no doubt of our sup-
> port for unification as the ultimate goal for Ire-
> land. . . . Until a political solution is implemented
> that is seen to be fair and even-handed by both
> sides, the search for peace will be in vain. Fifty-
> five thousand Americans died before we learned
> that tragic lesson in Vietnam, and four years of
> needless violence and destruction have passed
> while Britain learned that lesson in Northern
> Ireland.

In responding to Senator Kennedy we should repeat, as

Senator John F. Kennedy, first Catholic President of the United States.

previously noted, that we share his notion that Americans of various backgrounds and persuasions have a right, perhaps even an obligation, to speak out on Northern Ireland, and that the problems there are not exclusively the "internal affairs" of the United Kingdom. However, we would nevertheless encourage the Senator and those likely to listen to him to be very wary of ideas which, however attractive, would tend to commit American public opinion and diplomacy to one side of the dispute in Ulster. We are concerned, because in doing so the Senator may run the risk of continuing some of the less helpful tendencies of twentieth-century American internationalism.

If it is true that our heritage in the United States has been as a spokesman for "human liberty in the world," it should be pointed out that the world has not asked us to be that spokesman; it is a burden we have imposed upon ourselves. It is a responsibility we assumed because it accorded well with our naive conception of ourselves and the superiority of our institutions. Thomas Jefferson foresaw a time when the young, vibrant, and pure institutions of the United States would have to send their spokesmen back to Europe whence our immigrant ancestors had come, in order to redeem the old, decrepit, and decadent institutions of Europe. That time came during World War I, at least in the view of President Wilson, who saw American participation as vital because the struggle was one to save humanity: thus, it was "the war to end all wars," "the war to make the world safe for democracy." In World War II, America's participation as "the arsenal of democracy" was required to defeat international fascism; but that was only a prelude to America's postwar role as self-appointed spokesman of opposition to international Communism. Both American political parties have subscribed to that role, and they have given a general American commitment to the world.

President John F. Kennedy gave the most articulate rendering of that commitment in his inaugural address: "We will go anywhere, pay any price, support any friend, oppose any foe. . . ." Those of us who cheered the young President in 1961 did not realize, as perhaps even he did not, that having said that, the first steps toward our agonizing involvement in Vietnam—at least in our imaginations—had already been taken. Because of his assassination, Kennedy was not forced to encounter the contradiction that faced those who remained and participated in the "agonizing reappraisal" by the end of the decade. Having confronted ourselves in the rice paddies of Vietnam, many of us discovered that there was another American tradition that did not view the United States as the self-appointed "spokesman for liberty" or the arbiter for the problems of the world. John Quincy Adams believed that America should not go abroad in search of dragons to slay, because she would thus no longer be mistress of her own spirit. Herbert Hoover believed that toleration of differences in the world accorded better with the American character than attempts to impose American solutions by either military diplomacy or dollar diplomacy.

President Kennedy, perhaps as he matured in office, also caught a glimpse of the vision in his beautiful speech at American University in 1963, which was a model of restraint and toleration. In that speech he did not dwell on the divisions caused by the cold war, but he looked forward to a world at peace—a peace that would not necessarily be universal accord but a process by which all parties agreed to solve problems.

> With such a peace, there will still be quarrels and conflicting interests, as there are within families and nations. World peace, like community peace, does not require that man love his neighbor—it requires only that they live together with mutual tolerance, submitting their disputes to a just and peaceful settlement.

It would be a peace that would not require the repeating of the slogans of the past, but rather a realistic understanding of the present: "We must deal with the world as it is, and not as it might have been had the history of the past . . . years been different."

Senator William Fulbright's essay on Vietnam (The Arrogance of Power) reminds us that there are two traditions, two heritages, regarding America's role in the world. One tradition would have the United States assume the responsibility that the "right" things be done in the world, whether or not the rest of the world shares our definition of what is right, or whether or not the United States should be the vehicle for the accomplishment of such "justice." The other tradition would have America assume its responsibilities in the world in a spirit of sympathy, understanding, and toleration—a position that is not mere isolationism. The internationalists would have us believe that any lowering of the dominant American profile in the world would be a retreat to isolationism and parochialism. That is certainly a danger to be avoided, but it can be avoided if American leaders realize that the United States, a nation with a substantial number of its own problems, does not own the patent to the solutions of the rest of mankind's problems.

To Senator Edward Kennedy one could reply that the larger issue is precisely "what kind of foreign policy we want for America as we enter the final quarter of this century." The Senator warns that if we retreat from internationalism "we deny our heritage"; but that is only one tradition in our heritage. It is conspicuously ironic that the Senator invokes the "lesson" of Vietnam as the reason we should involve ourselves in Northern Ireland. One would have thought that the "lesson" of Vietnam would surely have instructed us to be wary of a blustering intervention into the sensitive relationships of a partitioned nation. In thinking thus, however, one is invoking the other tradition of our heritage, a tradition of toleration and restraint that commends itself for our consideration. Of course, in stating this position we should not overemphasize the antithesis between the two traditions. There are several examples of their compatibility, such as the Marshall Plan and the Berlin Airlift. But in both of those instances the United States was helping people confront a real and relatively clearly defined danger. Problems come when an outside power enters a nation's internal strife with prefigured solutions that do not accord well with the historic situation that produced the conflict.

The near future in Northern Ireland may well prove to be a watershed in the province's history. After a period of direct rule from London, the creation of a short-lived "new assembly" with a power-sharing executive, and a

Senator Edward M. Kennedy, Democratic Senator from Massachusetts.

further period of direct rule, a constitutional convention is now sitting in Belfast.

The burning question in Ulster today is whether or not the Protestants, mostly represented by the various factions of the Unionist party, can work together with the Catholics, largely represented by the Social Democratic and Labour party. This may be Ulster's last chance; for as Mr. Callaghan, the British Foreign Secretary, has said in London, "Britain cannot bleed forever." The London *Times* noted in its sensitive and sensible editorial (June 21, 1973) that "there are no soft options in Ulster," but rather difficult and painful steps toward reconciliation that will require herculean efforts of compromise, graciousness, toleration, and good will from all parties in Britain, Northern Ireland, and the Republic of Ireland. As Messrs. Wilson, West, Paisley, Craig, Fitt and Cosgrave try to guide their constituencies through the difficult months ahead, they deserve our sympathy, understanding, and prayers. It would be tragic if American interference at this most sensitive time in any way impeded efforts by the people of Northern Ireland to be reconciled to each other.

While Senator Kennedy is correct in his assertion that the international migration of Irish peoples has internationalized the problem of Ulster, and while many Americans, whether or not they are of Irish or British ancestry, are very interested in the outcome, and while many may share the Senator's general belief that unity in an all-Ireland republic may be the island's last and best hope, we must nevertheless maintain that there are inherent difficulties in approaching this situation with prefigured solutions, especially when they come from the United States in the name of "human liberty." Since Protestantism and Catholicism have become the badges for the sectarian conflict in Northern Ireland, we believe that it is important for persons who are committed Christians to join the debate. This is not to say that because we are Christians we have the answers; on the contrary, we are painfully aware of how difficult the answers are to grasp. It is to say that as Christians we should help in any way we can in the work of the kingdom of God, which offers men the potential of being reconciled both to God and to each other.

# 3 LIFE IN NORTHERN IRELAND

> There are two communities in Northern Ireland, different in their origins, nursing different historical myths, possessing distinguishable cultures, having different songs and heroes, and wearing different denominations of the same religion. Religion is the clearest badge of these differences. But the conflict is not *about* religion. It is about the self-assertion of two distinct communities, one of which is dominant in the public affairs of the province.
>
> — The Times, August 30, 1969.

"WHAT ARE THE PEOPLE of Northern Ireland really like?" Those who ask me this question often appear slightly skeptical about my reply. For in the opinion of most people the Irish, particularly those in the North, are a hard-drinking, fairly unpleasant lot who will revert to tribal religious customs at the drop of a crucifix. Nothing could be further from the truth. They are generally decent, hard-working, friendly people—good neighbors, whose main characteristic is their kindness. Their tragedy is that it is they on whom "the sins of their forefathers" are being visited. However, they are also an insecure people, and many of them do not really understand the interconnections between the spiritual, moral, and social values they prize. Nor do they understand the viewpoints of those who hold different values. Consequently, they have become insular and at times defensively aggressive, lest their inadequacy become exposed for all to see. In these ways they are really no different from people in the rest of Britain or, for that matter, anywhere else in the world.

The purpose of this chapter will be to consider the views, prejudices, and practices of average Ulstermen—both Protestant and Catholic. We will use these labels to identify them, bearing in mind, as the quotation from The Times indicates, that the conflict is not simply about religion, and bearing in mind also that there are broad spectra of opinions within both communities. We should realize, however, that any other labels would be equally misleading generalities. Through these "average" men the political, religious, social, economic, and psychological attitudes and behavior of Ulster's two communities may be described.

Some may argue that no such "average" person exists.

Certainly the events of the last five years have considerably changed people's outlooks, and today's average man is a very different person from the one of ten years ago. Secondly, many people born and raised in Northern Ireland may well point out that this or that "average" characteristic is not true of them. Nevertheless, it is often necessary to speak in general terms, provided, of course, they are as accurate as possible, in order that those who are not directly concerned in a given situation, and sometimes even those who are, can more readily understand the issues involved. And we feel that understanding of Northern Ireland and its problems is a paramount need today. It can provide the only basis for the dialogue and accommodation that are presently missing both in Ulster and Britain, and in Eire's dealings with Ulster.

## POLITICS

All the people of Northern Ireland are British. They owe allegiance to Queen Elizabeth II, are represented at Westminster, and pay their taxes just as do the people who live in Cardiff, Edinburgh, or London. This is a constitutional and political fact of life. Yet only the Protestants feel British—and this is another political fact of life. A survey, published in 1971 in Professor Richard Rose's book *Governing Without Consensus*, showed that about 70% of all Protestants approved of Northern Ireland's constitution; the figure for Catholics was about 30%.

Historically, as we have seen, the province comprises two distinct groups of people: descendants of the native Catholic Irish and descendants of the transplanted Protestant English and Scots. In Ulster today these divisions continue to be clearly apparent. The 1961 census showed that there were in Northern Ireland 413,000 Presbyterians, 345,000 Church of Ireland members, and 72,000 Methodists, as well as 498,000 Roman Catholics. The latter still resent the "invasion" that cost them their land; the others still despise the traditions and religion of the natives. Thus, the primary cause of tension was, and in a sense still is, <u>ethnic</u>. Unfortunately, this is not a situation unique to Ulster, as citizens of Spain, South Africa, Rhodesia, the United States, Russia, England, Australia, and India—to mention but a few—can testify. In Northern Ireland it just happens that the easiest peg on which to hang

The homes of the province proclaim their allegiance.

*Left.* A Catholic home in Derry displays pictures of both Pope Pius XII and John Hume, moderate leader of the civil rights movement and SDLP politician.

*Below.* Union Jacks and a picture of the Rev. Ian Paisley declare this to be a Protestant home.

these differences is religion rather than the more usual pegs of skin color or regional loyalty. This centuries-old ethnic division colors all contemporary thinking. One faction equates England's ruling of Ireland with colonialism, chauvinism, and economic subjection; the other sees it as an exercise in loyalty and in preserving national boundaries, coupled with an attempt to civilize the "natives."

History, therefore, plays a perhaps unduly large part in Irish politics, Yet the lessons it teaches are themselves often obscured by sectarian thinking. In some cases people are given different interpretations of the same event. To unionists, Connolly's socialism was simply a development of the anarchy of the French Revolution. To republicans it was the only sensible reaction to the exploitation of absentee English landlords. In other cases people, especially children, are taught only those aspects of history that are considered "beneficial," and events are seldom set in their full context. Thus, one group of children learns about Cromwell's massacres at Drogheda and Wexford, the callousness of the British government during the great famine, and the "thuggery" of the Black and Tans. The other group is nurtured on the glorious Protestant victory at the Boyne, the sacrifice of hundreds of loyal Ulstermen at the Battle of the Somme in 1916, and the treason of the Easter Rebellion in the same year.

It is hardly surprising that in such a blinkered society the dominant political issues are most frequently thought of in terms of security. Catholics in the North feel insecure because they are a minority; as a result they turn for help and moral support to their kinfolk in the South. And this action is immediately interpreted by unionists as an act of betrayal. Unionists feel insecure also, and for the same reason. They constitute a minority within the whole of Ireland and so look to Britain for support. This, in turn, is viewed by the Irish as the natural action of a colonial and puppet state. Thus, the cycle is completed and revolves remorselessly towards destruction.

But why should this be? Let us first consider the Protestant viewpoint. The Unionist party governed Northern Ireland from the time of its inception until the imposition of direct rule, and the ratio of Unionist members of parliament to nationalists, of whatever party, has always been greater than the ratio of Protestants to Catholics in the province. Such a situation caused no surprise in the first decade or two following partition. After all, Ulster was primarily established as a Protestant country for Protestants. (Monaghan, Donegal, and Cavan were excluded from the historic Ulster when the present Northern Ireland boundaries were drawn up, because the 1911 census indicated that the people in these counties were 74.7%, 78.9%, and 81.5% Catholic respectively. The number of Catholics these figures represented would have dangerously lowered the size of the Protestants' overall majority in the province.) Also, the early refusal of many Catholics to acknowledge the state's authority helped to reduce their representation. The continuing under-representation of Catholic interests, however, was due in large part to their disillusionment with the way the state has evolved, to the refusal of many to vote (Protestant view), and to political gerrymandering (Catholic view).

The reason for unionist dominance has been quite simply "the border." The Unionist party, as its name implies, stands for union with Britain. Over the years, the party has skillfully pre-empted the political middle ground. It has also so presented political issues that every decision has carried with it constitutional implications. That

Boys hoist the illegal Irish tricolour on a Bogside scaffolding. The children of the province grow up in an atmosphere where games and reality merge into one.

Headquarters of the Ulster
Unionist Party in Belfast.

is to say, support for the Unionist position has been coupled with the imperative of continued links with Britain. Support for any other position, no matter how plausible, has been projected as undermining the authority of the Unionist party—and thus the union—which alone could be trusted to preserve and defend the loyalists. Thus, for example, the Northern Ireland Labour party has languished because it has been unable successfully to separate industrial relations from the larger issue of the state's existence in the minds of most people.

Unionists have decried the notion that the Labour party can just seek to raise the lot of the working man, irrespective of his religion. Each Protestant vote for Labour splits the loyalist front, so the slogan goes, and may allow Catholics to assume power. Until the assembly elections, Ulster Protestants never dissented from this political theory. Consequently, every election has been fought ultimately not on social and economic issues but on the constitutional one. Faced with the choice of preserving or dismantling the state, or believing that they were faced with such a choice, Protestants voted the Unionist position. Safety could only be found in solidarity.

The *Belfast News-Letter* can claim with considerable justification to have faithfully reflected majority Protestant opinion through the years. The following excerpts from its editorial pages set the mood and illustrate this single issue theme on which elections have been fought.

- The issue at stake in this election must be apparent to all. Do the Ulster people still value their birthright? Are they still insistent on retaining their full partnership with the rest of the United Kingdom within the Empire? In neither case is the issue in doubt. There remains the question which tomorrow must settle: Is the Government that for twelve years has stood, and continues to stand, for the conservation of that birthright to receive a mandate not less emphatic than before. . . . The electorate must not be deceived by those who are not Unionist Party members or supporters. . . . Every such vote (for them) is a symptom of weakness and indecision and will be regarded as such by (Ulster's) enemies. (1933)

- From whatever angle the general election in Northern Ireland be regarded, the Constitutional question emerges as the governing issue. (1945)
- Today Ulster people go to the poll on an issue which admits of no compromise—whether they are to continue in Union with Great Britain or to be absorbed into an Irish Republic. Never throughout the long controversy has their position been challenged more directly; at no time has the need for an unequivocal reply been more urgent. (1949)
- Not the least disturbing feature of the present

1971 State opening of the Northern Ireland Parliament at Stormont Castle. Lord Gray of Haunton, then Governor of the province, opens Parliament in the name of the Queen.

*Above.* Carson's True Blues, one of the Orange Lodges, in an Orange Day parade through the streets of Belfast.

*Right.* An Ulster Loyalist, one of an estimated crowd of 50,000 gathered for a rally of the Ulster Vanguard Movement.

General Election campaign has been an increasing tendency to suggest that as Northern Ireland's position is now unassailable, the time has come when the Unionist electorate can dismiss its fears and with safety concentrate upon purely domestic issues. No more pernicious theory could be advanced; no policy is more fraught with danger. (1953)

● While the leader of the Northern Ireland Labour Party has declared that one of its objects is to preserve and strengthen the Province's link with Great Britain, the fact remains that it is challenging candidates whose attitude towards the maintenance of the Border cannot be called into question, and has abstained from opposing men who would like to see Ulster absorbed by an all-Ireland Republic. (1958)

The extent to which union with Britain and loyalty to

*Above.* Loyalist Protestants feel strongly about any moves toward ecumenism.

*Right.* Protestant fervour is not restricted to Ireland. Scots Orangemen rally at the annual Orange Walk in Edinburgh.

the crown have been made the preserve of the Unionist party was indicated by a 1966 survey. It showed that 82% of all Protestants voted, and 81% voted Unionist. Only 2% of Catholics voted Unionist, and 40% did not vote at all. Over the years unionism also became symbolically and actually linked with both the Orange Order and the existence of a separate government at Stormont. The Orange Order is deeply involved in the religious and political life of the community. Each Orange lodge has a chaplain, and its membership is frequently drawn from local church congregations, though there is no official link between the lodge and the church. Nevertheless, the lodges' strong religious emphasis is highly significant, not least in the eyes of Catholics. For the Orange Order is committed to the Protestant ascendancy, and phrases like "no surrender" and "not an inch" fall easily from the lips of its members. In fact, before joining a lodge a man must agree to "love,

uphold and defend the Protestant religion . . . [and] stren-
uously oppose the fatal errors and doctrines of the Church
of Rome. . . ."

The order's political influence is likewise considerable,
because membership in it is virtually a requirement for
Unionist M.P.'s and those aspiring to join their ranks. Perhaps it is only by insisting on this precondition that many
rank and file Protestants feel assured that their government will not step outside the primary objective of Or-
angeism: "to maintain the laws and peace of the country
and the Protestant constitution." Even those Protestants
who feel that the order is a divisive and negative force
would be quick to acknowledge its powerfulness. Stormont's importance, on the other hand, was both practical
and symbolic. Before its abolition it consisted of a fifty-two
seat house of commons and a twenty-six seat senate,
which had the power to pass laws for "the peace, order
and good government of Northern Ireland" (Government
of Ireland Act, 1920), subject to certain limitations. However, it was not only the laws it passed but also the fact
that it could pass them that was important to most
unionists.

The glistening white building in its immaculately kept
grounds, in which Ulstermen regulated their lives without
fear of political subjection, symbolized their independence from both Dublin and London. In the case of the
former, Stormont's very presence soothed their fears by
reminding and reassuring them of the continuing reality
of "the border." As far as London was concerned, Stormont was a bulwark: while it functioned, any attempt by
Britain to try to reunite Ireland could easily be thwarted.
It was the existence of these sentiments that provoked the
outcry from Ulster's loyalists when Stormont was suspended. All their anxieties about betrayal again flooded
to the surface. And subsequent statements by British min-
isters and ex-ministers concerning the eventual reunification of Ireland, an all-Ireland council, and even integration with Britain have positively accentuated the apprehensive and skeptical feelings Ulstermen have toward
British intentions.

Finally, it should be understood that the commitment of
Ulster's Protestants to their political heritage has not
been diminished by the present troubles. They are in no
mood to seek peace at any price. Even the most "ordinary"
citizens regularly combine expressions of dismay and
despair over their present plight with a steely determination not to give in to the IRA. This determination was

The defiant figure of Lord Carson stands in front of Parliament buildings, Stormont, solid symbol of Ulster's independence.

made clear by the large majority that voted in the 1973 plebiscite to retain the province's ties with Great Britain. Its strength, however, was more clearly revealed by Professor Rose's survey. He found that 52% of Protestants endorsed the use of any methods, including violence, to keep Northern Ireland Protestant. And 73% of the members of the Orange Order were in this category.

The other major factor reinforcing the Protestants' commitment is the belief that their position has been grossly misrepresented by much of the world's press. Repeatedly, they argue, newsmen have resorted to sloganeering, the use of emotive catch words—"civil rights" and "ghetto" are two that are particularly offensive—and oversimplifications. Protestants feel they have been invariably classified as "baddies" and Catholics, even at the height of the IRA campaigns, as "oppressed goodies." Such allegedly biased reporting has caused Protestants to close ranks, to feel that no one is concerned with discovering the truth or appreciating their legitimate viewpoint. Despite their contribution to Ulster's troubles, stretching back over fifty years, the Protestants argue that they have been more "sinned against than sinning." They believe that they should not be made scapegoats for the conflict, to which they are only one party. Neither the press, nor even British governments, should feel that easy solutions can be found by pressuring the Protestants to become the kind of people whom those not involved in the past or present of Northern Ireland would find more congenial.

Constitutionally, as we have said, the Catholics and nationalists who live in Ulster are also British. They too vote in Westminster parliamentary elections and had a say with Protestants in who was elected to Stormont and, more recently, to the new assembly. But they "feel" Irish. To them the border that divides "their" country is an artificial barrier that was imposed by Britain as an expedient reaction to Protestant blackmail. They want it abolished. Politically, the Catholic working man wants nothing to do with the Unionist party, because he believes it speaks against his interests. He wants political unity with the South for a whole series of reasons that can best be summed up in the word "Ireland." For to him Ireland is more than a geographical entity. It has a spiritual and cultural identity of which he feels a part; early made aware of this heritage, he wants fully to enter into it.

What Catholics see as the sham democracy of the North alienates them and strengthens their desire to be free. They know that they will be effectively excluded from governing in the foreseeable future. (This is being written at a time when "power-sharing" remains an unproved political concept.) Since the province votes along strictly sectarian lines (the Alliance party notwithstanding), and since Protestants outnumber Catholics by a ratio of

Many Ulster Protestants believed that the Civil Rights Movement was simply a Communist front. This banner, "Antichristian Forces Unite Communist and Catholics" is carried by Loyalists in a march protesting the activities of the Civil Rights workers.

Provisional IRA leaders at an unofficial press conference. Left to right: Martin McGuinneas, David O'Connell, leading theoretician and the man who attempted to smuggle arms out of Holland in 1971; Sean MacStiofain, ex-Chief of Staff; and Seamus Twomey.

roughly two to one, Catholics cannot hope to achieve political power. This political impotence has driven many to seek influence through organizations such as the CRA and the IRA. Even the occasional electoral victories of Sinn Fein candidates, who then refused to take their seats, only added to Catholic frustration by underscoring the essential futility of the republicans' position.

To Catholics, the first two demands of the CRA in 1968 really expressed the nub of their political problem. These demands were for the introduction of a universal franchise in local government elections and the redrawing of local election boundaries. They were made because, unlike the voting systems used in the two parliamentary elections, universal suffrage did not then apply in local elections. This fact formed the basis for the highly effective, but in view of the circumstances somewhat misleading, rallying cry "one man, one vote," which helped to endear the Catholics' cause to people throughout the world. In order to vote at the local level, an elector had to qualify as the owner or tenant of a dwelling house, land, or premises subject to certain conditions. This qualification had the effect of reducing those eligible to vote from about 900,000 to about 700,000. Now there is nothing in these restrictions of a political nature per se. The economic limitations were designed to express the sociological concept that only those with a direct interest in a community should be allowed a say in how that community is run. However, if we remember that Northern Ireland was established as a "Protestant" country, and that, generally,

Some of the men who have become legendary in the Republican Movement for their part in directing militant action.

*Left top.* Thomas MacGiolla.

*Left below.* Rory O'Bradaigh.

*Right top.* Cathal Goulding.

*Middle.* Joe Cahill.

*Bottom.* Sean MacStiofain.

more of the wealth belongs to Protestants, we can see that the effect of economic restrictions on voting will not be uniformly distributed throughout the community. Catholics will theoretically be disenfranchised more heavily, and this in fact was the case. Further, since local authorities control such things as housing, education, and social services, the disadvantage experienced by Catholics under these Protestant-controlled authorities could be severe. Thus, in a real sense Catholics felt themselves cut off from and unable to attain political power.

This feeling was increased by the alleged practice that prompted the second CRA demand. Many Catholics believe and claim that Unionists used their local council control to gerrymander local election boundaries. Carefully drawn ward boundaries could ensure Protestant control of a council even if the majority of the citizens in its area were Catholic. Barritt and Carter, in their excellent book *The Northern Ireland Problem* (1962), question the validity of these claims. By 1969, however, the *Report of the Cameron Commission on Disturbances in Northern Ireland* indicated that, in their view, a minority of councils were guilty of this practice. They made the following comment on one example of manipulation of electoral boundaries:

> The most glaring case was Londonderry County Borough where sixty per cent of the adult population was Catholic but where sixty per cent of the seats on the Corporation were held by Unionists. These results were achieved by the use, for example, of ward areas in which Unionist representatives were returned by small majorities, whereas non-Unionist representatives were returned by very large majorities.

In Londonderry County Borough in 1967, 14,429 Catholic voters and 8,781 other voters returned twelve Unionists and eight non-Unionists! Even though local election voting restrictions have now been removed and local election boundaries have been reviewed by the Macrory Committee, Catholics' feeling that they have suffered political discrimination has in no way decreased their aspirations for a united Ireland.

During the province's existence, the major political pressure in behalf of Catholics has been exerted by the Dublin government. It has never recognized the legitimacy of a separate Ulster and has continually championed the cause of its detached brethren. The government's refusal to act decisively against the IRA in its sporadic attempts

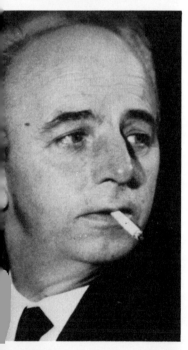

to "liberate" the North, and its intransigence over the question of extradition have left no doubt where its sympathies lie. Catholic political leadership in the North may even have suffered because of the tendency of the people to look to Dublin for guidance. With the emergence of the Social Democratic and Labour party, however, that leadership is firmly back in local hands. This, generally speaking, was the position in 1969. Protestants voted together—for Unionists—to ensure separation from the Republic and the maintenance of ties with Great Britain, while the Orange Order guarded the purity of the political faith. Catholics, if they chose or were able to vote, voted for an assortment of nationalist and republican parties whose common goal was to reunite Ireland and finally rid it of British imperialism.

Since 1969, political feeling has become further polarized. Protestants, outraged by the campaign of killing and terror, have become increasingly "right-wing." The solidarity of the Unionist party cracked in 1969 when official and unofficial Unionists stood against each other. From that split two groups have emerged. One, under the leadership of Brian Faulkner, seeks to continue traditional Unionist policies—once thought extreme by many, but in today's political climate offered as almost moderate. The other, led by Ian Paisley, William Craig, and an ever changing number of militant workers, not to mention Enoch Powell, is more adamantly loyalist and given to speculation about the possibilities of a unilateral declaration of independence on the one hand and total integration with Britain on the other.

Catholics, terrified by the brutality of the early Protestant attacks, initially welcomed the British Army as saviors. Not long afterwards, however, they turned to the IRA for protection and made both physical and political secession and the gun their political weapons. Eventually, under the tutelage of Gerry Fitt, John Hume, Austin Currie, and others, they were persuaded to transfer their allegiance to the SDLP. This allowed the SDLP to obtain about 30% representation in the since disbanded new assembly. By voting in such large numbers, Catholics firmly rejected an IRA call to boycott the elections. It would be dangerous to assume, though, that the IRA no longer enjoys considerable support.

Thus, politically speaking, Ulster is bitterly divided today and will remain so for some considerable time. The ability of the present constitutional convention to provide a viable forum for decision-making and power-

Gerry Fitt, leader of the Social
Democratic and Labour Party
(SDLP) and Westminister MP.

Edward Heath (then Prime
Minister) and William Whitelaw
(Northern Ireland Secretary of
State), with the Lord Mayor of
Belfast, visit the City Hall.

*Right*. William Craig, leader of
the Protestant Vanguard
Party. Once a hard-liner,
Mr Craig's conversion to the
idea of some form of power-
sharing has caused a reassess-
ment of the policies of the
United Ulster Unionist
Coalition.

sharing, the Whitelaw-Rees answer to Protestant power
concentration, is still to be determined. On its degree of
success may depend the very political future of Northern
Ireland.

## RELIGION

There are approximately two Protestants to one Catholic
in Northern Ireland, and just about everyone claims to be
religious. In the 1951 census, only sixty-four people out of
1,370,921 claimed to be atheists. In 1971, 86% of Ulster
people believed that God watches over what each person
does and thinks, compared to 49% with this belief in the
rest of Britain. A 1959 survey of Queens University students, who are perhaps as representatively religious as
any other group, showed that 94% of Catholics and 50-
55% of Protestants attended church. It would seem accurate to conclude that, if these figures are even reason-
ably representative of the community, the percentage of

Ulster churchgoers is very much higher than that in England. This may make it difficult for the English to understand why religion is so important to the Irish. And this importance becomes even greater when one takes account of religion's historical role in shaping Irish society.

People within both religious communities can be divided into two categories. There are those to whom the faith is real and vital: they have a personal knowledge of God that gives significance and purpose to life. Secondly, there are those to whom religion is little more than a social ritual and who seek only to identify with a particular church "brand name." The latter know little of what they are supposed to believe but are quick to recite the "errors" of the other man's creed. It is primarily they, rather than the former, who make religion the inflammatory point in the society. The Christians for their part are content, with some notable exceptions, to discuss and disagree on theology and church government.

Let us then first consider the views of the majority. The average Protestant, if he has any theological knowledge or understanding, sees himself and his beliefs in the tradition of the Reformation. In his opinion, Martin Luther was one of the most significant figures of ecclesiastical history. And he feels that in Luther's stand against Roman Catholicism his own freedom of worship was procured. That freedom having been established, he holds that certain doctrines naturally follow from it. These include the sole and sufficient authority of the Bible in all matters of faith and conduct, the right of an individual Christian to approach God directly, and the assurance that Christian believers—those who have a personal trust in Jesus Christ—can know God's forgiveness for their sins. Finally, the average Protestant rejects as unbiblical the role of tradition in the Roman Catholic Church, the idea of papal infallibility, the "theory" of the transubstantiation of the sacraments, and the right of the church to control private morals. All these doctrines, of course, are bound together theologically, though the vast majority of Protestants are not able to explain why this should be so. Nevertheless, they passionately believe them to be true. With the zeal of new converts (despite the centuries since Luther), they spurn, often with open hostility, the religious system from which they have been "freed." Rightly or wrongly, they see in the Roman Church an exclusivity and authoritarianism that fundamentally contradicts the tenets of their faith. As far as the church's relationship to the state is concerned, Protestants resent the Catholic position as outlined by the Most Rev. Dr. Sheehan in his *Apologetics and Christian Doctrine:*

> The Church, commissioned by Christ to preach the Gospel, and clothed with infallibility, can never be unwilling to suppress erroneous doctrine. The Church and every lover of truth must necessarily be intolerant of error.

This Catholic intolerance toward "error" was given more practical substance by Jesuit Father Cavalli in *La Civilita Catholica* in 1948. He wrote:

> In a State where the majority of the people are Catholic, the Church asks that error shall not be accorded a legal existence, and that if religious minorities exist they shall be accorded a *de facto* existence only, not the opportunity of spreading their beliefs.

Thus, the lines of religious dispute are clearly drawn, and their connection with Irish politics is quite obvious. In a united Ireland, Protestants would be in a minority and therefore vulnerable to Catholic pressure. Furthermore, because the Catholic Church is recognized in the South as the "State Church" (it was until recently accorded a special place in the republic's constitution), and because its influence and precepts still play a large part in molding Eire's public policy, Northern Protestants naturally feel that their most cherished beliefs would be undermined in any all-Ireland union.

The average Catholic sees his religious faith validated by two thousand years of history and tradition. He traces his church establishment back to the direct command to Peter from Jesus himself that the apostle should be the rock on which the Christian church should be built (an interpretation hotly disputed by Protestants). As a consequence, he sees no inconsistency in allowing those who have followed Peter's example and have been directly instructed by God to educate and teach him what God expects of him. Nor does he have any reason to think that the Pope, whom he believes to be Peter's direct successor, should be in any doubt as to what is the mind of God. On the contrary, Catholics find the social and religious services of their church both helpful and reassuring. And above all, they believe its teaching, so obviously linked to the Bible and the church's tradition, to be true. It is hardly surprising, therefore, that they should view Protestants— who, after all, deserted the church, not vice versa—as being in error. The fragmentation of Protestantism is just

what they would expect to result from the holding of such heretical views.

In his book, Dr. Sheehan gives a balanced statement of the Catholic viewpoint.

> No man . . . who, on coming to know the true Church, refuses to join it can be saved. Neither can he be saved if, having once entered the Church, he forsakes it through heresy or schism. . . . He who severs himself from the Church severs himself from Christ, and cannot be saved, for in Christ alone is salvation. . . . [God, however,] will not condemn those who through inculpable ignorance are unaware of His precept, who serve Him faithfully according to their conscience, who have a sincere desire to do His will, and therefore, implicitly, the desire to become members of His Church. . . . [However,] in view of the fact that the Church stands plainly before the eyes of men like a city on a mountain top, that the words of her ministers have gone forth to the ends of the earth, we do not venture to say that such cases are typical of large numbers. We are certain, at all events, that for men deprived of the abundant graces at the disposal of those who belong to the visible membership of the Church, salvation is not easy.

From our brief survey we can see that the theological differences between Protestants and Catholics center on the view each holds of the Bible. All Protestants affirm the uniqueness and all-sufficiency of Scripture. The Catholic Church, in contrast, places itself alongside the Bible as the means of conveying God's revelation to men. This doctrinal variance, so unimportant to nonreligious people,

Religion plays a vital part in everyday life in the province as well as being a focus for divisions amongst the people.

*Left*. A shrine to the Virgin Mary with the inscription "Hail Queen of Peace" stands intact in the heart of the Creggan estate.

*Right*. Bible texts worn unashamedly at a public meeting.

remains the primary unresolved issue of Christendom. And from it these two presently irreconcilable traditions flow.

There are three major areas in which the theological differences already described are translated into emotionally charged social issues. These are education, interfaith marriage, and general morality. We shall consider each of them in turn.

Catholic and Protestant children are educated quite separately in Northern Ireland. A survey in 1960 showed that 41% of the school population was Catholic and 59% Protestant (this compared with 35% and 65% of the population respectively). Ninety-eight percent of all Catholic primary school children attended Catholic schools. After the eleven-plus examination, the religions were still kept apart in different secondary and grammar schools.

Ulster's segregated education is entirely due to the insistence of the Roman Catholic Church. It does not reflect any unwillingness on the part of the Northern Ireland government to discharge its responsibilities to one section of the community. In fact, the Government of Ireland Act prohibits the endowment of any religion and any preference or privilege, disability or disadvantage, to anyone on account of religious belief. From what has been said we can see that it would be impossible to teach in secular schools a religion that would be acceptable to everyone. The Catholic Church has made its position clear in the Catholic Canon Law, which includes the following statements:

- Parents have a most serious duty to secure a fully Catholic education for their children. . . .

- Catholic pupils are not to frequent non-Catholic schools or neutral schools or schools that are open also to non-Catholics. Only the Ordinary of the place where the school is situated is competent to determine, according to the instructions of the Apostolic See, in what circumstances it may be tolerated for Catholics to attend such schools and what safeguards are to be prescribed against the danger of perversion. . . .

Thus, the church's requirement that Catholics be educated in Catholic schools is uncompromising. And because of the dominant influence of the Irish Catholic Church over its people, its wishes have substantially been carried out. Interestingly, evidence is now available, perhaps for the first time, that this segregated education is widely unpopular. Professor Rose found that 65% of all respondents in his survey were in favor of educating Protestant and Catholic children together, although five-sixths of them had themselves been educated in segregated schools. Among Catholics, 69% approved of integrated education—in flat contradiction to the views of the Catholic hierarchy.

Quite understandably, segregated education is viewed differently in the two communities. Catholics see it (or saw it) as a natural extension of what they believe. To them education involves more than merely learning the three R's; it includes training the will and developing spiritual and moral values. They consider it vital that children appreciate the complementary nature of what they learn and what they believe. In fact, many Catholics would go further and say that they want their children to have a Christian education, as opposed to the amoral, secular education offered by the state. (Their reasoning is almost identical to the reasoning of evangelicals in the United States who send their children to Christian schools and colleges.)

Protestants also believe in the unity of God's revelation and the need to develop spiritual understanding, but they emphasize the role the church and family should play in teaching that to their children. They view the desire for Catholic education as nothing more than a means of indoctrinating the children to accept socio-religious theories and historical interpretations that will eventually bias them against the state. They also see it as one more example of the Catholics' refusal to become integrated into the state's systems and further evidence of their anti-social behavior.

Whatever the reason for Catholics' compliance with

their church's views, three consequences of immense social importance flow from separate education. First, it is perfectly understandable that Catholics should want to live near the schools their children attend. In fact, many cannot afford to live far from them. Nevertheless, this proximity increases the likelihood that the two communities will live in isolated enclaves apart from each other, and this situation naturally fosters sectarian feeling. Secondly, children, during the most impressionable and formative years of their lives, have no opportunity to meet those whose backgrounds are different from their own. There is no way for them to learn that the others are human beings of equal sensitivity and with equally genuine aspirations. Thus, the myths and prejudices of unenlightened and fearful people are perpetuated from generation to generation. And although students of strong and no religious conviction go to Ulster's two universities, by then it is often too late for any radical change to occur in the thinking of even this minority of the people. The third consequence of separate education is that it provides a means for those so inclined to covertly discriminate in employment. Let us offer an illustration of what form this may take. If a graduate of one of Belfast's grammar schools applies for a job in Northern Ireland, the first thing his prospective employer will request is his academic record —a perfectly legitimate request. Yet the very name of the applicant's school declares his religious position with a high degree of accuracy, and this information can then be used as a basis for discrimination. How bright the prospects for peaceful coexistence in Ulster can be while children are educated separately is a matter of considerable doubt.

The second controversial issue that stems from Protestant-Catholic theological differences is that of interfaith marriages. Such marriages could provide one means of truly integrating the two communities; yet few take place. The Catholics' attitude toward them, following naturally from what they believe, was set forth as long ago as 1564 in the Council of Trent. Since 1908, the Catholic Church has required that such marriages be solemnized in one of their churches and that both parties signify their agreement to the following points:

(i) There shall be no interference with the religion of the Catholic party or his (or her) practise of it.

(ii) The Catholic party shall endeavour in every reasonable way to bring the non-Catholic partner to the faith.

    (iii)  All the children of the marriage shall be baptized and brought up in the Catholic faith.

    (iv)  The parties shall not present themselves either before or after the Catholic marriage before a non-Catholic minister of religion for any religious ceremony.

[There were some minor modifications resulting from Vatican II.]

The requirement of Catholic education is generally included under the third of these points. Such a declaration is understandably resented strongly by Protestants. To them its rigidity and arrogance, as well as its theology, deny the whole basis of marriage, which is mutual sharing and responsibility. They also point out that, as in education and morality, it is not they but the Catholic Church that, by its rules and regulations, destroys the concept of normal community relations. Such few interfaith marriages as occur are consequently subject to all the pressures of a society that recognizes no compromise position. And these pressures are universally understood. A survey of Queens University students some years ago

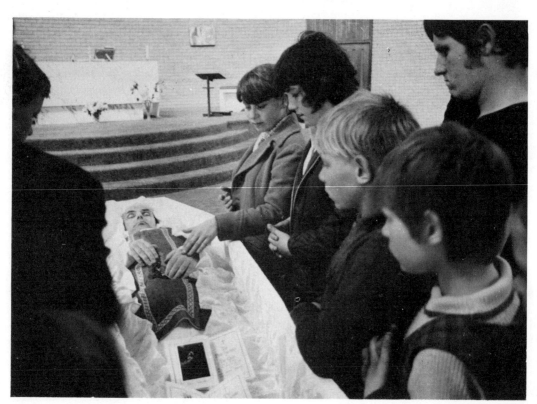

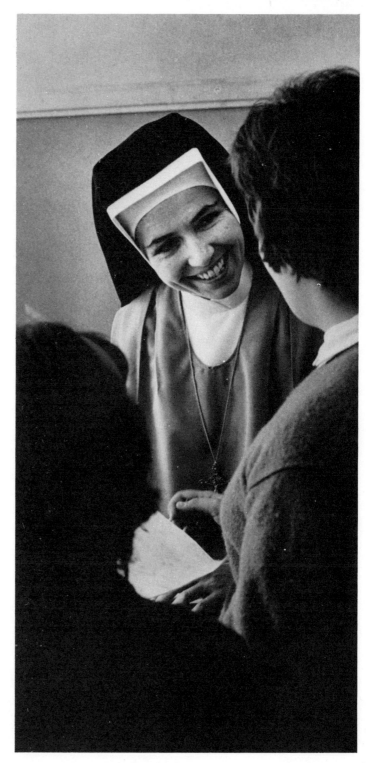

To Catholic children, religion represents a whole way of life.

*Left.* Children file past the body of their priest, Father Mullan of Ballymurphy, killed by a sniper while administering the last rites to a dying man.

*Right.* A teacher-nun talks to pupils at a Roman Catholic school.

showed that, although seventy-eight percent claimed to have friends of the opposite faith, ninety-six percent were against intermarriage between members of the two communities.

The third socially divisive issue arising from the theological divide involves the different standards that govern the private, "moral" lives of the people. With varying degrees of enthusiasm, most Protestants accept such procedures as divorce and artificially induced contraception as an often necessary and unavoidable part of their humanity, and they regulate their lives accordingly. However, not only does the Catholic Church not support such policies; it actively seeks to prevent the Irish government from adopting them. The most famous example of this type of ecclesiastical pressure involved legislation that the then minister of health in Dublin, Dr. Noel Browne, proposed to introduce in 1950. His Mother and Child Bill included free maternity care and education in childbearing, aspects of which offended the church. Dr. Browne, believing that there was nothing in the bill that contravened the church's teaching, refused to withdraw it, and he was subsequently forced to resign. This involvement of the church in the private lives of its members as an extension of its pastoral concern is a completely acceptable activity to many Catholics, though their numbers may be decreasing. On the other hand, such direct moral persuasion is alien to the Protestant tradition. Hence, fear of Catholic-inspired, government-enforced morality is to Protestants another good reason for resisting the establishment of a united Ireland. Likewise, the fact that the political power of the Catholic Church is so great that it could cause the Dublin government to retreat is a specter that haunts most Protestants.

Finally, these different moral standards give rise to real community tensions. Catholic families are often very large and as a result are entitled to a higher proportion of state subsidies than their actual numbers might suggest. This is a continual source of irritation to Protestants, who mutter darkly about Catholics "sponging off the state" and fear that they will eventually be outnumbered in the province simply by being outbred.

Religious differences are thus central to the whole "problem" of Ireland. Yet they are not the only issue, despite what the media would have us believe. Neither are they as insignificant as many conservative Christians would have us think. Religion, along with politics and economics, is a practical factor that divides the population and keeps it divided. Nevertheless, there are many Christians on both sides of that divide, and in this fact lies both the hope for and the tragedy of Ulster. (We will deal with the hope in the next section.) The tragedy is that these Christians generally do not recognize each other's existence. (We say "generally" because recently clergy have begun to get together informally, and Christians in both communities have had common charismatic experiences and prayer services.) That is to say, they have allowed doctrinal differences to assume greater significance in their thinking than the love of God and the unity of the Spirit, which bind both together in the true body of Christ. As a result, Christians have done little to moderate religious intolerance. To the extent that their attitudes reflect the inability of each one of us to show God's love to those with whom we disagree, we all stand condemned.

## ECONOMICS AND SOCIAL HABITS

The two communities in Northern Ireland are inclined to live quite separately, especially in the towns. Perhaps it is worth pointing out, however, that this separatism, though undesirable, is not necessarily sinister. People naturally tend to live near those institutions that occupy a major place in their lives—churches, schools, and places of work. In addition, all of us choose as friends and neighbors people with whom we have things in common. A Catholic Bogside or Protestant Sandy Row is no less preferable in principle than a Jewish Golders Green in London or an Irish district of New York or Boston. They all reflect the human tendency to seek congenial surroundings. And the reasons governing this desire need be no more insidious than those which cause towns to have a rich section or a wrong side of the tracks. This inclination of people to live "with their own kind" means that the two communities also socialize separately. There are sectarian pubs and clubs that by choice as well as location cater almost exclusively to either loyalists or republicans. In both cases the appropriate cultural heritage and the version of Irish history acceptable to the patrons are extolled, often in songs whose words are at best highly offensive to the other side. Fortunately for community relations, like attracts like and complete mayhem is thus averted.

The social differences between the two groups are numerous. One of the most obvious is the divergence of their attitudes toward Sunday. Ulster Protestants are fairly puritanical in their outlook. They dress in their best clothes to go to church, and they generally do little else for the rest of the day. Many would not even work in their gardens on a Sunday. This practice stems from their belief in the ethic of rest on the Sabbath, combined with a strong temperance background. It was brought into sharp focus a few years ago by a furor in Belfast over whether or not children's swings in public parks should continue to be chained up from Saturday evening until Monday morning, as was the custom. Catholics, on the other hand, have a much more flexible approach. They are quite prepared to use Sundays for recreation, provided they have first attended mass. As a result, their sports events, entertainments, and local dances are commonly held in certain parts of Belfast, while the rest of the city is completely closed.

Province-wide, music and arts societies and professional (though usually not amateur) theater groups are mixed, as are such sports as soccer. And boxers are loudly cheered or booed regardless of their places of worship. Rugby and cricket tend to be games that Protestants play; Gaelic football and hurling are decidedly Catholic.

Northern Ireland's economic progress over the past twenty years has been impressive. The government has attracted many new industries to the province by offering financial incentives. This successful policy has ensured a steady increase in manufacturing output. However, the

Unemployment in Northern Ireland is greater than in any other part of the United Kingdom, and adds to community tension. A Catholic father, reviewing his son's prospects said, "When he grows up in Derry, he'll run as a messenger boy like I did. There'll be no jobs, there's no chance. But he's going to fight for work anyway."

problem of persistently heavy unemployment has so far defied solution. Consequently, although the annual rate of growth during 1950-62 was greater than in the rest of the United Kingdom, and real income per capita rose by about one-third, it was still 25% below the national average. Within the community, Protestants are better off than Catholics. (It should be remembered, though, that such a statement is based on average earnings and total unemployment figures. There are also many poor Protestants, but there are fewer middle and high income Catholics than Protestants.) Yet such a situation is not in itself evidence of financial malpractice. The bulk of Northern Ireland's wealth, both industrial and personal, has always been Protestant owned. Similarly, a majority of the province's leaders in all the major aspects of its life are Protestants. Thus, there has been an uneven division of the economic cake from Ulster's inception. That it should still be so merely reflects how inadequate normal economic forces are to produce economic equality, especially if contrary forces are also at work.

The following figures, quoted as examples of this economic disparity, are all drawn from Barritt and Carter's book *The Northern Ireland Problem*. The authors surveyed 2,481 people in Portadown in 1960 and classified them according to the five social class divisions (for employment) used by the registrar-general for England and Wales. Thirteen percent of all Catholics appeared in the top two categories, 55% in the bottom two. Comparable divisions for Protestants were Presbyterians 24% and 26%, Church of Ireland members 24% and 33%, and Methodists 21% and 21%. In 1959, of 740 people who held grades from staff officers up to permanent secretaries in the Northern Ireland Civil Service, 694 or 94% were Protestants. And in the same year a survey of the province's trade unions indicated that 20% of branch secretaries were Catholics and 80% Protestants. However, in the Amalgamated Transport and General Workers Union, with its large unskilled membership, 46% of branch secretaries were Catholics. Comparable figures for the Amalgamated Engineering Union and the Association of Supervisory Staffs, Executives, and Technicians were 12% and 9% respectively. While all these figures may have changed somewhat in the intervening years, the overall balance of wealth has not.

To offset the impression that the Catholics' economic difficulties are all of Protestant making, we should remember the other factors that are involved. Catholic families are generally much larger than Protestant ones, and therefore a given wage buys less per capita. Secondly, any disparity that exists between Catholic schools and state schools tends to favor the state system. Children going through the latter, mainly Protestants, are better equipped to compete for top jobs in the economic marketplace. Thirdly, a higher proportion of Catholics are unemployed because a higher percentage of them are unskilled or semiskilled. Towns such as Londonderry, Newry, Strabane, and Limavady, all heavily Catholic, have always been near the top of the unemployment tables. Each of them is on or near the geographical perimeter of Ulster and far from United Kingdom markets. Consequently, they are not attractive to industrial concerns and investors. How hard the government has tried to overcome this natural handicap, considering the religion of the local citizenry, is a hotly disputed issue. Nevertheless, the advent of large British and foreign firms to Ulster, wherever they are located, must eventually benefit the whole community. Such firms are unencumbered by historical religious preferences and refuse to discriminate.

## PSYCHOLOGY

Fear is a predominant emotion in Ulster today. Nobody knows where the next bomb will go off or who will be its victims. People's nerves are constantly "on edge." Some psychiatrists say that many of the province's children and old people will never fully recover from the emotional trauma of the past few years. Yet fear is only one of two related emotions. The other is insecurity, and it lies at the very heart of the Irish problem. People in both communities feel that the principles they believe in and stand for are being called into question by events beyond their control. As a result they have reacted desperately, using extreme measures, in an attempt to protect the things they hold dear.

Let us consider the Protestants' feelings. They have three main concerns. First, they have little confidence that the rest of Britain understands their problems or is particularly committed to the cause of retaining Ulster within the United Kingdom. Most Protestants fervently believe that they are involved in a struggle against the forces of tyranny, anarchy, and Communism. And they are convinced that if such forces succeed in Ulster they will soon move against the rest of the United Kingdom. Yet they also know that many in Britain do not see things their way. To loyalists, the disbanding of the B-specials (in

The Ulster flag is raised alongside the Union Jack over Belfast City Hall, symbolizing the upsurge of Protestant nationalism as well as dependence upon Britain.

whom most had unquestioning faith and whose demise was felt to be a blatant example of political skulduggery), the desultory prosecution of the IRA by the army, the moves to try to have British troops recalled by an increasing number of English people, and the détente between British and Irish political leaders are all indicators that Britain's resolve to see the conflict through to a satisfactory conclusion is weak. Having endured many hardships to defend their British heritage, the loyalists feel betrayed because they realize that their fellow citizens will not support them unreservedly. The upsurge of Protestant support for a more hard-line position is evidence of the growing distrust with which English politicians are viewed. Recently, much of the Protestant antipathy toward the Liberal party (due to its previous attempts to introduce home rule) has been transferred to the British Labour party because of its statements about Ulster, its leaders, and its place in a united Ireland. At the same time Conservative party politicians have also fallen from favor.

Historically, the Conservative party has supported union with Britain, as indeed it still does. So when the government at Westminster closed down Stormont in 1972, assumed direct control of Ulster's affairs, insisted on political power-sharing in the new assembly, and dared to intern loyalists, the province was stunned—all the more so because the decisions were made by Conservatives. These decisions have so undermined the confidence of many loyalists that they no longer feel able to trust any English politicians or those who work within their guidelines. The recurrent talk of an Ulster unilateral declaration of independence is one result of this distrust; the demand for the return of Stormont is another. Only by following men who have proved their dependability, when so many others have proved untrustworthy, will Ulster Protestants feel secure.

Protestants generally do not so much want total independence as they dread the possible alternatives. At the moment, they feel unable democratically to influence their destiny. Their demand that there be no power-sharing in any new governing body, or, alternatively, for an executive with a large Protestant majority, really expresses their fear that unless they control the apparatus of power they may be sold out. Their opposition to a Council of Ireland stems from the same fear. Until a system is devised that provides the reassurance that a majority of them need, they will not seriously consider the province's future. And in the final analysis this need for reassurance may prove to be paramount. The irony of the present situation is that Protestants will not understand that their intransigence serves only to alienate the British and thus works against the very things they so desperately want.

The second insecurity is economic. The Protestants' dominance in Ulster rests in part on the fact that they have always controlled the economy. Traditionally, that economy was based on linen, ship-building, and agriculture. However, all of these industries are now declining, due to world-wide competition. Linen has been supplanted by man-made fibres; ship-building has decreased, but other countries have modernized their yards more quickly and now attract an increasing share of the business; small acreage farming simply does not pay in the modern world.

The consequences of these changes in Ulster have been high unemployment and continuous massive infusions of capital from Westminster. Neither of these factors has boosted Protestant self-confidence. The former is not only socially undesirable; it also increases economic pressure by raising the social security budget. At the same time, the unemployed—a high proportion of whom are Catholics —have the necessary time and motivation to foment trouble. Secondly, Ulster's financial dependence on Britain is now so great that the province has effectively lost economic control, and therefore political control, of its own future. This realization increases the Protestants' feelings of political insecurity, an insecurity supplemented by the difficulty in enticing replacement industries to a violent and divided land.

Finally, Protestants consider anyone who advocates or works for a united Ireland a direct and personal threat. This goal remains offensive and totally unacceptable to them for the political, theological, and social reasons already explained. And it may be that the strength of their feelings is increased by the suspicion that their refusal to compromise and join forces with the South is a losing cause. History seems to indicate that many movements similar to that for a united Ireland have eventually succeeded. Whatever the reasons, the Protestants' militant anti-Catholicism is bolstered by fear that the tide of social history will engulf Northern Ireland too. The insecurity that this uncertainty breeds, the belief that they are alone and caught up in a conflict they may not be able to win, could yet drive the Protestants to the ultimate extreme of total civil war in a last desperate attempt to secure the peace with justice they so passionately want.

Northern Ireland's Catholics are unhappy because they see themselves as second-class citizens in an alien and hostile society, and they point out that their physical safety was seriously threatened in 1969. While they may regret the loss of life resulting from IRA activities, many defend it as the only agency able and willing to protect them. In their view, even the army, whom they initially welcomed as liberators, turned out to be nothing more than repressive government agents. The insecurity of their status as Ulster citizens is frequently brought home to them. Within the framework of the law they are treated equally; yet they maintain that this equality does not obtain in practice. *The Cameron Commission's Report on Disturbances in Northern Ireland* stressed the role of local government grievances in formenting trouble. It commented on:

Personal support for the Rev. Ian Paisley. His unequivocal stand helps to combat the insecurity many Ulster Protestants feel.

(1) A rising sense of continuing injustice and grievance among large sections of the Catholic population in Northern Ireland, in particular in Londonderry and Dungannon, in respect of (i) inadequacy of housing provision by certain local authorities, (ii) unfair methods of allocation of houses built and let by such authorities, in particular, refusals and omissions to adopt a "points" system in determining priorities and making allocations, (iii) misuse in certain cases of discretionary powers of allocation of houses in order to perpetuate Unionist control of the local authority. . . .

(2) Complaints, now well documented in fact, of discrimination in the making of local government appointments, at all levels but especially in senior posts, to the prejudice of non-Unionists and especially Catholic members of the community, in some Unionist controlled authorities. . . .

(3) Complaints, again well documented, in some cases of deliberate manipulation of local government electoral boundaries and in others a refusal to apply for their necessary extension, in order to achieve and maintain Unionist control of local authorities and so to deny to Catholics influence in local government proportionate to their numbers. . . .

(4) A growing and powerful sense of resentment and frustration among the Catholic population at failure to achieve either acceptance on the part of the Government of any need to investigate these complaints or to provide and enforce a remedy for them. . . .

In order that the above quotation not be misleading, one

must be careful to note that the grievances in (1) were "in respect of certain local authorities" and the complaints in (2) and (3) were against "some" local authorities. Such authorities, it was made clear, were a minority. However, it is a sad fact that the actions of this minority have produced widespread resentment far beyond their local boundaries. Nor is this surprising if one believes that oppression by legally constituted authority is one of the most insidious forms of human debasement. Although these criticisms were accepted by Stormont and action was taken to correct them, the bitterness and frustration they caused cannot be banished with the stroke of a pen. Nor is it reasonable that Protestants should be indignant over the continuing resentment, bearing in mind how long the abuses were allowed to remain unchecked.

The initial use of the Special Powers Act almost exclusively against Catholics heightened the insecurity they already felt. To them internment was the ultimate weapon

Bad living conditions contribute largely to the continuing problems of the community.

There are no playing fields or parks for the children of the Bogside. Catholics claim that the Protestant minority in Londonderry held on to power by gerrymandering, and as a result Catholics were crammed into certain wards of the city.

of a tyrannical government determined to suppress their legitimate, but in some cases violently illegal, opposition to that government. And the more recent jailing of Protestants has in no way assuaged their anger. Thus, the time came when even moderate Catholics found themselves driven to extremes—into the arms of the IRA—because they had no one else to trust. It could well be argued that the SDLP's contribution to peace has been its ability to reassure Catholics that their rights and their future can be protected legally and democratically.

It is axiomatic among many Catholics that economic history is repeating itself in Ulster. Just as England kept Ireland in economic subjection for centuries, they believe, Protestants are trying to keep them poor also. Many of them resent having to depend on the state and its social services for survival. They resent it first because the social security payments are vitally necessary to many of them. Yet Catholics are constantly aware that the payments are drawn from a community purse that is Protestant controlled. They may be subconsciously afraid that in a direct confrontation these necessary funds would be withheld. Secondly, they resent being dependent on subsidies from a state whose very existence a large number of them would like to destroy.

Those desiring work would claim that in seeking jobs they encounter employers with the mentality represented by Lord Brookeborough's remarks (cited earlier) or the mentality of the person who placed the following advertisement in a Belfast newspaper a few years ago: "Wanted—Reliable cook—general. Protestant (Christian preferred)." Catholics do "look after their own" also; they simply have less scope in which to do so and therefore come out of the battle of segregated economics less successfully. There can be little doubt that there are too few jobs with prospects of advancement to significant seniority and real fulfillment for Catholics. This constitutes a major factor in undermining their commitment to the province.

Finally, Catholic insecurity stems in part from their desire, latent or overt, to be part of a united Ireland. The clamor for instant reunification has diminished lately on both sides of the border, for political and economic reasons. The latter are particularly difficult to overcome with respect to the standards of living and social services available in the North and South. Northern Catholics would be much worse off economically if Ireland were to be reunited tomorrow. Nevertheless, the long-term desire of the people's hearts appears to be unshaken. And this eats away at the roots which a number of them have genuinely tried to put down in Ulster. For it is humanly impossible for a person to commit himself emotionally to one goal while at the same time he is striving to achieve an opposite one. Such competing loyalties invariably breed insecurity.

From Ulster's inception, when Catholics refused to cooperate in the founding of the state, they have generally held back part of themselves for Ireland. On the whole, they have not strived to be assimilated into the province, preferring rather to retain a separate and corporate identity. From their point of view, this desire to live lives centered in the church rather than the state and to aspire to a united Ireland is perfectly understandable and legitimate. However, it is equally understandable that it has evoked deep suspicion and resentful anger in those to whom the state means so much. Because of these attitudes, Ireland's future cannot be isolated from her past, regardless of how much any of us wishes it could.

The essayist Robert Lynd once wrote that all history is but a repetition of the same story with variations. In one important respect this was true of Catholics after the riots of August 12-14, 1969. In 1914, Irish politicians agreed to defer home rule, but some of their rank and file members refused to follow their lead and staged the 1916 rebellion. In 1921, the politicians accepted a political solution to the

Irish problem, but a large sector of their constituents would not accept it and resorted to violence. In 1969, the official IRA in the North was advocating political change and eschewing violence. Yet the very violence of August 1969 undermined its authority; out of the ashes of Bombay Street arose the provisional IRA, who like their predecessors in 1916 and 1921 rejected words for the persuasion of the gun. Never again, they vowed, would Catholics try to accommodate with the hated Protestants; now they would take what they wanted by force. What has happened since that night is too painfully fresh in the memory to bear repeating in detail.

- The B-specials were disbanded and the police disarmed over Protestant protests.
- IRA gunmen took to the streets in a chilling battle with the army.
- The Ulster Defence Association became increasingly militant.
- More and more British troops went to Ulster— and were killed.
- Parts of Belfast and Derry became "no-go" areas and were subsequently "liberated" in Operation Motorman.
- Ordinary, harmless people died.
- There were allegations of and inquiries into army and police brutality.
- There was "Bloody Sunday," when citizens of Derry lost their lives after the army took offensive action to disperse crowds and seek out gunmen.
- There was "Bloody Friday," when Belfast suffered a reign of indiscriminate bombings.

Long Kesh prison camp, where many IRA and some Protestant terrorists have been interned.

The presence of the British Army in Northern Ireland. Paratroopers frisk Bogside rioters at gunpoint. Ordinary city streets are occupied territory.

*Right top.* Troops try to maintain good relations with the people whenever possible.

*Below.* Human reactions among the troops in action. A young trooper in tears is led away by an understanding superior.

This is a people's war.
*Left.* Girls armed with a revolver and an American Armalite rifle play their part in the guerilla warfare. A grim masked figure guards the barricades in a city street. A boy wearing gas-mark and badge prepares to throw his handmade petrol bomb.

And the innocent are often the victims.
*Above.* A woman whose hand was injured in a bomb blast is helped away by a member of the Royal Ulster Constabulary. Peter Gallaher carries the coffin of his baby daughter Angela, killed by a terrorist's bullet.

- People hoped and then were disappointed when ceasefires lasted only a few weeks.
- There was and is internment.
- The government at Stormont was suspended, and a British minister of state was appointed to oversee the province.
- More people died.
- There were the Catholic rent strikes, tartan gangs, Vanguard, the Loyalist Association of Workers, the Catholic Women's Peace Committee, Sean MacStiophan's hunger strike, the Darlington Conference, the border plebiscite, the Abercorn restaurant bomb, backlash, Ulster freedom fighters, Communist arms, a new government in Dublin, the Price sisters, tar and feathers.
- The new Northern Ireland Assembly saw the election of three main political groupings, Unionists, Conservative Unionists (Paisleyites), who were

against some of the British proposals that established them, and the Social Democratic and Labour party, the near unanimous voice of the Catholics. The moderate Alliance party substantially failed to draw voters away from their sectarian past, and the IRA was nowhere. The assembly failed and direct rule was reintroduced.

- The IRA bombing campaign moved to England.
- There were resentment, bitterness, and violence, endless discussion and argument, and millions of pounds' worth of damage.
- But overshadowing all else, hundreds of people were killed, maimed, and injured.

Life in Northern Ireland continues to be complex and unyielding. Two groups of people, with loyalties that affect their very beings, find themselves at loggerheads. They neither understand nor trust each other and make little attempt to do so, for each in his own way feels vulnerable. Perhaps it is unreasonable to expect that an eight-hundred-year-old problem will be solved in the space of a few months. Yet the suspicion lingers that unless Protestants and Catholics, Irishmen and Englishmen, stop blaming each other and start examining and reassessing the relative importance of the principles they hold dear, Ireland's future must remain shrouded in gloom and uncertainty.

The bombing campaign moves to England. The scene in Oxford Street, London, after a bomb exploded in a store.

# 4 THE RELEVANCE OF CHRISTIANITY

*THE REAL POLITICAL* questions facing Ireland today are similar to the ones raised in America more than a century ago: What rights should a substantial and permanent minority possess in their dealings with the majority? Is democracy as we know it in Western civilization sensitive and flexible enough to protect minority interests? How can two communities, whose views are largely mutually exclusive, and yet who are forced to live together, reach a political accommodation acceptable to both? We believe that the only way in which such disparate groups can live together peacefully is through a willingness to accommodate and to compromise with each other. That necessity was finally recognized by Irish migrants and native Yankees in nineteenth-century America. It has still to be learned by their kinfolk at home during the latter part of the twentieth century.

The conflict in Northern Ireland is a microcosm of the difficulties of life in the modern Western world: the tensions that occur when the historic force of migration brings together people of different religions and races; the distortions in men's relationships when they respond to the competition for material goods in a society that places a high value on their attainment; the problems of operating a democracy when minorities seek to change the society by violent means. How Christianity fares in that context should be of interest to both Christians and non-Christians in Northern Ireland and throughout the world, because for all parties the question is the same: Does Christianity have any relevance?

We believe that Christianity *does* have a profound relevance for Northern Ireland, as it does for all mankind. Our aim in this final chapter is twofold: to suggest that a society of greater justice will obtain in Northern Ireland insofar as Christianity, as opposed to religion, becomes a predominant influence in the province; and to suggest that Christians should function "in the world" in order to witness to God's justice, the sort of justice he requires in his created world.

## I

In an effort to understand Christianity's relevance to the future of Northern Ireland we must begin by considering the political options proposed for the province. Some of the options command more support than others, but listing all of them reveals the wide variety of opinions that currently exist.

   (a) a unilateral declaration of independence by Ulster, leaving no political ties with either Britain or Eire

   (b) a return to the pre-1968 status quo, i.e., effective government solely in Protestant hands

   (c) a total integration of Ulster with the rest of the United Kingdom, in the manner of Wales and Scotland

   (d) the establishment of an executive within a Northern Ireland in which Protestant and Catholic participation would be proportionate to their respective political strengths.

   (e) a federated all-Ireland republic in which regional parliaments in Belfast and Dublin would retain substantial control over regional matters, while both would yield other powers to a federal parliament in regard to "national" matters

   (f) a socialist all-Ireland republic in which the traditional politics of both Belfast and Dublin would be entirely swept away

   (g) a total integration of Ulster with the rest of Ireland under a liberal, secular constitution

Throughout this book we have tried to portray objectively the views of the two sides in the conflict as fairly as possible. We have no intention of departing from that practice at this stage. Nevertheless, a few comments on each of these options from a Christian perspective is appropriate.

There are two peoples living in Ireland, each of whom has historic identities, rights, and interests that must be safeguarded constitutionally. If they are not so protected, the integrity of the individuals in one or both groups will inevitably be undermined. We believe that such a damaging process is a denial of the whole basis of Christianity. As a result, Christians should feel unable to support any political arrangements that do not uphold all aspects of human dignity.

In view of the annual grant from the British exchequer of around 400 million pounds (one billion dollars), it is highly doubtful that Ulster could sustain independence —proposal (a)—especially since it has always been assumed that such an independence would be Protestant dominated as would be the arrangements envisioned in proposal (b). Proposal (f) is supported by only a small minority of extreme republicans. Christian concern, should

A soup kitchen for all comers, during the famine in 1847, run by the Cork Society of Friends (the Quakers).

any of these proposals be adopted, would center on the social and constitutional arrangements likely to prevail under them. The new constitutions would probably not recognize the need to give full civil rights to all people. In fact, for the new state to survive under these proposals, its constitution would almost certainly have to suppress a sizable permanent minority and deprive them of effective means of legally influencing their destiny. Christians, however, must oppose the notion that numerical superiority and might make right.

Any of the other four proposals might, in principle, be acceptable to Christians, depending on the details that ultimately emerged. Proposal (c) has the advantage that it would more effectively guarantee the "Britishness" of Ulster on the one hand, and the civil rights of its minority on the other. Its drawback is that many persons in the rest of Great Britain would see it as blocking their desire to be rid of Ireland once and for all. Proposal (d), which was essentially the assembly system plus representation of the more loyalist elements, and (e) both recognize the

The church is intimately affected by the conflict.

*Left.* A local church becomes a temporary mortuary.

*Right.* A church is vandalized.

essential differences existing among Irish people. In different ways they seek to bring the two groups together while allowing both to retain their historic identities, rights, and interests. Finally, proposal (g) would require a much greater degree of separation between church and state in the Irish Republic than presently obtains. If this were successfully accomplished and accompanied by economic measures to ensure that Ulster people suffered no decrease in the standards of their social services, then in principle there would be no Christian basis for opposing this proposal. Its adoption, however, is not now a viable alternative, irrespective of whether or not it should ever be so.

Having said this, we would like to reassert emphatically that we have no prescription for the political and social future of the Irish peoples. We say only that, given the historic presence of two peoples on the island, the only way in which they may begin to live together in peace is to acknowledge that they are different peoples, and to recognize and guarantee constitutionally that the aspirations of both communities, if they cannot be mutually realized, can and must be accorded equal and legitimate redress of grievances. If Ireland is to have a future, some consensus

must emerge in which majorities of the two peoples decide that they can live and work together.

## II

As Christians we believe that all men are created in the image of God, and although the fact of sin has tarnished that image, it has not been erased. This belief is so basic to Christianity that all Christians, regardless of sectarian differences, must surely share it. Thus, if men bear the image of God, they all have equal worth in his sight. God is not a respecter of persons: from his viewpoint we are a community of equals. The Decalogue given in the Old Testament was intended to guide us in our communal living and to provide for us a framework within which we are all accountable to God. The New Testament extension of the law by Jesus Christ expresses accountability not only to God but to each other. We are instructed to do to others as we would have them do to us, and to love our neighbours as ourselves. There is no suggestion that God expects some people to be accorded greater or lesser respect or dignity than others.

On the other hand, while men are equal they are not the same, and we should value individual differences as assiduously as God does. Therefore, when men come to organize their societies, they must preserve man's created equality as well as his individual differences. A just society will not admit to one faction holding predominant sway over another, nor to one faction requiring the others to reject the differences that stem from their humanity. God abhors tyranny, whether it be the tyranny of the bomb and bullet, of discriminatory legislation, of intimidation and coercion, or of the denial of freedom of worship. God requires justice, and justice cannot coexist with tyranny, although the way in which God's justice is applied will certainly vary with time and place. Whatever the form of social order, however, Christians are by the very nature of their faith committed to promote justice; to work for the equality of men, while safeguarding their individuality, both of which are precious in God's sight. With specific reference to Northern Ireland, it goes almost without saying that Christians should support those constitutional forms that would promote justice, and totally reject any and all forms that would limit or prevent it.

We realize that human sin works against the accomplishment of justice on this earth. Consequently, social justice will be more nearly approximated as men are changed through being reconciled to God by Christ. As previously noted, Ulster has a higher percentage of church-going people than most other parts of the world. Why then has all of Northern Ireland's religion not caused an improvement in social relations over the years? Why has it instead become the axis of the conflict? Critics might well scoff, pointing out that we are suggesting that "religion has failed — give us more religion." Yes, religion *has* failed. What we are calling for, however, is not more religion. We are rather calling for Christianity, for religion and Christianity are not the same thing.

There are many critics of Christianity who believe that we would do better to forget religion and live together in peace, rather than be the kind of "Christians" who cannot live with each other. We have heard several people suggest that Ulster would be much better off if Christianity were abolished. Television documentaries, shown in both Britain and America, spoke of "Christians at war," and it may appear to many people throughout the world that this phrase sums up what is happening in Northern Ireland today. Such a viewpoint is mistaken, again because religion is not the same thing as Christianity.

Defining a Christian is not difficult. He or she is one who believes Jesus' claim to be the Son of God. He has new life in Christ, depending for this and for forgiveness for his sinful past on the death and resurrection of Jesus Christ, living it out in daily faith in God, in fellowship with others in the church, and in his whole daily life and pattern of thinking. The Spirit of God dwells in him and becomes the motivating force in a life dedicated to serving God in whatever area of life is his calling, and in all his human relationships.

Defining a "religious" person, however, is more difficult. For reasons not altogether clear, there is a large number of people who either agree to church membership or give nominal assent to the "belief system" of Christianity without considering the claims of God on their lives. It is not our purpose to judge these people, whether in Ireland, Britain, or America; we only observe that they exist—a fact Jesus anticipated when he noted that there

Refugees from the fighting, of whatever party, can find safety in St Clement's Retreat House, Belfast, run by Catholics.

would be on the final day many pseudo-believers who would protest vigorously their religious loyalty.

The fact is that substantial confusion exists in the minds of many persons, both in Europe and America, both inside and outside the church, on this matter of distinguishing between "Christian" and "religious." Also, the universal usage of the terms "Protestant" and "Catholic" in Northern Ireland, without regard for theological accuracy, tends to mask the reality that in both groups there are Christians as well as religious people. In both Protestant and Catholic religious groups one can identify (a) religious church-goers, (b) Christians, and (c) those who seldom if ever attend church. The last, while essentially irreligious, will happily accept a denominational label because they believe it describes their heritage. The first are the large number of "religious" people who would call themselves "Christian" (and would call Ulster a "Christian" nation), but whose definition of Christianity does not intersect with the biblical one.

We would like to emphasize that we believe these divisions occur within *both* Protestant and Catholic groups; and because this is so, it is invalid to portray the religious/ Christian dimension of Ulster's problems in simple sectarian terms. Even less acceptable is the suggestion that Christianity is at the root of the conflict; indeed, we would suggest that precisely the opposite is so. Unfortunately, however, these distinctions are not always clear in the public mind, and if Christians do not make them clear, Christianity will continue to be brought into disrepute by the "religious" connections of Northern Ireland.

## III

The New Testament makes it plain that Christians are required forthrightly to identify themselves with Christ and his righteousness. This is more than ever essential in face of the necessity, if occasion demands, of disassociating Christianity from those acts performed in the name of religion. All the pressures within any church group are to conform to the majority opinion, to avoid conflict which might divide the fellowship. The result can be a ghetto situation. But this will not do. The rigid religio-sociological barriers must be broken down so that Christians can have fellowship with one another. Christians must cross sectarian barriers — and many are doing so, despite misunderstanding and acrimony; despite the fact that any move toward the "other side" in a tense situation such as that in Northern Ireland, even on an individual basis, often renders a Christian doctrinally and politically suspect in the eyes of both his friends and his enemies.

The historical, social and political barriers which restrict the scope of Christian fellowship and cooperation, while fully understandable from the human point of view, run counter to the declared purpose of God. By the inflexible separation of the Christians of Northern Ireland into Protestant and Catholic groups the body of Christ has been divided — and this worldwide division tears relentlessly at the oneness and unity that all believers should enjoy in Jesus Christ. We recognize, of course, that the theological and doctrinal differences are real and profound and cannot be wished away by desires for Christian unity. Indeed, it is precisely the depth and breadth of those differences, when allied to political principles and practices, that have created a situation in which many Christians have become isolated within their own sectarian communities. However, Christians are committed to breaking down the barriers, to working for new social structures which make Christian fellowship — and indeed normal human relationships — possible between the two communities. Real differences exist and cannot be ignored, but Christians have a unifying factor: those who love and trust in Jesus Christ share "one Lord, one faith, one birth." They are required to seek areas of reconciliation in which this pre-eminent fact can be given practical expression. Christian believers are the best hope for Northern Ireland because they and only they, both Protestant and Catholic, have a bond that genuinely transcends sectarian strife.

Protestant and Catholic Christians in Ulster, contrary to popular opinion, are not entirely divorced from one another. There are many good neighbours and friends who pay scant attention to each other's denominational affiliation. Some Protestant and Catholic clergymen and laity, for instance, have begun informal prayer together. Members of both groups have met, worked and discussed together at Corrymeila. And the charismatic movement has challenged traditional attitudes in both communities. All of these interactions tend to reduce the barriers between the communities, and through these and other activities can be discerned the brightest rays of hope for Northern Ireland. This hope is not necessarily for ecclesiastical union, and certainly not for a Protestant return to the fold of Rome. It lies, rather, in the fellowship of groups of individual Christians and in the outpouring of the Spirit of God in the hearts of those who love, trust, and seek to obey God.

Corrymeela, originally conceived by Presbyterian students at Queen's University, is a community dedicated to reconciliation in Northern Ireland.

*Right.* Archbishop Donald Coggan with children from Belfast during a recent visit.

*Below.* A work-camp in progress.

Under a simple wooden cross, Catholics and Protestants meet and begin to understand one another, and accept that each is a person "made in the image of God".

Nonetheless we must all confess as Christians that very often our quest for doctrinal truth has not been balanced with a desire for the grace which characterized the Master we seek to follow. We do not have a winsomeness of spirit toward those who disagree with us. We show little loving tolerance toward those who interpret Scripture differently from us. The meekness, kindness, and generosity exemplifying Jesus' attitude toward his "enemies" is sadly an attitude that is imitated very poorly by his followers. In a situation where doctrinal issues are hotly debated — as in Northern Ireland — the graceless tendency we all recognize within ourselves is frequently taken to its extreme.

The world has a right to look for evidence of a God-centered and God-controlled life in every Christian. It is this which has to be added to the Christian's claim to have a distinctive message if the world is to recognize that Jesus Christ is Lord. Only then will people be able to tell real Christianity from Christless religion, something which is little more than a sociological category, and whose adherents are basically no different from the rest of humanity.

**IV**

But what if many of the "religious" people in Northern Ireland do not turn to the "newness of life available in Christ"? Does this make Christianity irrelevant in Ulster? On the contrary. All Christians, as we have already stressed, are by the very nature of their faith thrust into the social and political arena and must work for justice within it. It is not a matter of *either* preaching the individual gospel of salvation *or* working for social justice. The Christian is called to do both.

In the Sermon on the Mount, Jesus described Christians as "the salt of the earth" — a description which does not allow us to opt out of society. We have no choice in the matter. Christianity entails not only an individual's personal relationship with God but also involves the whole of his life on this earth. There are no distinctions because no human activities are more or less important in the total witness that Christians should bring to the world. God's sovereign purposes are here and now advanced by and through the total witness of his people. As his people, therefore, Christians must witness to God's grace and his kingdom, which will surely come. This kingdom is not merely a spiritual one confined to men's hearts. The Christian message points to a kingdom which will eventually be a whole new creation. It will lay claim to every aspect of human life, including political structures. As Richard J. Mouw has written in *Political Evangelism:*

> The New Testament's use of a political metaphor to describe the sum of God's redemptive purposes indicates that the total transformation of all things which God intends for his creation includes a transformation of the political realm. . . . The political sphere is not merely an area in which a Christian *can* be a witness; it is one in which we are *called* to proclaim the liberating power of the gospel.

A word of caution is in order here. It is easy for any person to sit in judgment on other people. Most of us can see the flaws in others while overlooking our own glaring faults. Yet Jesus commanded that we not judge others lest we ourselves be judged. Thus, it is not our purpose to criticize or censure the Christians of Northern Ireland. Any conclusions that we may draw concerning their attitudes and behavior are based on the premise that, if Christianity has relevance for Northern Ireland, it must apply to the observers as well as to the observed. When we engage in the quest for Christian social justice, we must be careful not to preface our own ideas with "thus saith the Lord." As Christians, we must recognize our own fallibility, and we should not dogmatically identify specific proposals for Northern Ireland's future as the will of God. Both the goal and our method of seeking it should reflect the character and teaching of God and should accord with his revealed purposes. The only political and social systems Christians can support will, by their nature, allow people to be treated equally and fairly and will recognize their individual and collective differences. In the final analysis it must be the peoples of Northern Ireland who come together in some workable consensus on which a majority of them agree.

Finally, we say: Let there be peace in Northern Ireland. Even as we acknowledge that peace is more likely to come as individuals begin working together as Christians, rather than as Protestants and Catholics, we also plead that all Christians—in Ulster, Eire, Britain, the United States, and Canada—begin praying for and witnessing not only to individuals but to institutional structures about the liberating power of the gospel. If such collective witnessing could begin, we would all be closer to the day in which we will no longer have to bear the burden of Northern Ireland. In pointing to the coming kingdom of God, we will be pointing to a political and social situation in which the kingdoms of the world will become the kingdoms of our Lord and of his Christ, and in which every knee shall bow in declaration of Christ's lordship, and in which there is no Greek or Jew, no Protestant or Catholic, no bond or free, but his people will be a fellowship that will "glorify God and enjoy him forever."

# SUGGESTIONS FOR FURTHER READING

Barritt, D.P. and Carter, C.F., *The Northern Ireland Problem*. London: Oxford University Press, 1962.

Beckett, J.C., *A Short History of Ireland*. London: Hutchinson University Library, 1973 (5th ed.).

Boyd, A., *Holy War in Belfast*. Dublin: Anvil Books, 1969.

Duffy, J., *The Irish in the United States*. Belmont, Calif.: Wadsworth, 1971.

Handlin, O., *Boston's Immigrants*. Cambridge, Mass.: Harvard University Press, 1959 (rev. ed.).

Kennedy, E.M., "Ulster is an International Issue," *Foreign Policy*, Number 11 (Summer, 1973), 57-71.

Mouw, R., *Political Evangelism*. Grand Rapids: Eerdmans, 1974.

*Report of the Cameron Commission on Disturbance in Northern Ireland*. Her Majesty's Stationery Office, 1969.

Wallace, M., *Northern Ireland — Fifty Years of Self-government*. Newton Abbot: David and Charles, 1971; New York: Barnes & Noble, 1971.

Wittke, C., *The Irish in America*. Baton Rouge: Louisiana State University Press, 1956.

# The Third Brother

ALSO BY THE AUTHOR

*Twelve*

# The Third
# Brother

A novel

by

Nick McDonell

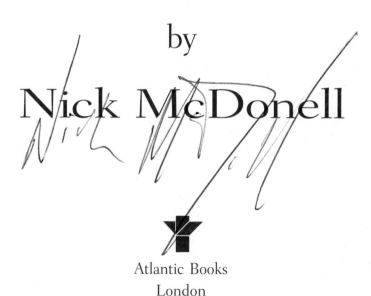

Atlantic Books
London

First published in 2005 in the United States of America by Grove Press, an imprint of Grove/Atlantic, Inc.

First published in Great Britain in trade paperback in 2006 by Atlantic Books, an imprint of Grove Atlantic Ltd.

9 8 7 6 5 4 3 2 1

A CIP catalogue record for this book is available from the British Library.

Trade paperback ISBN  1 84354 477 6

Printed in Great Britain by MPG Books Ltd, Bodmin, Cornwall

Atlantic Books
An imprint of Grove Atlantic Ltd
Ormond House
26–27 Boswell Street
London WC1N 3JZ

To my mother

# The Third Brother

# PART I

*Mike was privileged and troubled at the same time. He knew that if you grow up with money you don't think about being rich, and that the same is probably true of courage. But if you grow up with lies, you find out that some lies become true. Mike knew this, too, and so did not lie. Except to himself, about his parents.*

*They were husband and wife but sometimes mistaken for siblings. They could have been carved out of the same piece of alabaster. Mike inherited the long high planes of their cheekbones, and he loved his parents in a very conscious way. They were both troubled themselves, and their trouble accelerated Mike's childhood. He had seen them at their worst, violent and irrational, naked in public, smooth features contorted. In his reckoning as a young man, though, they were fine, and he had decided, in the face of their madness and addictions, that he loved them. And his life was his own.*

# 1

The summer is dragging for Mike as he rises, by escalator, out of the cool subway into the Hong Kong heat. He is too tall, out of place as he crosses the jammed street to Taikoo Tower, where he has been working for six weeks. Seems like a year. The tower looms over him, silent workers and pulsing technology, a kingdom of itself above the Hong Kong streets. Mike doesn't like the skyscraper—it has become predictable—but he is grateful for the air-conditioning. Everything inside the tower works. Outside, not. His job, his internship, is at a news magazine that he had never read until the twenty-two-hour flight from New York.

Mike has several bosses at the magazine, but the reason he has the job is that the managing editor, Elliot Analect, is a friend of his father. Analect even looks like his father, Mike realized when they shook hands. All of those guys look alike, all tall, clean, white guys who have known one another for decades. They were in the same club at Harvard, wore the same ties. And then they went to Vietnam and almost all of them came back. Growing up, Mike didn't see his father's friends much but he had the sense they were in touch. So when it was time for his first internship, the summer after his freshman year, Mike was not surprised that he ended up working for Analect. He was glad, at least, that the job was in Hong Kong and not in midtown Manhattan.

As a summer intern, Mike seldom gets out of the office, spends his days wading the Internet. He is doing research, mostly for Thomas Bishop, one of the magazine's correspondents. Mike has a view of Analect's office and sometimes watches his father's old friend through the smoked-glass walls, but they have had little contact since that initial welcome handshake. And the most excitement Mike has had was when Analect abruptly spoke with him in the hallway, promising to take him out to lunch at the end of the summer. Strange, Mike thinks, and wishes there was more for him to do. As he surfs the Internet he thinks about fathers and sons, and how friendship does not necessarily pass down. Mike has already seen this often among his friends and their fathers.

So Mike is glad when the assignment comes, even though he is very surprised. He had been watching again, and Analect had been standing in conversation with Bishop for nearly ten minutes. Mike had been looking closely through the glass—he sensed the men were angry with one another—when Bishop suddenly turned and opened the door. Mike feared he was caught, but then Bishop waved him into the office and Analect asked if he wanted to go to Bangkok. "Help Tommy with some reporting," as he put it.

Bishop nods slightly at Mike. Bishop is a small man, with fat features and prematurely graying black hair.

"The story is backpacker kids going to Bangkok to do ecstasy," Analect says. "Just don't get arrested."

"He doesn't want to have to retrieve you," Bishop says.

"It's really just a travel story, is another way to look at it," Analect goes on.

"Just a travel story," Bishop repeats, chuckling.

"You're their age," Analect continues, "the backpackers'. You'll be good at talking to them. Ask questions. It can be your story too. And one other thing I've already explained to Tommy . . ."

Mike catches Bishop rolling his eyes.

". . . I want you to find Christopher Dorr."

Mike can't place the name.

"He used to do a lot of the investigative pieces Tommy does now," Analect says, looking straight at him, seeming almost to ignore Bishop. "He's been in Bangkok for a while, I think. It'd be good for someone from the magazine to look him up."

Mike tries to decode this and can't. Analect tells him again to stay out of trouble and that Bishop will take care of him. It seems to Mike that Bishop is pleased to have the help, but that there is more to it. When they are leaving the office, Analect tells Mike to wait for a moment, and when they are alone, he tells Mike that Dorr had been a friend of Mike's father, years ago. That they had all been good friends, actually, the three of them practically brothers, and that Mike's father would be glad for news of Dorr.

Mike looks out the window. He notices for the first time how really extraordinary the view from Analect's office is. Mike can see the whole city, enormous and smogged and throbbing. For a moment he can't believe the sound of it doesn't blow in the windows. But Analect's office sits quietly above it all, humming coolly. Mike is suddenly uneasy, with only the inch of glass between the two of them and the loud, empty space above the city. He looks back at Analect, who is frowning.

"Dorr and your father were sparring partners, when they boxed back in college," says Analect.

Mike looks back out over the city. He knew about the boxing, but his father had never mentioned Dorr. It all surprises him, but maybe it's just seeing his own features reflected in the glass, and the long drop to Hong Kong from fifty stories up.

# 2

When Mike was a small boy, his parents often entertained. In New York City in their world, they were famous for the dinners they gave in their big beach house at the end of Long Island, especially Thanksgiving. Mike remembered the candlelight and gluey cranberry sauce, which he would wipe off his hands into his hair. His older brother, Lyle, remembered the same things. There were servants, who disciplined Mike when his parents did not. One Filipino lady in particular boxed his ears. When he was older he remembered how it hurt but not her name. Their parents gave these dinners several years in a row. There were mostly the same guests, adults who would tousle Mike's fine but cranberried hair, and their children, a crew of beautiful, spoiled playmates whom Mike assumed he would know forever. He still saw some of them, at parties and dinners of their own on school breaks. At hearing that one or two of them had slid into addiction, Mike would remember chasing them through his mother's busy kitchen. His mother was never in the kitchen, of course, but it was definitely hers. Small paintings of vegetables and an antique mirror hung on its walls.

When dinner started, the children would go to the playroom and eat with the nannies. They lounged on overstuffed couches, watching movies until they fell asleep and the nannies went outside for cigarettes. Lyle especially loved these dinners and made a point of talking to everybody, lingering in the dining room rather than watching movies with the other children. He loved listening to adults talk. So did Mike, but he knew he didn't understand the way his older brother did.

The adults sat and drank wine and laughed and smiled at one another in the fall candlelight. Many of them had started families late or had been married once before and had only recently started new ones. Jobs were interesting; there was much travel. There was a lot to talk about, and the subtext was that they were lucky to have the lives they had. Mike remembered everyone being very happy.

Before one of these dinners, Lyle decided that he and Mike would be spies. Lyle had gotten a small tape recorder, only a toy really, for his birthday earlier that fall. Their plan was to hide it in the dining room to record the dinner conversation. While the servants were setting up, and Mike's mother was upstairs dressing and Mike's father was out walking along the ocean, Lyle and Mike secured the tape recorder under the table with duct tape.

As the guests arrived and had drinks, the boys slid between them and crawled under the table and switched on the recorder.

They were very excited all through dinner, but they didn't tell any of the other children what they were up to. By dessert, Mike couldn't wait any longer. He wanted to go get the recorder. No, said Lyle, they'll be there for a long time. Let's just look.

When they peeked around the dining room door, Elliot Analect saw them and held up the tape recorder, which he must have found much earlier, maybe when he first sat down. Analect wasn't a regular guest at these dinners. He was usually abroad somewhere. At that point he was a correspondent in East Asia, and Mike's father was especially glad to have him for Thanksgiving. Mike's mother didn't like Analect. Mike didn't know this the way Lyle did, but he had a sense of it too.

When Analect held up the recorder Mike knew instantly they would be in trouble. He saw the way the adults laughed but didn't think it was funny. One of them, drunker than the rest and not a very good friend of Mike's parents, was even a little angry. Mike remembered that he worked for one of the networks. Their mother was embarrassed and that always made her cross as well. Mike's father called the boys over and tried to set things right by giving them a talk, in front of everyone, that was both funny and serious. Analect removed the tape from the recorder and put it in his pocket.

# 3

On the flight from HKI to BKK, Mike asks Bishop about Christopher Dorr.

"A crazy fuck," Bishop tells him. "Won awards. Then just stopped filing, so the magazine stopped paying him. I won't bullshit you, I never liked the guy much."

Mike doesn't know what to say.

"Analect's the one that lost him," Bishop goes on. "He should check in on Dorr himself."

Mike looks out the window at the flat turquoise sea below. He wonders if Analect has spoken to his father since he arrived in Hong Kong. No, or his father would have said something. But then they haven't talked much since Mike left. Mike knows there were some things his father never talked about. His life before his children wasn't a secret; it just never came up. Mike always thought that maybe this was because his father hadn't wanted to end up in banking but did anyway. Mike thinks if he talks to Dorr he'll know a lot more about that.

"You don't have to worry about Dorr," Bishop is saying. "Just fill your notebook with stony backpacker quotes and we'll have a week in Bangkok. Pretty girls in Bangkok. You'll have a blast."

Mike keeps expecting Bishop to give him specifics about what else he wants for the story but he never does, just sleeps most of the three-hour ride. Mike looks at Bishop and thinks that if you sleep on a plane you could crash and be unsure whether you are dreaming until you are dead. Mike isn't worried about the specifics. He figures he'll get whatever information he needs when the time comes. Bishop has already told him they'd have the place wired because of some friends of his who are based in Bangkok.

"You'll like them," Bishop said, and then called them the "flying circus."


Following Bishop, Mike sails through Bangkok customs on a tourist visa. The room is hot but the lines are short. Customs officials in lizard-colored uniforms slam their stamps, and the pale Europeans and Americans in bright, patterned shirts sweat in line and shuffle through.

As they clear, Bishop tells Mike that in Bangkok it's easier to be a journalist if you're not a journalist. "You'll see what I mean when you meet the flying circus," he says. "They get away with anything."


On the way in from the airport, Bishop tells Mike to take the night off, check out the city. He is going to meet his "best girl" and, in fact, is going to be spending most of his time with her. He needs a break. This is good for Mike because he will get to do most of the reporting. Of course Bishop will write the story in the end; Mike just has to find the stony quotes. They both get a week in Bangkok and he will make sure they share the byline. "It'll be a good surprise for Analect, but you really have to do it yourself," says Bishop.

Getting out of the cab in front of their hotel, Mike knows that Bishop is going to ditch him. What the hell.

# 4

Mike knew something strange and probably bad had happened that Thanksgiving. Everyone went home earlier than usual. Lyle was miserable, almost in tears, and Mike tried to comfort him. Mike often felt that he did not see problems his older brother saw.

As the two boys lay in their bunks that night, Lyle in the top, they heard the sounds of an argument coming from their parents' room across the hall. Eventually the sounds would become so familiar that Mike never remembered a time when he had not heard them, but this was one of the first times. Lyle climbed down to investigate. Where are you going? Mike asked, watching his brother's legs swing out into dark space. Lyle didn't answer, though, just crept across the hall and listened at his parents' door.

Mike pulled his covers up over his head and tensed his small body. Then he got out of bed and went across the hall too. He saw Lyle there, lying on the floor with his ear to the bottom of the door. Their parents were really yelling now and their voices seemed very loud in the hallway. Mike lay next to his brother and tried to listen, but Lyle pushed him away. Go to bed, Lyle said, in the way their parents often ordered.

Mike wouldn't go. They began to tussle but froze when they heard the argument stop. Their parents had heard them. Lyle grabbed Mike and they ran back to their beds. Their parents opened the door but didn't catch them.

Mike waited until his older brother fell asleep and then went and listened at his parents' door again. He couldn't tell what they were talking about, but he heard Analect's name. After that night he was always a little suspicious of Analect, although he could not say why, exactly.

# 5

The hotel is white with a revolving door. It is jammed in among the hostels on Khao San Road. As he is checking in, Mike overhears a paunchy Brit describing the hotel to his wife as "the best place to see Bangkok from the street." Mike doubts that. His room is on the third floor, small, with a shower and satellite television. A baseball game is on when he walks in. He looks out the window down the length of Khao San Road vibrating in the heat.

Across the street from the hotel is a row of cafés. They are all different, Italian, Thai, American, and so on, but they are really all the same, like everything else on Khao San Road. Mike figures that every backpacker in Southeast Asia starts and ends here. He sits down at the closest café and orders a beer, and a backpacker kid, twirling his dreadlocks around his ringed thumbs at the next table, asks him how it's going and joins him.

"Fine," says Mike, "how about you?"

"Good except the cops are fucking everywhere," says Dreads.

Mike hasn't seen any cops except those directing traffic.

"You just get here?" asks Dreads. Mike tells him yes and then Dreads gives him three minutes on the wonders of Thailand. Getting high on the beaches, riding the elephants up north, getting high on the elephant rides, dancing in the clubs. This is exactly what Analect said would happen. It's easy for Mike to talk to this kid, who keeps bragging about the club he is going to later. Like any middle-class stoner from back home, but somehow transformed by heat and distance into a legitimate denizen of this strange locale. Mike thinks it's as though someone dropped a tropical urban bomb on the mall he slouched through every day.

"Want to come get fucked up?" he asks Mike.


So Mike goes to the club, Z Club it's called, and stays all night, wondering at first if he is really working or just having another green beer. It's a dance club, could have been London or Paris or New York, where he's from, but Mike doesn't really know because he doesn't go to clubs.

The strobes illuminate the dancers in smoky flashes, sunburned Europeans and black Africans so dark they almost disappear. Where are those guys from? Mike wonders. It's like they're from the surface of the sun. Mike doesn't dance. He stands at the crowded bar drinking beers, and then sometimes he walks to the wall and leans there drinking, watching the sinuous dancers. He is trying to pick up the signals, what is what, trying to pick out the tourists from the locals. Easy. Tourists talk to him because he looks like them. A South African relates how a woman shot a dart out of her pussy the night before at a club in Patpong.

Three dumpy Kiwi girls pull him to a couch and talk to him about how cheap everything is in Thailand and how much they like it that foreigners come up and talk to them. In the end they tell him he's cute and they'll look him up when they get to New York at the end of their holiday. At first Mike thinks maybe this would be fine. Maybe he wants to fuck one of these girls, or even all three at once. But not really. He has a girlfriend, Jane, back home, and that was complicated enough already. Plus he is working, isn't he?

# 6

During his freshman year, Mike sometimes studied in a wing of Widener Library named after the nineteenth-century historian Robert Benson Ames. The name meant nothing to Mike when Analect told him to look up Christopher Dorr, but then it did because on the Internet he found out that Dorr's full name was Christopher Ames Dorr. Mike wondered if the two were related. Probably, he figured.

Supposedly the Ames wing was haunted, and there was a tradition, a joke really, about making Phi Beta Kappa or something if you had sex there when you were a freshman. When Jane visited him over a long weekend that fall, he mentioned this to her and she said it sounded like a good tradition. Mike said he only mentioned it because it was so ridiculous, but then he was pleased when Jane insisted on seeing the library. After all, it was very old and very famous. So she and Mike walked through the stacks, talking in low voices as the motion sensors clicked and lit lamps above the rows of books they passed, until they found a place.

Jane froze while they were having sex. The light in the next aisle clicked on.

"Did you hear that?" she whispered.

Mike became very serious, as if he were almost expecting something.

"Breathing," said Jane. "But I didn't hear any footsteps."

She kept a straight face. Mike thought she might really be scared and he hurried to pull himself together. He even took her by the hand and started to lead her out of the aisle. When they were three rows away and hadn't said anything, Jane couldn't contain herself anymore. Her laughter overwhelmed the quiet of the library. "I knew it," she said. "You really thought there might be a ghost."

But Jane didn't get it. It's not that Mike believes in ghosts, it's that he knows you can be haunted.

# 7

By midnight, Dreads has a whole backpacker crew gathered around him, eyes flooding from the ecstasy. Mike watches them dance, bumping into one another, stopping only to pull beaten water bottles from the pockets of their cheap linen fisherman's pants, just purchased on Khao San Road. Dreads is straight Khao San. Mike doesn't really want to talk to Dreads anymore. What he wants to do is find Dorr. He wants to impress Analect, not Bishop. He wants to meet this man who boxed his father.

At 2 A.M. the strobes stop and the PA blares that it is time to leave. This is exactly Mike's story, backpacker kids and how the government is cracking down on the ecstasy scene, instituting a two o'clock closing time. People begin to filter out. Mike starts to go with them, but Dreads hands him another beer and tells him to relax. "No worries man, what'll they arrest us for?"

For being stupid, thinks Mike.

The PA fires again: "THE POLICE WILL BE HERE IN FIVE MINUTES . . ." and then it becomes garbled and everyone is leaving. Mike is tired but Dreads says he knows a place they can go to and tells Mike about an apartment, just a few blocks away. Dreads gets excited talking about how the apartment is like a secret society of cool backpackers where there is always good hash. "Plus," he explains, "there are always girls there, white girls, you know? Not that the Thai girls aren't totally cool."

Mike looks at Dreads and knows that he is afraid of Thai girls.

Dreads keeps talking about the apartment and the "rad old guy" whose place it is. "And you should see his hookup," says Dreads as they walk out, "an older chick with red hair, so hot."

Outside, Mike sees two monster sports cars, hundred-thousand-dollar, 4 million baht, candy-colored, speed machines. Their brown, hair-gelled drivers open the doors and white girls with blond hair and slender bodies get in. Mike hadn't seen them inside. Probably rich Indian or Bengali kids, on holiday. They are loud, speeding into the night.

The walk to the apartment is longer than Mike expects, and Dreads talks the whole way, bragging about drugs. As a kind of experiment, Mike tells him he is doing a story about kids coming to Bangkok just to get high.

"Cool," says Dreads. "You can write about me."

# 8

The day before he left for Hong Kong, Mike was worried. For a day and a half his parents had not been speaking to each other with such cruelty that Mike became apprehensive about their future and the future of his family. Worrying slowed him down, though, so he tried to think of better times.

He thought of his mother skiing in Sun Valley, Idaho. She blew great powdery swaths of snow into the air as she raced down the mountain in front of him. She skied beautifully. He saw men watch her, in her yellow snowsuit, as she flew past them, and he was proud of her. She encouraged her sons to go full speed down the slopes. Why turn? she liked to say.

Their father asked her privately if she was crazy. They'll get hurt, he said. They're already berserk. But she brushed him off and told the boys very theatrically to snowboard like young gods racing in the sky. Mike and Lyle were more or less invincible on the mountain, and they raced and slipped through the pines at full speed, and even invented an out-of-bounds run on the back side of the mountain that they jokingly called "young gods."

The next year their father was injured on an icy inter-
mediate run early in the morning on the third day of their trip.
Only Mike saw him go down, breaking his arm in the kind of
surprising fall an athlete takes at fifty. After that, Mike never
thought of himself as a young god racing in the sky but, rather,
as just a person much younger than his father. Just very young.
This happened to Mike a lot when he started remembering
the times he'd had with his father as a kid.

# 9

Mike follows Dreads up a narrow staircase. The apartment is in a peeling building over an Internet café. Dreads knocks on the door and says his name. Locks shoot and click before the door swings open. There is a mountain of backpacks just inside the door, and Mike has to step around the framed, zippered burdens.

"Welcome," comes an Australian accent.

Several kids look up at Mike; they're all pierced and a little raggedy but too white and western to be really ragged. They sprawl on the floor or lounge on wooden benches along the walls, an audience. The Australian sits on a cushion in the middle of the room. He has frizzed, gray hair and wears a vest but no shirt, lots of chains. He looks twice as old as most of the kids and seems to Mike to weave like a snake charmer. He is holding a joint.

"Mike," says Dreads, sweeping his arm at the Australian, "this is the famous Hardy."

"So, what brings you to Bangkok and would you like a pull?" Hardy asks.

"I'm fine, thanks," Mike says.

"He's a reporter," says Dreads.

Stupid, thinks Mike, but he sees some of the kids get more interested.

"Well, not much going on around here," Hardy says, evenly, producing a lacy bra from under his cushion. He begins to play a kind of cat's cradle with it between his fingers, joint at his lips.

"For a travel magazine," Mike says. "Just a good vacation, really."

"I'm sure."

Mike nods. Hardy studies him and says, "Did you know there is a doctor in California who has a cure for cancer?"

Mike doesn't say anything and a girl in a pirate bandanna whom Hardy calls Lucy rises from the heap of kids at his feet and makes her way through a beaded curtain to the kitchen. Mike is careful not to stare at her long, tan legs rising up into her cutoff jeans.

"We only started getting cancer recently," Hardy continues. "It was you Americans, treating everything. But this stuff . . ." Lucy Long Legs is back with a bowl of noodles and a pair of chopsticks and sits down between Hardy's legs. ". . . this stuff is just about as organic as you can get."

Mike asks him how long he's been in Bangkok. Hardy wraps his legs around Lucy Long Legs and puts down his joint. She feeds him some noodles.

"He's been here going on fucking twenty-two years," Dreads says.

"Can't trust a single motherfucker in this whole town," Hardy says through a mouthful of noodles. "Never could."

Mike asks if Hardy can point him to a place where he might score some pills. For the travel story. Mike doesn't want the pills, he just wants to ask for them.

"No problem, somethin' like a couple pills," Hardy says, and resettles his crotch before continuing, "How about a girl, too? Local, the real Thai experience. I've got just the one."

"No thanks," Mike says, noticing that Hardy is slurring his words. How high is this guy? he wonders.

"Yeah, a girl can be trouble," Hardy goes on. "She has you because you want to fuck her, so she drugs you and pinches your schwee, or she is set up with a cop and they shake you down. Happened to me three or four times, but I been here going on twenty-two years now."

"Cops were coming to the club," Dreads volunteers. "That's why we left."

Hardy nods knowingly. "They lock the door and make everybody piss in a cup," he says. "It's not the same here, not like it was in the old days."

Mike looks at Hardy and thinks about how he never wants to have any *old days.* But "Yeah," he says. "I'm on the lookout for a friend of a friend who was here back then. His name is Christopher Dorr, American reporter guy. He's supposed to be living in Bangkok somewhere."

"Dorr, yes, can't say I know him personally, though." Hardy pulls on his joint again. "But I reckon I've heard of him. Then again," he exhales, "every other bugger you meet is looking for his contact, isn't he? A lot of stories out there."

"Far-out," says Dreads.

"Long-lost fellas who went to earth," Hardy says, smiling.

"Went to earth?" Mike asks.

"Like me," Hardy snorts. "Went to earth and now I eat fire." He sucks down to the end of the roach and then flicks it up in the air, smoking, and catches it in his mouth. The backpackers almost applaud. Hardy swallows.

Way over the top, thinks Mike. He looks at Hardy carefully and decides that he is very high, but not necessarily from the joint.

"There are, at any given time, some fifty righteous men on the planet," Hardy says. "These righteous don't know it, but if it weren't for them, God would blow the whole place to hell. And here's the catch, see: as soon as one finds out he's one of the chosen, he dies and somebody else, some other righteous soul, takes his place."

The sprawled backpackers are captivated. Lucy Long Legs is indulgent but interrupts. "Do you want to watch a movie?" She rises from Hardy's crotch and rummages in a cabinet.

A stir of approval from the backpackers and Hardy picks *Casablanca*. Mike leans against the wall, sometimes watching the movie on the little television in the corner, but mostly watching Lucy Long Legs as she nods out on Hardy's lap. Blond hair spills out from under her Jolly Roger bandanna and Mike sees a tattoo on her ankle. She looks very young.

# 10

Mike's father, Mike's mother, Elliot Analect, Dorr, and Dorr's twin sister were all students at Harvard when they met. The three boys were roommates but they shared more than an address. They all wanted to be writers and were very competitive, especially Mike's father and Dorr. As freshmen, all three became marginally famous for driving Dorr's beat-up 1953 Chevy convertible down the frozen Charles River, past the boathouse where the Radcliffe winter formal was taking place. The story was that they put down the top just as they came into view, just before the car broke through the ice—and therefore just in time to allow them to escape. This was not exactly true.

The Holworthy boys, as they came to be known, after Holworthy Hall, their freshman dorm, became very close during the four years. At the end, they were something like brothers.

Mike's father and Dorr often sparred in the late afternoon and then went for a drink or several afterward. Dorr was a great talker and a decent boxer. These fighting and drinking sessions were Mike's father's favorite times. Dorr had schemes, places to go, women to fuck. He was exuberant and frequently drunk, and Mike's father envied him for the way he didn't seem to think too much about anything. Spending time with Dorr turned Mike's father into a heavy smoker.

Analect was never as close with Mike's father and Dorr. He did not drink as much and did not box at all. Unlike them, Analect had grown up with both of his parents. He was a third-generation legacy at Harvard and, by the time he was eighteen, already very good at not fucking up, something that saved Dorr and Mike's father from expulsion on several occasions. Thinking about this, Analect decided it was a trade-off he was willing to accept: two real parents for two fake brothers.

# 11

The movies run late and the morning seeps through the shuttered windows. Mike says "Thanks for your hospitality" to an unconscious room as he picks his way through to the door.

As he opens it, a Thai man is opening it from the other side. Mike apologizes across the languages and brushes past him. The Thai man stands in the doorway and takes a small package wrapped with rubber bands from the pocket of his jeans and wings it at sleeping Hardy's forehead. The Thai man reacts with a high-pitched laugh and is following Mike down the stairs before Hardy registers the whack.

Down on the street, Mike wonders where to go for a cab. The Thai man walks quickly to a parked motorcycle, turns, and calls back to him.

"Taxi? Taxi! Cheap." He is wearing a blue vest with a number and an advertisement for a taxi service on it. His movements are quick and jerky as he gestures for Mike to get on behind him.

"How much?" Mike asks, as he approaches the bike.

"A hundred and twenty." The Thai man bounces up and down on his seat, gunning the engine.

How much is that? Mike wonders. Whatever. "Sure," he says, getting on the bike.

The driver offers him a helmet, which he declines, and they are off. Mike is glad for the handholds at his side so that he doesn't have to hold on to the driver. The motorcycle flies and weaves on the wide boulevards and sends the cloth of the produce stalls flapping as they shoot the alleys.

They join a wide line of bikes at the first light they don't make. Mike looks over to the next motorcycle and sees a Thai girl. She is wearing white sweatpants and a T-shirt, and long black hair hangs in a shimmer between her shoulder blades. Her complexion is dark and clear like tea. She has a bundle of something at her chest that Mike can't quite see.

The girl suddenly catches Mike looking at her and smiles a shy, sweet smile that surprises him and snaps his head back to looking straight ahead. The light changes and the girl speeds forward, hair blowing out behind her, leading the charge of the motorcycles into the morning. As Mike catches up he sees that she is holding a naked brown baby.


When Mike sees the baby he is distracted, so he doesn't see the crash coming.

The driver is gunning. Mike has never been on a bike like this before. It is much faster than he imagined. And then, just as the slow skid begins, Mike realizes what made him nervous about his driver. His eyes. The driver is high.

Mike tries to lean into the skid or away from it; he doesn't know, just tries to exert some force, change it. The bike is almost scraping his leg on the cement. Mike wants to turn it all down, like a radio. Horns bleat, cars veer out of the way. Mike's mind ricochets off the instant possibilities of hitting the car they just cut off or of being broadsided by another. He grits his teeth and holds on. This might be it, he thinks, for the first time in his life. It's a sickening realization, a deep and awful nausea that he feels, death maybe, flying underneath him. And then it all stops.

On the other side of the intersection, the driver looks around as if he has lost something. He is speaking to himself in Thai and all Mike can say to him, tapping him on the shoulder, is, "Khao San Road?"

They take off again, and looking down at his pant leg, Mike sees that it did scrape, and there is blood, running in smudges, down to his ankle.

Mike's hotel is either right here or down at the other end. He has the heady feeling of a wild night, danger that has passed. He can look anyone in the eye and tell them—I was out. I was doing something. I did not just stay in my room and watch TV the way I wanted to. I did not just cross the street and drink beer until I got sleepy. I did not just chat with backpackers or visit a temple a couple minutes from the hotel. I went out there. I talked with Hardy and saw Lucy Long Legs and almost died on a motorcycle. I went.

The hotel, it turns out, is right in front of him.

# 12

"Don't forget," Mike's father told him on the way to the airport, "Hong Kong is only eighteen hours away."

Mike drank a beer with his parents at an empty airport bar. His mother remarked that time always seemed to stand still for her in airports. "Time and space," she said, "are in the same continuum. This is not space," she went on, sweeping her arm over the plastic bar, "so there's no time."

Mike's father rolled his eyes. Mike laughed and sipped his beer, but he was thinking about all the planes his mother had missed. When she ordered shots of tequila, he said he wanted to go to the gate, even though he had plenty of time. He shook his father's hand and kissed his mother on the cheek and promised to be in touch. They told him not to worry about staying in touch. "We'll be OK," said his mother.

"Regards to Analect," said his father.

Mike walked away toward the gate. Looking over his shoulder, he could see his parents at the bar. They looked ridiculous, still not talking. The bartender placed two shot glasses in front of them, and Mike saw his mother pull one of the glasses to her lips and throw the shot down her throat. Her head jerked back like someone had punched her in the chin. He had never seen his mother drink a shot before, and in that instant he thought of all the drunk kids at school, sweating and red-faced, going shot for shot across dorm desks.

His mother looked at his father and at the shot still in front of him. He did not look at her. Then she took his shot and drank it in one long, slow sip, and Mike saw his mother call the bartender over again.

# 13

Mike wakes up as the sun is going down and looks at the evening sky, thick and red, out his window. He wants to wolf down the candy bars in the minifridge, but he knows this would show up on the magazine's bill and he doesn't want to look like he was just hanging around the hotel.

He goes to the café across the street and has an evening breakfast of rolls and noodles with a French paraglider girl who just walks over and sits down next to him.

"I'm leaving in a few days," she says.

"Where are you going?"

She is headed up north to Chiang Mai to go parasailing or hang gliding and to otherwise get high. They smoke cigarettes and drink coffee together.

"I know some good bars around here," she says.

Mike wants to go to one of her bars and tell her his story of last night. He is about to suggest they do this, go to a bar, when she says that Thailand has expanded her consciousness and brought her closer to God. Not really God, but the state of truly organic being. She can actually feel her aura expanding, right now.

Mike goes back to his room and writes this down in his notebook. He realizes Bangkok is probably full of these people.

There is no message for Mike on his cell, no message on his room phone. He wants to tell Bishop about his night with the backpackers and how, maybe, Hardy is the center of the story. But Bishop is not in his room. Mike knocks, waits for five minutes, and knocks again to be sure.

No surprise, thinks Mike, as he walks back down to the lobby. Bishop told him he'd be making up for lost time with his girl. Mike thinks she must be Thai. He imagines a woman putting on her best yellow dress and red lipstick and rushing in white high heels to meet Bishop at a bar he has gone straight to after dropping Mike off at the hotel. Maybe they know Bangkok very well and love it together, and take long walks through the winding streets that smell of peanut and sweet smoke. But Mike knows, from the way Bishop said "best girl," that this is not how it is. Mike hopes the woman in the yellow dress makes good money, whoever she is. This is what Mike is thinking as he crosses Khao San Road.

The road is crowded, always. It is crowded with *farangs*. It's famous for this. "A *farang*," Bishop told Mike, "is a Caucasian. Especially like you," he said.

Mike is not hungry, but for something to do he orders a bowl of noodles from a street vendor and watches the lady crack an egg into boiling water. Bishop had warned him about street noodles. "Sometimes they get you and sometimes they don't," he said. "It can take a couple days. But that's how Bangkok is, it sneaks up on you."

Behind the street vendor, the motorcycle taxi drivers are lounging, smoking, and looking at backpacker asses browsing the cheap hemp clothing. Next to the motorcycle taxis an old man sits at an easel, the way an old painter might sit along the East River in New York. He is making fake IDs. These are not driver's licenses—like the ones Mike's friends back home get so they can buy beer—but international student IDs, passports, and documents to get discounts or through borders in the north. Very poor fakes. As the woman hands over the egg noodles, Mike realizes that he should have checked at the desk for messages. He eats his food quickly and returns to the hotel.

The lobby is empty and Mike's shoes are loud on the hardwood floor. He asks the two pretty Thai girls behind the front desk if there are any messages for him.

"No, no, sorry."

"Are you sure?"

"No, no, sorry." The girls are about Mike's age and smiling at him unhelpfully. He knows they will chitter when he turns to go.

"How about for my friend Mr. Bishop?"

"Oh, but I am sorry, we cannot show other guest messages."

Mike knows what he has to do and smiles big but sad at the girls.

"But he's my boss, and I'm supposed to be arranging his meeting, and the people who sent the message didn't know my name."

The girls smile and laugh. This *farang* could be trouble. He's cute, though, and maybe a big tipper. They show him the fax that came in for Mr. Bishop.

The message reads: "Forty-four Bar @ Soi 4 Silom 9:00 you owe me. MB."

Mike imagines with dread trying to relay this address to whatever driver he recruits and wonders what is owed.

# 14

Mike's grandfather died in World War II, leaving Mike's father as the last scion of a San Francisco import-export family. The family thought Mike's grandmother was not quite up to standard, a charity case their lost son would have gotten over if he hadn't died on the beach at Iwo Jima. She raised Mike's father while warring with the family in their big house in Pacific Heights, and by the time Mike's father turned eighteen, he was glad to leave for college.

Mike's mother was from New York. She met Mike's father on the first day of college and everyone said they looked alike. Her father was a councilman whose roots in city politics could be traced back to Tammany Hall. She inherited the ability to talk to everybody like they were the only person in the room. She graduated at the top of her Stuyvesant class.

Dorr and his sister were the exotics. They grew up Catholic in New Orleans and were orphaned at age twelve. Their parents died in a fire, which Dorr said, when he said anything about it, was set by the ghosts of slaves. From then on, they lived with a widowed aunt. The siblings were very close but never incestuous. Trust funds paid for Harvard.

It was Analect's idea that the five of them have brunch every Sunday. The tradition started at the end of freshman year. His joke was that he liked to have his omelet with two eggs and two sets of twins. They all drank Bloody Marys. A lot of the things they wound up doing were Analect's idea.

# 15

Mike hopes Bishop will show up but knows he won't. He waits anyway, sitting across the street from the hotel at his café. He orders Coke after Coke. They come in tall, narrow glass bottles, different than in the U.S., and he tries to pace himself. As he watches for Bishop walking in or out of the hotel, he thinks about Christopher Dorr. Makes up stories, actually.

Maybe Dorr was a spy, had a cover as a journalist, but was actually working for the government, bugging hotel rooms, assassinating warlords, fucking cultural attachés. Shit like that. Or maybe he had become consumed by his own writing and couldn't be bothered with the journalism anymore, rising at dawn every day, punching at a steel typewriter on some overgrown roof garden. Why not? His piece on the Wa was beyond journalism. Or maybe Dorr had finally realized he was a woman and was right now at a club in Patpong in high-heeled boots and purple makeup. Whatever. Mike would find his body, hot with bullets, in a bloodied bathroom and have to go after the killers. Maybe he had married a wealthy dope-dealer widow and spent his days watching animated movies on thick carpeting with his young stepchildren—and the hell with Analect and all the rest of it. All bullshit for sure.

Analect had said that he and Dorr and Mike's father were like brothers once, but Mike's father had never talked about it. Mike thinks about this. Why didn't his father ever say anything? He had always spoken freely about Analect. Maybe there was an argument. Mike imagines the three of them drunk and arguing about nothing, like some of the popped-collar fools he goes to school with. The argument is so loud they can neither remember nor forgive it the next morning. The argument is about money or women or God or art or sports but really is about which of them is the best, because they all know that one of them is but they don't know who yet.

Maybe none of it is important. Maybe they weren't at all like brothers, and Analect just said they were. Or maybe brotherhood is completely gaseous, and theirs dissipated thirty years ago in the air behind jet planes and thrown wedding bouquets. Mike doesn't know.

It gets to be eight o'clock and Mike has called Bishop's cell phone and left another message, but there is still no sign of him. It is so hot, even in the breezy night, that Mike is sweating through his shirt. He knows that he will have to go to the bar by himself.

A "soi" is a road Mike thinks he remembers, but he has no sense of distance yet in Bangkok. The motorcycle taxis are right there, handy. But maybe he should walk and find a cab at the end of the road. No, he decides, what are the chances of two motorcycle skids? He approaches the pack of lounging drivers and shows one of them the address. As the driver makes a display of looking at it, Mike realizes he cannot read.

"Soi Four, Silom," says Mike, and the driver nods vigorously. Mike looks into his eyes for maybe a moment too long, weirds the guy out a little, but he has to be sure.

And then the wonder of a clean motorcycle ride through Bangkok. Mike leans into the turns, watches the city slide past him. Wild dogs everywhere and carts of rice and vegetables. In one neighborhood, bald men in red robes. Buddhists, but out at night? Maybe Dorr has become a monk, solitary even among the red robes, and is marching home from prayer to sleep on a yellowing woven mat. Mike wishes he could stay on the motorcycle all night and all day, never have to talk to anyone, just soak it all in at high speed. If he could only see it all in motion, he thinks, he could have the insight without the fear, the trip without the nerves.

The story without the work. Mike wonders if Analect knew this would happen.


Mike gets to Silom Road in twenty minutes. It's only eight-thirty and he doesn't want to be early. Then, swinging his leg over the back of the motorbike, he hears a rip.

"Ha." The driver points at Mike's ripped pant leg as Mike pays him. Mike nods and laughs, but he is thinking Goddamn it, because he has ripped his expensive New York no-pleat safari pants right up the inseam. His father got him those pants.

Mike looks up and down Silom Road, sees Soi Four and walks down the smaller street looking for any numbered building. Where is 44? He can't find it, but then, at a dead end, a sign that reads .44 Bar. The .44 Bar. Like a gun. Good.

To kill time, Mike walks back to Silom Road looking for new pants in the stalls that line the sidewalk. It is hard to walk in the crowd. He is not really looking for pants. He is looking for the version of himself that does not arrive too early.

He goes from stall to stall and all the pants are either a bad color or a bad cut or stop above the ankle, fisherman's pants. Hemp. A woman catches his eye and points to a bunch of metal rings on a string. They have designs painted on them, like the rings Dreads had on his thumb. Maybe no one will notice his pants.

Mike decides he wants a beer and to hell with not wanting to arrive too early in ripped pants.

# 16

The first real conversation Mike could remember having with his mother was about ambition. Before, there was only the buzz of childhood, and this conversation remained with him like a kind of demarcation. Mike was in sixth grade and had failed a test in Latin that day and he had never failed before. He cried in private before dinner, in hot frustration, and his mother caught him and decided to take him out—on an expedition, she called it—to calm him down, so that he wouldn't beat himself up the way Lyle always did. Lyle made himself sick, she said, doing schoolwork. Mike's mother was determined that her second son be more comfortable.

"Can't let the same thing happen twice," she said to Mike's father.

"Don't think too much," Mike's father said over his shoulder, loading the dishwasher. This pissed her off and she slammed the door. He finished the dishes because the maid was off the next day, and then looked in on Lyle, who was hunched over his trigonometry like a hawk protecting carrion.

\*    \*    \*

Mike and his mother sat listening to a street jazz quartet in the plaza at the World Trade Center. Mike's mother said the weather, which was clear, made her want to fly up and see her floating reflection in the high windows as she listened to the hard bop. She hated to fly but now she said she wanted to.

This didn't cheer Mike up. He was still frowning. So his mother described to him how everybody failed sometimes. She pointed to the musicians.

"That's all improvisation is," she said, "a series of exchanged failures. No one ever gets it right. You think you get one thing, but then you find out you missed something else. You think you studied enough, but then you find out you haven't."

"Lyle never failed a test." Mike was still very frustrated. "Did you? Did Dad?"

"Your father's not always right," she said without meaning to. "Neither is Lyle," she added quickly. But Mike heard what she had said first, and that was part of the demarcation.

"I don't know why, Mike, but most people, most of the time, fail. Nobody gets what he or she wants. Everyone thinks they will in the beginning but then they don't. Usually they don't have enough money, so they aren't free. Sometimes they have the money but it doesn't matter because they aren't as successful as they should be. Or *think* they should be." Mike's mother went on and on until Mike realized that she wasn't talking about him and his test; she was talking about something else entirely. Mike interrupted her.

"*O di immortales! In qua urbe vivimmus? Quam civitatem habemus?*" he said.

"What?"

"It was on my test today. It's the only thing I got right."

"What does it mean?"

"O immortal gods! In what city do we live? What society do we have?"

She looked at her son frowning on the bench next to her and began to cry.

"I'm OK about the test," Mike said, "really, it's OK."

"I know, Mike," she said, and pulled herself together. "I was just so proud of you, just now."

Mike knew that wasn't why she cried.

# 17

The .44 Bar is an English-speaking pub, paneled in dark wood, with a football match droning on the one television. Mike goes to the bar and orders a beer. He wants to order right, in case anybody's watching. Nobody cares, he reminds himself, scanning the scattered groups of expats. Nobody looks like an "MB," no lone journalist waiting for Bishop at the bar.

However, in a booth near the pool table Mike notices a redheaded woman and a blond man with his hair topknotted like a samurai. They are laughing about something and watching a small but very tough-looking black guy with a shaved head handily beat a very much larger man at nine-ball. Mike remembers the hookup that Dreads told him about, the redhead, but then lets it go when he remembers something Bishop told him about everyone in Bangkok looking like a dope dealer if you're looking for one.

Mike edges down the bar and hears something from the redhead about tiger teeth, smuggled aphrodisiacs in a false-bottomed boat. Mike can tell that the redhead is pissed off about something and decides that, whoever she is, he would never want to cross her. Then suddenly she laughs again. Her anger was just part of the way she was telling the story. The guy in the topknot gesticulates like a conductor as he starts talking, something about a particular cop and the gusto with which he is celebrating the birth of his first son. He is the cop to go to these days because he is in such fine spirits.

Mike wishes Bishop would show up. He orders another beer and moves closer to the booth to hear better. The topknot guy pulls up his legs and sits cross-legged and straight-backed with a new story. "So the soldiers walk us in and take off the blindfolds and the general is standing on one side of a little glass coffee table and he's tiny, like this, full uniform, the whole thing, dress for the camera, and Harrison . . ."

The bald guy playing pool, Harrison apparently, nods to confirm the story.

". . . Harrison has got that fat motor drive of his with the 85x150 zoom hanging over his shoulder. And as he reaches out to shake hands with the general the strap slips somehow . . ."

Harrison wears a small, tight grin and sips his drink.

". . . and the camera crashes down on top of this glass table-top and shatters right through. So we freeze and every guy in the room has his gun pointed at us . . ." Topknot imitates the sound of a gun cocking. It's remarkably realistic.

". . . everyone is dead silent for a second, and then the little general, he just goes, 'hahahaha,' and all the rest of them start laughing too, 'hahaha.' And we're looking at each other, laughing our bloody arses off, 'hahaha,' and then we all sit down and have beers."

Mike is thinking how it all sounds like something out of a

comic book when a strong finger taps him from behind, not on his shoulder but exactly on the tip of a vertebra. Mike spins.

It's the leathery bald guy, Harrison. "Do I know you?" he asks.

Mike knows instantly that Harrison has caught him eavesdropping. His heart thuds in his chest and he concentrates on speaking slowly. He introduces himself and explains that he is looking for a reporter with the initials *MB*. The topknot guy laughs behind him.

Mike turns again and feels his face warming, the last thing he wants, and now the redhead is staring at him, too, and he knows he is blushing.

"Mickey Burton," Topknot says, "at your service." He sticks out a hand from his cross-legged seat and cocks his head at Mike. "I was expecting Tommy Bishop."

"I'm his assistant."

"Really?" Burton asks. "Hilarious. You better sit down and have a drink. Welcome to the flying circus."

# 18

There, sitting around the table, Burton formally introduces Mike to the redhead, Bridget, and the giant, Paul, and again to Harrison. They are all freelance but not broke. Burton rattles off résumés that sound to Mike right out of Kipling, except these are set in East Timor or involve going into the jungle with the death squads or, most recently for Burton, watching a Buddhist temple blow up in southern Thailand—"idol arms flying through the air."

Burton goes on and on. Bridget is from Sydney and is working on a photo book about endangered animals, how they are poached and smuggled all over Southeast Asia and Africa. Paul recently returned from chasing pirates across the South China Sea and is working on his own book about how modern piracy is a billion-dollar industry. Burton is hypnotic, practiced, and self-deprecating as he describes their exploits, but when he gets to Harrison's story, Harrison stops him and redirects the talk to Mike.

"What's your story?" he asks, and Mike is surprised by how interested they all seem. They pay close attention as he explains how Analect sent him with Bishop. It's as if he were just as compelling as guns in the jungle. It's kind, Mike thinks, but it's also spooky.

"I get it," Burton says. "Shrewd, shrewd Analect. You can pass for one, so you set up a bunch of backpackers for Bishop. A bit of a travel piece. And you're his decoy."

That last word surprises Mike. Paul sits down heavily next to him and leans in. "Sounds like a bullshit story," he says, in an Eastern European accent Mike can't place.

"Ecstasy's not so bad a story, you see." Burton laughs, as if translating. "But it's a bit of an easy thing to come in here looking for, and Paul's a bit perturbed on account of your focus on that, given the other pill story."

"*Yaa baa.*" Mike wants them to know he knows something, that he did his homework.

"But do you know about the silence killings?" Burton asks. "That's what's been happening in Thailand. Hundreds here, maybe more up north."

"Toxic Thaksin," adds Bridget.

Mike knows that Thaksin Shinawatra is the prime minister of Thailand.

"Did your man Bishop tell you what he was up to tonight?" asks Burton.

"No, I haven't spoken to him since we got to the hotel."

"Have you checked in with Hong Kong? Analect would probably like to hear from you." Burton fingers his topknot with a tan, veined hand. "What did he say to you, actually?"

Mike tells them that Analect also told him to look up Christopher Dorr. This produces looks of surprise between Bridget and Burton that they quickly gloss over. But Mike notices, and is glad he did not tell them Dorr was a friend of his father.

"Let's have another round and think about this," says Burton, and goes to the bar. Bridget is staring at Mike again. He smiles and looks down at his empty bottle.

"So what are you planning on doing, Mr. Mike?" Bridget's voice is low and even.

"Well, I'm not sure," he says, feeling himself blush again. "I suppose I'll keep working on the story myself and wait to hear from Bishop. It's really just asking backpacker kids questions."

"It always turns more complicated than you think," she says, looking at Mike over the forest of bottles on the table.

Mike knows this already.

# 19

Mike's parents' house on Long Island was constructed of old beams, and the cedar shingles were gray and weathered by nearness to the sea. The living room smelled of dry wood and salty air, and also candles. Mike's mother adored expensive candles, and she burned them constantly, especially over the winters, which was strange for a woman who claimed to be so afraid of fire. She said the house would go up like a box of matches if they weren't all very careful.

One winter night, the living room fireplace spat an ember onto one of their mother's small Persian carpets. She had been alone in there all evening. The boys had eaten with their father and he had already tucked them into bed. He was in the kitchen making a drink when he heard his wife scream. The boys ran to the stairs a moment later and saw their father spraying the rug with a yellow fire extinguisher. The gray exhaust overwhelmed the whole room and seemed overcompensation for the circle of black ash burned in the rug. Mike's mother was sobbing and yelling at her husband. He sprayed the rug a last time, sprayed the fireplace, and then put down the extinguisher and looked at her.

She screamed, how could he not have noticed? Was he drunk? Did he maybe even want the house to burn down, so that he could start again somewhere else? None of this made sense to Mike and Lyle, but they didn't forget it. Their mother was in only her robe, and it kept slipping open. She didn't seem to care. And somehow her nakedness, combined with her yelling, paralyzed the boys on the staircase. It took their father a few moments to register their presence and then shepherd them back up to bed. Turned out she was drunk.

# 20

"Come with us, will you?" asks Burton, almost too politely. "You really ought to. We're going to my place. I've also got just the thing, a good contact for you, a police lieutenant. I'll write down his number."

"Maybe I should leave a note for Bishop," says Mike.

"I wouldn't worry about him," says Burton. "In fact, I'd forget about him."

Mike feels like he's been adopted, or at least let in on some kind of private joke. And no one has said anything about the rip in his pants.

"Thaksin wants every drug dealer in the country dead," says Bridget. "Come with us and we'll tell you about it. You don't want to write a backpacker story."

"You'll see," says Paul. "Cops on dealers, dealers on dealers." But Mike can see in Paul's dilated eyes that he's not sure about the invitation. "I'll meet you there," Paul continues. "I have to make a stop."

Mike notices, following Paul out the door, how heavy and high his shoulders are, how big his fists—how enormous the man actually is, like a bouncer headed for work, going into the neon lights of the Silom district.

It's strange, suddenly piling into a car with these new people, driving off with them through the warm rain in the Bangkok night. Mike admires the way Burton directs the driver. The rain splashes and crystallizes the light through the windows of the damp cab. No one speaks. Mike is in the backseat between Harrison and Bridget. She looks out the side window, and Burton and Harrison stare straight ahead; they are all quiet for a moment. Harrison strokes his bald head and closes his eyes. Mike is acutely aware of the point at which his leg leans up against Bridget. She smells of sweet pepper. Mike is keyed up and a little drunk and feels good. He says something like thanks for taking me around, then feels it was premature for thanks.

"Oh please," says Burton.

Bridget nods, though she is still looking out the window.

# 21

Mike's father, Dorr, and Analect were all in love with Mike's mother, but it was his father who had her first. Neither of them had been in love before. They had sex everywhere, including the library. The affair was even fiercer because of the tension between Mike's mother and Dorr. Analect saw what would happen a long way off.

Over Thanksgiving break their senior year, Mike's father found out that she was cheating on him with Dorr. Boston was three hours into the first snow of the year. Mike's father had the cab turn around halfway to Logan when he heard on the radio that all flights were grounded because of the storm. He had been dreading San Francisco anyway. He returned to Lowell House and there they were, drunk in bed together. No one knew what to do.

Mike's father found Analect in a bar on Mass. Ave. Analect pretended to be surprised and lied that he didn't know anything about it.

By the time the snow stopped falling, Mike's father had slept with Dorr's sister as revenge.

# 22

A refuge from the wild traffic, up a road in some corner of the city. Gardens and houses, no carts on the side of the road. Getting out of the cab, Mike sees an elephant fountain spraying water from its trunk. Burton's apartment is behind the elephant in a compound originally occupied by French soldiers. Up the wide stone stairs, five flights of them, Burton's door is painted blue.

The apartment isn't huge but it has two long couches, a television, a bar, books. One wall is covered in hanging two-foot lengths of yellowed rope. A terrace and a hot tub. Burton pours drinks for everybody and the four of them simultaneously light cigarettes.

Mike asks about the rope, testing the feel of it against his knuckles.

"Conceptual decor," says Burton.

"Those are all from boxing matches along the Burmese border," says Harrison. "They wrap the rope around their hands."

Mike knew that already, but he isn't sure how.

Paul arrives shortly, carrying clinking bodega bags of green-bottled beer. He walks in talking, as if to announce himself with some kind of monologue. Mike feels like he's heard it all before, even though he hasn't. "The problem in Thailand," says Paul, "is not *farangs*. Yes, *farangs* are annoying. They visit just to fuck the women. Some maybe go to earth and stay, OK. I'm a *farang*." Mike wonders if anyone besides him is listening. "But the real problem," says Paul, "is Thais who want to be *farangs*. Bananas. Yellow on the outside, white on the inside. They fuck up the system. They say they're cleaning it up but they are the dirtiest."

Mike sees that Paul is particularly upset by the notion of dirty.

Mike sits in an easy chair watching Burton chop white pills into halves. Paul eats a whole one and Burton eats a half. Mike is surprised by the lack of ceremony, especially compared to the way he's seen every stoner back home get high—so very, very carefully.

"Have you ever taken ecstasy?" Paul asks.

"No," says Mike.

"Man, watch out," Paul says. He sighs and suddenly seems very tired. Mike realizes Paul is either drunk or high, probably both. "The fucking cops are everywhere," he says, "but don't worry, it's always too early for dread."

Mike has no idea.

Burton looks at him. "Would you like a pill, Mike?"

Mike shakes his head. Not now, he thinks. Sometime, maybe soon, but not now.

Burton has changed into a loose shirt and great baggy silk pants. He sits on a footstool next to Mike's chair. His blond hair is now let down from the topknot and loose about his eyes.

"I tend not to do hard drugs."

"You've tried some, then?"

Mike smoked weed occasionally back home. It made him stupid and slightly sleepy and he usually did it with Jane and they would fuck and watch a movie.

"Yeah, I had a bad time recently."

"What happened?" Burton asks, and Mike is not surprised, somehow, by how easily the lies come.

"I'd been smoking and drinking with my girlfriend and some people at a party on the roof of this building, and I think there must have been some weird shit in the weed, because it made me sort of nuts."

"That's no good," Burton says, tapping down a cigarette.

"I know," continues Mike, "made me want to jump off the roof." He says this half solemn and half not, like someone, he thinks, who is too cool to brag about nearly tossing himself off the roof but who is too honest to lie about it. Burton seems to be taking him at his word. They all are. Of course they are, Mike thinks. Why wouldn't they?

"Well, we won't let you jump off the roof."

They all talk to Mike about why he should do ecstasy. Why, Mike wonders. But they are very civil about it. Ecstasy is not like weed that will make you jump off the roof. It's friendlier. And we're all here. Couldn't be a safer place.

Mike thinks that, beneath it all, they are asking him a question. But what? And then suddenly he thinks of the girl on the motorcycle carrying the baby. Maybe he's high already.

The pill feels chalky for a moment on Mike's tongue and then he swallows.

# 23

As soon as Mike decided to take the internship in Hong Kong, his mother gave him a picture of the family. In it, Mike, his parents, and Lyle stand at the seashore near the house on Long Island. They look like catalog people, handsome and expensive, posed and shot.

Lying in bed a week before he was to leave, Mike held up the photograph to a lamp. He was wondering what his life would be like in Asia. The lamplight shone through the silver gelatin print, and Mike could see through himself. He could see through his blond hair and white teeth. He could see through his parents with their arms around each other, and his frowning brother. He could see through the sky behind his family and the sand they stood on.

Mike was determined that his life in Asia be good and simple. That it be the start of his life, Mike's life, and not be a crazy life. But as he looked at what was actually just a snapshot and saw his family ghosted by the backlight, he suddenly understood something new and it unsettled him. What Mike saw was the potential for craziness in himself, just like it was there in all of them.

# 24

Mike is high. He looks around the room and is struck, in the self-conscious and lengthy realizations of his synapses, by how ordinary everything is. Mike is beginning to suspect that he is himself as much a cliché as his new reporter friends. But he feels good. He thinks of the girl on the motorcycle with the baby and what she would say if she could open his head with a crowbar and read his thoughts, which roll around like so many ball bearings in there. Maybe she would ask him to marry her. Maybe she would rob him. Both appeal to Mike.

"Do you know an Australian named Hardy?" Mike asks Burton. It's like he can't help himself.

"Total stoner lech," says Burton, beginning yet another monologue. "His father was a lawyer but he grew up poor in Sydney because his father was obsessed with the Aboriginal women, wanted to fuck every single one he saw, and so his practice was dedicated to Aboriginal land preservation and he never made any money. Father and son started smoking hash together when he was twelve, which could have been good or bad depending on how you look at lawyers, because young Hardy was himself considering the law until his father was murdered and ritualistically mutilated in the outback by a cuckolded Abo. Poor Hardy, in rage and grief, left his beloved Australia and, not surprisingly, was broke upon arrival in Bangkok. But Bangkok being what it was then, he was able on that first afternoon to get fed, laid, and housed. Good place, he thought, so he stuck around, moved a little dope, just enough to get by. Life was easy and hazy, and mostly he fucked backpackers, boys and girls, because, as he saw it, somebody had to. Now it's twenty years later and he keeps a crash pad to fuck the backpackers. Been in love with Bridget for years."

"How do they know each other?"

"Everybody knows everybody here and I think I fancy a soak," Burton says. "Have you thought about the hot tub? It's quite lovely. And there's the quite lovely Bridget sitting in it."

Mike follows Burton's gaze to the terrace, where Bridget and Paul are waving to them from the tub.

Mike strips out of his ripped pants to his shorts at the edge of the hot tub. The tub is deceptively large and deep, with submerged benches.

"Will you look at that, Paul?" says Bridget. "Look at Mike."

Paul looks at Mike and Mike looks down at his own chest, his hand absently scratching.

"He's in such form!" says Bridget. "Look at his stomach."

Mike goes red in the face as he lowers himself into the water. So ordinary, it's like he's at home. He remembers blushing in other hot tubs. It's the drugs, Mike suddenly thinks. What kind of asshole feels fucked with because he's in good shape?

"I bet you were an athlete," Bridget tells him. He says he was, just stopped playing when he got to college. Could have played.

"Were you that good?" she asks him.

"Fastest white kid in the city," Mike hears himself say, then feels very stupid, very young.

"How old are you, Mr. Mike?"

"Nineteen."

"Oh, I knew it." Bridget brings her hand up to her mouth, teasing him. "You're just a baby!"

Mike wants to tell her he likes the world probably as much as she does. Paul, staring up into the night sky with his wide, pale arms stretched out along the edge of the tub, tells him he has a rip in his trousers. So they noticed, thinks Mike. Of course they noticed.

Burton calls from the kitchen for Mike to come and help with drinks. Mike steps out of the tub with the certainty of Bridget's eyes upon him. If only she had to get out of the tub before me, he thinks.


Mike likes making drinks with Burton in the kitchen. He looks at the newspapers on the bar as Burton breaks ice with a small steel mallet. Mike reads about world leaders embroiled in war and torture. The Republican candidate for president of the United States is a deeply religious man and is quoted as saying that God is on his side. This is not cool with Burton, who, tapping the paper with an angry finger and shaking his head, breaks off to go piss.

Mike picks up the mallet to test it and it feels good in his hand. He lights another cigarette and reads the bookshelf behind the bar. Some books he doesn't recognize about Southeast Asia and drug smuggling, and high fashion, and a couple he knows from his first-year philosophy course, St. Augustine, Kierkegaard.

Suddenly, Bridget's voice, sticky and harsh, comes from the terrace. She is swearing and calling for help. Mike looks and sees her straining in the tub, sees her body and her freckled breasts roll up over the top and her red hair falling in her eyes, and then she braces her knees and drives her hips forward, calling for help, pulling, afraid.

"Burton," she is yelling, "come on, you idiot."

Mike runs and sees that she is trying to pull Paul from the bottom, where he is sitting cross-legged, like a submerged Buddha. His hair floats like a pale lily pad just beneath the surface. Harrison and Burton both rush up behind Mike and together they haul the enormous Paul from the tub. He splutters and hacks, eyes closed as they get him onto a chair on the terrace. Mike noticed earlier that the chair's back is made of wrought iron angels. Paul is still coughing as he opens his eyes.

"I didn't realize he had been down there so long," says Bridget, calm now. "I was looking off the other way and then I looked and realized he was there at the bottom."

Paul's long, pale face has a blue cast and his eyes stare out into nothing. Burton leans down into his face, patting it gently and then less gently.

After another minute or two, Paul seems to focus on Burton.

"What happened," asks Burton. "What happened, Paul?"

"It felt so good, I didn't want to be coming up."

This sounds very spacey to Mike, as if through an airlock.

"It felt like being in chocolate mousse."

Harrison walks back into the living room and starts reading the paper.

# 25

Mike remembers the time Lyle burned himself with a bottle rocket. They were at the beach with their parents and a friend of Lyle's who was visiting for the weekend. The sand was cool on their feet and the June sky was cloudless. They had a small bonfire, and were sitting on blankets watching as Mike's father roasted yellow bell peppers and hot dogs on metal skewers for lunch.

The friend was describing his father to Mike and Lyle, and their parents were listening even as they had their own conversation, which is something they learned to do as parents. Mike and Lyle learned to do the same thing as children. The friend was joking about his father, a television writer, describing him as an artist shamed and oppressed by the wealthy financiers who worked in the same Midtown tower where he had his office. Mike and Lyle were both nodding and laughing at the notion. Then their mother interrupted them and said to the friend, "That's called a fish-out-of-water setup, and I believe any number of very successful sitcom writers keep offices in Midtown."

"No, I guess you're right," said the friend. "I know."

They finished eating in silence and looked out at the ocean. Then Mike's father told the boys to go look in the trunk of the car. There was something for them in there. At a newsstand in Chinatown he had bought a coffee can full of bottle rockets. Mike and Lyle and the friend ran to the trunk and then down to the water to set some of them off. Lyle was especially jumpy because his parents were arguing over the fire behind them. The bottle rockets punctuated their argument with short, screaming hisses and weak pops.

Mike remembered that one went off in Lyle's hand. He couldn't tell how it happened, because Lyle was being so careful. But it looked like Lyle held it too long, like he wanted to see what would happen. The rocket shot up like a cartoon insect trying to burrow into the bottom of Lyle's chin. And then it exploded. The bottom of Lyle's face turned black and swelled immediately. Their father ran down to the water and grabbed his son, stroking his hair as he looked at the burn. He picked up Lyle and carried him to the car. "I'm taking him to the hospital, stay with Mike," he said to his wife.

Lyle, through the pain, was glad to be with just his father in the car. It was better to be with just one parent than two. Mike, with his mother, was thinking the same thing. "Divide and conquer" was their joke several years later.

Years later, Mike and Lyle would be drinking in the co-op of that same friend, and the friend would be telling the bottle rocket story, and Mike would say quietly, he thought, to his brother, "You set that thing off into your chin."

"Hey, yeah," the friend said, "I always remembered it like you were trying to fucking blow your chin off."

"I'm just bullshitting with my brother," said Mike.

The friend thought, not for the first time, that the whole family was crazy.

# 26

The night is over. The first color of the day is rising into the sky. Mike is tired and sweated out and a little high still, and he is sitting outside with Burton. Bridget has gone into the bedroom and closed the door. Paul has fallen asleep inside, watching television. Harrison walked into the bathroom a few minutes earlier and Mike hears the shower raining behind the door.

Mike lights one last cigarette and looks out at the coming morning, much clearer up here than the day before on the street. He wants to keep talking to Burton but doesn't know what to say, other than to ask some lame question about credentials.

"What?" Burton asks, with one eye open through the veil of blond hair. His head is nodding and weaving.

"Don't I need credentials or something like that to talk to that cop you mentioned?"

Burton blows his hair out of his face and trains his one open eye on Mike. "Mike," he sighs, very tired, "don't worry about the cops."

Burton nods out, and Mike is thinking about how exhausted he is too when Harrison appears on the terrace beside him. He is freshly scrubbed and doesn't look tired at all.

"How about we go out," he says. "I'm hungry. You hungry? Eat off the booze. Breakfast beer. Introduce you to the Grace."

Burton is completely passed out now but Mike says thank you to him anyway.

# 27

The Grace Hotel is an air-conditioned tower with a bar in the basement that never closes. It's famous for this. The bar's walls and ceiling are blue and yellow tile and the light is soft but fluorescent. The floor is not sticky and the bartenders are jaded Thais wearing hotel badges. It is impossible to tell when the sun rises because there are no windows. All very obvious. There is also a bowling alley.

"I hate this place," says Harrison.

Then why are we here? Mike wonders, as they step out of the way of a tiny Thai girl and a Brit in an orange, tie-dyed shirt. The girl trips as she passes and Mike sees a small, brown breast pop out of her dress. As Harrison leads him to the bar Mike notices a group of prostitutes in one corner who are taller and whiter than almost everybody else in the room. Mike thinks they look Russian, although he knows no Russians. A couple of them have red hair, he notices.

"Not for your story," says Harrison, as he orders beers, "but interesting."

Mike decides the prettiest girl in the place is a tall Thai, who does little talking but lots of hair mussing. She wears jeans and a white blouse cut in a deep V. She has three drinks from three different men in front of her and is sipping from each of them. Unlucky that she has ended up at the Grace this late, Harrison explains. She has to make up time.

Mike goes to the bathroom and when he returns Harrison is talking to a Thai girl whose back is to Mike. She is small, wearing a silver, almost metallic dress that stops just above her knees. From the back she looks the way the girls Mike grew up with did when they were twelve or thirteen and trying to look older. Her hips are so narrow. But when she turns, he is startled by the heavy makeup and the way she stares at him. Mike thinks she is probably his age.

Harrison calls her Tweety.

"Always flitting in and out of trouble," Harrison says, smiling at her.

Mike extends his hand and Tweety takes it in both of hers and leans forward and kisses him on the cheek, saying something to Harrison in Thai. He says something back to her and Mike is surprised to hear the sharp language come so easily out of Harrison's wide mouth.

"Harrison," Tweety says in a high voice, "you have very handsome friend."

Harrison grunts and sips his beer. "Mike is doing a story on pills," he says.

"A reporter?" Tweety says. "But you look so young."

"I'm barely doing it." Mike can see the bags under her eyes.

Harrison explains that Tweety is a very good translator. Tweety nods at the praise. "Maybe I could translate for you," she says and puts her hand on Mike's arm.

Mike tells her that the club kids all speak English.

"Many stories," is all she says.

"Better stories," Harrison says, seriously. "Tweety lives in Khlong Toei. That's one of the neighborhoods where Thaksin is cracking down. You've seen a lot of pills, haven't you, Tweety?"

Tweety's expression hardens. "I have seen," she says.

Mike realizes Harrison is trying to help him and that they are talking about *yaa baa,* not ecstasy.

"What do you think?" asks Mike. "The government is too rough?"

"Many stories," she says, again.

When Mike asks Tweety if she has heard of Christopher Dorr, she is startled and looks at Harrison, whose expression doesn't change. Mike himself is a little nervous about his question and watches Harrison for a sign. Nothing. Finally, Tweety says yes, she knows Dorr. He is a reporter, but she has not seen him in a long time. She looks past Mike at an expat in a pinstripe suit just down the bar.

"Another *farang* asshole," Tweety says. She now seems a little drunk. Mike asks her again about Thaksin and his crackdown.

"Even this place, the Grace, was raided, " she says, loudly. "They made everyone pee in cup. Many are careful about coming now, too high."

The expat in the suit overhears this and is unsettled. "What's that?" he wants to know. "You say they'd make me piss in a cup?"

Tweety smiles at Harrison, who nods down the bar.

"Really, they make you piss in a cup?" the man asks again. Then he comes out with it, of course. "I had a tab of E last night."

Harrison shrugs to show that this is nobody else's problem, and the man pays up quickly and leaves. Of course Tweety meant for him to hear.

After another drink, Mike asks Tweety if she could help him meet Christopher Dorr.

"No, I do not see him anymore," she says. "But maybe I translate for you."

"Finding Dorr is where I could use some help," says Mike.

"It is not a good story," says Tweety.

# 28

Mike's girlfriend, Jane, was a very good student and also good at sex, a combination that Mike's father once told him was not unusual. She was studying classics and was a fine translator. Sometimes she quoted the *Iliad* to Mike in bed, in Greek. They had never had an argument. One time Mike asked her if she thought that was strange.

"Why would we argue?" she said. "We never do anything wrong to each other and we're rich white kids at fancy schools." Mike found that answer very unsatisfying but didn't tell her.

Before Mike left for Hong Kong, he and Jane had re-affirmed that they would remain faithful to each other. Jane was going to Greece for the summer, and they had a loose plan to meet up somewhere in Europe in early September before they went back to school. They would race to bed and then linger in cafés and talk about their adventures. They were both a little sad because they knew they would potentially meet lovers on their travels. But they were also both slightly nervous and so were glad to have each other as anchors. Or something.

Mike and Jane did not like talking about their relationship. Many of the people they knew at college liked discussing and dissecting romances. Mike and Jane weren't interested, and this was part of why they had been together since those Fridays in high school when they talked all night about their families. The other part, of course, was that both sets of parents were crazy. Mike told Jane that life with his parents was like bad weather that came and went, and she told him about her father cheating on her mother and her mother taking him back, time after time. Later, it would occur to both of them that they had been so concerned with their families that they really hadn't thought much about each other, and they would regret this. By then, though, it wouldn't matter.

# 29

When they leave the Grace, the sun is all the way up and the heat burns down. Harrison takes Mike to a restaurant that is a single room off an alley. It is tiled and cool, with a stove and sink and refrigerator and two tables. They sit with beers and Harrison tells the man at the stove what food they want. Rolls come, along with cold noodles and fried vegetables spiced in egg. Mike realizes he is eating too quickly. And that he wants to know more about Tweety.

"Tweety seems like an interesting hooker," he says, with instant regret.

Harrison does not seem to notice, just eats his noodles. "She likes journalists," he says finally. "Wants to be a writer."

"Can that happen?"

"You never know," says Harrison.

"She's really a hooker?"

"She does a lot of things, works as a translator and a fixer sometimes."

"You use her?" Mike asks.

Harrison trains his eyes on Mike. "We helped her get started doing it way back," he says. "It's not really that unusual and she's quite good. Burton and I have this story going that Tweety's helping with right now, actually. Her brother runs pills on his bike. She's introducing us to him and he's supposed to connect us to a factory. Good pictures, maybe."

"She didn't seem to like Christopher Dorr," Mike says.

"Do you know why Analect asked you and Bishop to find him?"

Mike shakes his head. "Bishop said he disappeared."

"Not exactly." Harrison lights a cigarette and shoots his eyes at Mike again. "Analect burned him on a source that year on the Wa story. Some people died."

"That's why he disappeared?"

"You'd have to ask him yourself."

"I'd like to."

"You've got your own reasons."

"I read the work."

Harrison chuckles at this and inhales hard on his cigarette, as if an important decision has been made, and then relaxes. Relaxes for the first time since they met seventeen hours ago, it seems to Mike. Not a lot, just that his shoulders ease a little.

"Fair enough," says Harrison. "I can introduce you if you want."

"Thank you," Mike says. "That would be great."

How does this work, Mike wonders. What will I owe him?

# 30

Mike wakes up, still a little buzzed, as the sun is going down. He slept on top of his bed again. He showers and then empties his pockets. In one pocket he finds the number of the police contact Burton gave him. He should call right away, but he doesn't want to pick up the phone. He doesn't know why but he's not ready. After a meal, he thinks.

He takes care dressing, much more than he does at home. What a joke, he thinks, a new expat anticipating the worldly glamour of foreign sidewalks where no one is looking. He can dress like a movie star. He leaves his clean, light shirt open an extra button, revealing the undershirt beneath. He does not shave. He combs his hair back and rolls up his sleeves. A clean, broad white guy in good clothing. I am not an easy mark, he thinks. He hopes.

Downstairs, Mike leaves another message for Bishop at the desk and tries him on his cell phone. No answer. He connected himself without Bishop. He has friends now, a number of his own to call.

The rain comes as he sits down to noodles at the café across the street. It's suddenly cooler and the sky darkens. Mike eats slowly and drinks a green-bottled beer, realizing that he is hungover, and becomes daunted because he has to call the number he got from Burton and he is not a real reporter. He is just causing trouble. He wonders what Dorr is doing right now. Maybe Dorr is like his father. Maybe, now that it's evening, Dorr is sitting down with a Scotch on the rocks and reading a favorite novel again. Maybe he is writing a new story. Mike has no idea—Dorr could be doing anything. Mike is sure only that they'll both be surprised if they meet. Fine.

The rain comes in a torrent. The noodle vendors flee the streets with woks held overhead. The café customers slide their chairs under the awnings. The motorcycle taxi drivers lean against the wall and smoke cigarettes. Mike sees the fake-ID guy packing his easel into a suitcase with his pens and razors, and decides suddenly that he must catch him and have a press credential made. No time to get change, so he leaves too much cash on the table and rushes off after the ID guy, who is now disappearing down an alley.

Around the corner the man steps into a doorway. When Mike catches up he sees two old women squatting in a tiny room. Their creased cheeks are red from a small fire.

The old women stare out at him and Mike makes a hurried half-bow and backs away.


Mike walks through the rain to his table at the café. He is soaked. His plate and money and beer are gone. He pulls his chair even farther under the overhang and lights a cigarette.

Then, across the street, he sees Bridget and Paul, and jumps up again. They are walking under a great black umbrella and do not seem surprised to see Mike.

"Khao San Road is not New York," says Bridget. Mike is not sure what she means by that. He's always running into people he knows in New York.

"Where are you going?" asks Mike.

"A sex show," Paul laughs. "Where else on Buddha Day?"

"It's a kind of holiday," Bridget tells Mike. "Everyone is supposed to be in prayer, around little fires. You should come with us."

They are doing a story for an American men's magazine. Paul is the one who got the assignment.

"It's embarrassing," says Bridget, "but it will help finance the animal book."

"Isn't life grand?" says Paul.

It occurs to Mike that they might have meant to run into him.

# 31

Mike follows Bridget as she navigates her giant umbrella down a narrow alley. The alley is not wide enough for the three of them to walk abreast. It's like walking in a sweating water pipe. Mike is thinking that he would like to go back to his hotel room and sleep. But he also likes being with Bridget.

The bar is shut behind a corrugated metal door, like a garage. And it's paid off tonight, like every night, Bridget explains, Buddha Day or no Buddha Day. This place never gets busted. Just watched. Paul makes a phone call and they wait until the door begins to rise with a grinding sound.

"Get in quickly," Bridget tells Mike.

A yellow light spills out into the gutter, casting a glow on their shoes. Paul squats in first, and Mike follows Bridget as she ducks under the metal curtain that closes on the concrete behind them.

The club is dark with spotlights above a stage. They sit on stools at a raised table. The bar is crowded with Northern Europeans, tall and blond, mostly overweight like at the Grace.

There are also tight groups of Japanese businessmen drinking whiskey at tables close to the stage. The Thai girls are all light and thin as birds. The waitresses are distinguishable from the hookers because their English is less good. The hookers sit between the Japanese businessmen or stand with the Europeans at the bar and sip glasses of sweet cola. The men buy them drink after drink. Occasionally, if the girl is on good terms with the bartender and she looks at him as he pours for her, he will put some whiskey in the drink. Even after they go to a room with a man, they come back to the bar and drink more colas.

At one end of the stage, under hard white light, a Thai woman is reclining on a lawn chair. Mike heard about this in high school. On either side of her, a girl in sequined panties holds one of her ankles. The woman on the chair is naked and Mike looks at her carefully in the lull after Bridget explains the girls' drinks. Her pussy is shaved and Mike tries to gauge his feelings, create some silent understanding with himself. So what? So this is part of my life. I do not want to fuck this woman. I want to, what, save her?

Mike drinks his beer and watches as the woman on the chair makes a squealing noise and thrusts her hips. The girls seem to be pulling her ankles like levers. A dart flies from the woman's vagina across the room into a target. Cheers erupt from the Japanese businessmen. The Europeans at the bar guffaw and the hookers between them laugh politely. Bridget sneaks pictures and Paul goes to the bar for another round. Mike looks at Bridget and decides it might be easier to watch this alone.

The woman shoots another dart from her pussy, this one into a balloon on the other side of the stage. Pop. She puts in another dart and pops another balloon. Paul returns with drinks.

Mike notices a pumped-up young man with a handlebar mus-
tache leaning against the far end of the stage, sipping a beer.
He is wearing a sleeveless shirt. Mike sees the tattoos of a South
Pacific tribe wrapped around a thick bicep. He is laughing and
looks ridiculous, like those models in Dutch beer ads, thinks
Mike.

The woman shoots another dart but her aim is off this time
and the dart sticks the handlebar man in the arm. The man
bellows and drops his beer. Welcome to the tribe, Mike thinks,
and wonders how often this kind of thing happens and whether
it's part of the show for the *farangs*. Probably not. Holy shit,
people are saying, but some are laughing.

The man is yelling, "What the fuck, what the fuck!" The
woman in the chair jumps up and disappears behind the bar.
The prostitutes look like they are going to cry, their thin faces
shaking and pinched. Trouble is coming, maybe, and they are
afraid and hope it does not come down on them. They press
themselves more tightly to their Japanese businessmen or tall
Europeans. Safety with the customers. The customer is always
right.

"I would be catching a cab to a hospital," says Bridget,
aiming her camera at the handlebar man.

Mike thinks the guy will tell the story only if he doesn't
get a disease.


Paul is still laughing when a high voice calls to him from behind. *"Paul,"* the voice flies, and Mike knows he's heard it before. They turn and see Tweety coming toward them from the
pool table just behind them. Paul stands and she throws her

arms around him. Bridget, too, seems pleased to see Tweety and they kiss on the cheek.

"Have you met Tweety?" Bridget asks Mike.

"We met last night," Mike says. "This morning."

"With Harrison," says Tweety, nodding very brightly.

Mike looks at Tweety and remembers what Harrison told him about her, that she wants to be a writer. He wonders what her story would be if she could write it right now. Mike remembers something else Harrison told him about her, that she is a roamer, a girl who does not belong to a particular club but works several.

"What are you doing here," Tweety asks him, "in this dirty place?"

"Working," Paul volunteers, "on his travel piece."

"Oh, no," Tweety says, giggling.

"And we must have a quote from you," Paul smiles. "Here, why should Americans come to Thailand?"

Tweety deliberates, staring off toward the stage for a moment, and then, with great seriousness, brings her voice down a notch. "Thailand is the most beautiful country in the world."

Mike cannot tell whether she is joking or not, but he knows that they are all playing some kind of game.

Paul and Bridget clap and laugh. Mike makes a study of the pool game so he doesn't have to look at Tweety, but after a moment she leans close to his ear. He can feel her light breath on his neck. She puts her hand on his arm, gripping him as if to tell a secret. He bends down to hear, to be closer to her.

"Can I go home with you tonight?"

There is something in her voice Mike has heard before. From Jane, maybe? He laughs, but feels terrible and hypnotized.

"Thank you," he says, "not me." He smiles the whole time he speaks, as if this were really funny.

Tweety leans closer and asks again using the same words and breathes again into his ear and puts her hand on his thigh. Mike catches Bridget looking away as he laughs again, and says, "No thank you, Tweety."

Tweety pouts and backs off and starts to banter again with Paul, who starts hugging and touching her. Mike shrugs and Tweety smiles meanly at him and puts her hand on Paul's thigh.

Mike tries to watch the pool. Two guys who look like twins start running the table. They are Thai, and distinguishable to Mike only as white T-shirt and blue T-shirt. They hover like dragonflies, and sink or miss at will, yelling in triumph, cracking the balls and disorienting the *farangs*.

Their behavior is "not in Thai character," says Tweety to no one in particular. "Those boys."

Mike wonders if they might be on *yaa baa*.

Suddenly Bridget is whispering in his ear and he can feel her breath the way he felt Tweety's. It startles him.

"Relax, Mr. Mike," she says.

# 32

On a vacation in California, when Mike was only five or six, the family passed through a ghost town. At least that's how it seemed to Mike. It was really just a small cannery town called Moss Landing. Mike and Lyle both remembered short trawlers bobbing in the oily harbor. It was a Sunday morning, and the main drag was closed up, except for a weird old antique shop and the gas station. Their mother walked in on a whim while their father was getting gas, and the boys followed her.

Mike immediately found the most interesting piece, which was a 1971 Nikon Nikkomat. The camera was in bad shape with what looked like a bullet hole through the casing, small and circular in front and blooming out like a metal flower in the back. Mike put his little finger in the hole and then showed the camera to his mother. She bought it and told the boys not to mention it to their father and gave it to him for his birthday later that summer.

From then on, the camera sat on Mike's father's bookshelf. At first it was out of Mike's reach. When he was tall enough to get it down, he often played with it. When he was older and stopped playing with it, he still took it down and turned it over in his hands. His mother forgot all about it. His father only occasionally looked at it. Of them all, only Mike valued the camera, having spent his childhood pretending to die as a war correspondent shooting combat pictures with it.

# 33

A uniformed policeman slides in under the metal guard. He is skinny, with a thin mustache, and has a gun on his hip. He narrows his eyes and customers at the bar stiffen. He scratches his chin with his truncheon. The hustlers disappear up the back stairs.

The cop accepts a beer in a coffee mug, bowing slightly. Mike was never afraid of the police until he arrived in Bangkok. He didn't have to be. No cop had ever looked twice at him before. It's different here. He wishes he did not have the ecstasy residue in his blood. But when he looks around at Tweety, he realizes he is nervous about the cop for the wrong reason. Mike fears getting arrested for something he did, when the thing about cops in Bangkok is what Mike is now reading on Tweety's face. Cops here can do whatever they want. But then, after Tweety gets a good look at the cop's face, she is herself again, telling dirty jokes to Paul. Maybe they all know this cop, Mike thinks. Probably.

The hustlers reappear and the *farangs* around the table laugh at their coming and going and coming. The hustlers laugh with them. They have been winning what will be seven thousand baht off some guy from London. Taking turns letting him win, winning it back bigger. The guy is getting frustrated but orders another drink and keeps playing. Finally his American friend says no more games and stands as if to fight with the hustlers, which confuses them. The American is heavy in tapered jeans and cowboy boots.

The hustlers ignore him and play a game between themselves, putting on a show, wielding their cues like long wands. The American asks them where they think they'll be in twenty years, as if that will settle things, or at least make them feel bad. But then one of the hustlers, the better one, gets to talking. He has a daughter. No, he doesn't have a daughter. His fourteen-year-old wife is pregnant, that's it. Made good money tonight. Good money. Lotta fun. Only played at 20 percent. His eyes are whacked out.

The American says fuck you and turns his back to the pool table and starts flirting with Tweety, whom Mike assumes he knows from other nights. Tweety flirts back even though Mike is sure she doesn't want this guy. Something is not right. The American keeps asking Tweety if she wants another drink. She says she has a drink. The American grabs Tweety's arm, lets go, and then grabs it again. Tweety is laughing and wincing at the same time, and says she cannot go home with him. Finally the American gives up, but he wants the last word.

"All right, Tweetybird," he drawls, kissing her hard on the forehead, "that's OK. But don't ever ask me to buy you a drink again."

Mike and Paul both stand up off their bar stools. Bridget backs up a step and readies her camera.

"Do you all hear that?" the American says to the bar, enunciating, not smiling, "I'm never buying her a drink again. As long as she understands that, I'm fine."

"I think she understands," says Bridget.

# 34

There was one night when everyone in his family went to jail except Mike.

Lyle went first. He was rarely drunk, but sometimes he took walks with a bottle of bourbon, late at night. He enjoyed how the cab headlights seemed to soften at 3 A.M., how the only people he saw on Fifth Avenue were couples coming home. He grew warm, with heavy steps. Have a swig, sit on the fountain in front of the Plaza, stroll into Central Park and take another swig. Sometimes he brooded, especially if his parents had been crazier than usual, but usually he just allowed the city's shapes to float in and out of his mind. He was careful to be discreet and he was lucky.

But that night he got picked up. Public urination, open container. Bad judgment, he knew. But man, he thought, sometimes you just have to go. Everything was so awful when he was drunk and arrested. Worst of all, his parents would have yet another fight over whose fault it was. Lyle looked so down in the yellow fluorescence of the precinct station that the desk sergeant told him, "Don't worry, kid, it's just a fine."

Lyle knew that, just a fine, but when Mike came to pick him up at the station Lyle couldn't stop apologizing.

"What a hassle," he kept saying. "I know it's not a big deal, but what a hassle. Sorry, Mike." Mike didn't want to hear it. He hated when his brother apologized.

Mike insisted on being there with Lyle to explain to their parents the next day.

The boys told their parents at the dinner table. Take-out pizza off fine plates with good red wine and candles, because their parents had just gotten back from Long Island. Mike felt sorry for his brother, who wolfed his pizza and slurped his wine. And Lyle felt worse for Mike because here he was about to wreck it all for his brother, when for once their parents looked OK, even cheerful around the table.

Lyle told them, and Mike added how the cop had said it was no big deal.

"You're a good brother, Mike," said his father. "I just hope you weren't scared," he said to Lyle. And it seemed that was all he would say.

Their mother shook her head, but she was smiling. Mike could see that she would have been angry at other times, but now she wasn't. She almost laughed, and she said to Lyle how low-rent it all was.

"I know," Lyle said, "I'm really embarrassed. It'll never happen again."

"Oh, Lyle," their mother said, "don't worry about it. Your father went to jail for drunk driving last night." And then she blew out all the candles and left the table.

*　*　*

When they heard, they both imagined one of those green back roads out on Long Island and their parents driving home from a dinner party in some big house. No streetlights, so if their father turned off the headlights by accident when he meant to signal, it would be terrifying for their mother. And she would have a lot to say, in the car. Their parents were not the same in the car as they were at the dinner parties. Probably they had too much to drink. And a cop pulled them over.

The boys were sure there was never any real danger, because their father was a great driver. Both boys had ridden with him after a beer or a few and were never afraid. He would never let anything happen to them or their mother. But then Mike's mother had been so belligerent with the cop, when she saw that he would arrest her husband, that he arrested her too.

# 35

Mike is woozy from the beer and feels a cold sweat on his neck as he watches Tweety disappear with a squat man in a leather biker vest. Mike wonders if the guy walking up the stairs, holding Tweety's hand, is a dwarf.

"That's her uncle," says Bridget, "and her pimp sometimes. Only family she has in Bangkok, except for a younger brother."

"Little guy," says Mike.

"People are afraid of him. Makes it easier for Tweety to fuck people for money."

"Why are they afraid of him?"

"He's a thug," Bridget says, almost brightly, "from a drug operation up north."

Mike doesn't want to think about Tweety anymore. Dancers are now sliding up and down a row of poles, naked except for purple garters and red feathers in their hair. Mike thinks they look like pistons of flesh going up and down.

The American comes back and Mike watches him tap his pointed boot at the bottom of the stairs, impatient, waiting for something. And then Tweety's pimp uncle is back too, and they are talking. Mike points this out to Bridget, who, he realizes with alarm, is also drunk. She runs her long, pale fingers through her bright red hair and smiles mournfully at Mike.

"Poor Tweety," says Bridget, "she always knows."

"It's her business," says Paul, clearing his throat, "but that American looks awful."

"We should do something tonight," says Bridget. "I'm going to buy her out."

Paul shakes his head as Bridget walks over to the uncle and the American.

"What's she doing?" Mike asks.

"Who knows," says Paul, looking at the ceiling and lighting a cigarette. "Who knows life?"

Mike gets up and follows Bridget. They are all by the wall, in the shadow under the staircase. Mike comes up behind Bridget just as she is saying that she will pay double what the American is paying. The uncle likes Bridget's offer and apologizes to the American, pointing to another girl across the room who might replace Tweety.

"We had a deal," says the American. "I already paid."

The uncle apologizes, but says he is a businessman and offers the money back.

"This is bullshit," says the American. He is sweating and the blood is going to his face and he is stomping his cowboy boots. He even spits on the floor.

"What the fuck are you doing?" he demands, jabbing a finger at Bridget. "You can't have her. You won't even fuck her."

"How do you know?" says Bridget.

Mike notices Tweety, crouching on the staircase, watching.

"Fine, goddammit," says the American. "I'll pay the same."

"Come on," Bridget says, "there are so many other girls here. What difference does it make?"

"Fuck you," says the American. "You want to pay more?"

Bridget doesn't have any more money. She looks at Mike and he nods. His good leather wallet is full of money. He can feel Tweety's eyes on him as he hands it to Bridget. The American yells, "What is this shit?" and starts jabbing his finger at Mike. "She's for you?"

Mike doesn't say anything. The uncle quickly takes Mike's money from Bridget. The American whirls and calls Tweety a little bitch he didn't want to fuck anyway.

When the American turns back to get his money, the uncle is gone.

# 36

The fight starts like a fight between children, with shouting.

"What kind of con is this?" the American yells, pushing past Bridget and punching Mike clumsily, but with the full force of his shoulder. Mike sees the punch coming. The fist expands until it's all he can see, but he's too slow from the beer to slip it. It hits Mike in the nose and bright red blood flows over his lips as he stumbles back like a tripping dancer.

The cop drinking from the coffee mug sees Mike get punched and puts down his beer. The American is now on top of Mike, clawing into him. Mike feels his heat and weight and the hair on the American's forearms rubbing in the blood on his face. Mike flails his arms, but the American has a hand under his chin and is pushing back, trying to hit him in the temple with his other hand. "Oh shit," Mike hears Bridget say.

Paul starts to pull the American off, but the cop pushes him away and clubs the American hard on the head. Mike hears the cracking sound and coughs on the floor, scrambling to get up as the American blacks out.

The cop chatters furiously at Mike, who doesn't understand.

There is blood, slick and matte in liquid tendrils, dripping down the cop's wooden club. The cop is pushing Mike, and Bridget tells him to just get against the wall. Paul is on his cell phone. The cop cuffs Mike and then puts handcuffs on the American, who is still unconscious on the floor.

The cop scowls at Mike and is taking his radio from his belt when Paul says something in broken Thai to him. A name. He is giving the name of another cop. You know? He is on his way here, wait for him. When the cop hears this he cracks Mike in the spine with his club. The shot feels electric and hot up into Mike's neck. He has done that before, thinks Mike.

The cop orders everyone back. Only Paul is left close enough to Mike and the American to translate. Mike looks at the wall. He can feel his heart pounding and hears the cop and Paul parlaying. He strains to listen. He wishes he could understand the cop's radio. He knows suddenly that his fate crackles along those shortwaves. He wishes that it had all gone differently, but when he looks into the wall, he realizes with a strange surge of happiness that it's all just totally fucked. He imagines the horrors of prison in Thailand. He keeps his eyes open and isn't panicking and this gives him confidence. Let's just see how far it can go, let's see how much trouble a white kid from New York can actually get into. Is there a hole in the world so deep that my father can't track me down and pull me out?


Someone bangs on the metal door. Mike is straining to see, twisting his neck for a sliver of vision behind him.

Another cop has arrived, a lieutenant, and somehow Burton is right behind him. Mike thinks it's as if they came together. He sees them over his shoulder and sees how the lieutenant intimidates the uniformed cop. The lieutenant looks like a pig. This pig lieutenant was my contact, Mike realizes.

The uniformed cop relates what happened with deference to the lieutenant and the lieutenant grunts. Mike feels the flow of the narrative, where the American punched him, where the cop swiftly subdued the troublemakers. Mike darts a look up the stairs, searching for Tweety. She is gone from her perch.

Mike listens to Burton and the lieutenant talking as the cop uncuffs him.

"How's your new son?" asks Burton. "All his sisters taking care of him?"

"I don't like having to come out in the rain," says the lieutenant. "I like to stay dry."

"Of course," says Burton.

"It is too much trouble," says the lieutenant, and he turns abruptly to leave. Everyone in the bar is watching. The uniformed cop looks at the unconscious American and calls for another coffee mug of beer. The lieutenant ducks under the metal door.

Burton claps an arm around Mike's shoulders. No worries. He is smiling and reassuring, but Mike knows he had to use a favor. When Mike starts to apologize, Burton says, "That's what they're for, those kind of favors. I'm just glad everyone was in a good mood. It could have been tricky with that lieutenant." Mike wonders what kind of tricky Burton means.

"Let's go for a drink," Burton says and leads Paul and Mike out the front door of the club. Mike notices that the patrons pretend not to look at him now. He sees their fear of him and his companions, their awe of trouble survivors. He likes it.

Following Burton around the back of the club, Mike sees a wooden staircase to the second floor, crowded with Thai girls. Some are wearing robes. Some at the top by the door, just towels. There must be a dozen smoking and chatting and looking tired like nurses outside an ER.

Paul and Burton smile and say hello to the nearest girls. Before Burton can ask about them, Bridget and Tweety emerge from the door at the top of the stairs. Mike thinks it's strange to see Bridget there. He is even more unsettled by Tweety, who is now wearing simple jeans and a T-shirt, instead of the uniform of the whore. Mike also notices her skin, how clear it looks without makeup, how soft.

"Ready?" says Burton to Tweety.

Tweety nods and smiles without opening her mouth, as if steeling herself for something that will hurt but is good for you, like a shot.

# 37

Mike's mother took her boys to the Central Park Zoo only once. It was very early on a Saturday morning, and she had woken them up and rushed them out of the house. Even in the rush, Mike saw his father asleep in his suit on the couch in the living room. Mike's mother was pretending to be cheerful, and he and Lyle were both uneasy about this. They didn't know what to say and were careful not to irritate her.

"Relax," she said in a flat voice when they walked into Central Park at Sixty-fourth Street. "We're going to the zoo, not school." She bought them fleshy hot dogs for breakfast from a vendor with a cart, another surprise because they were not allowed to eat street food. Mike and Lyle would remember all of this vividly, because it was unusual to be with their mother any Saturday morning, but mostly because they had then gone to see the polar bear that was famous for being depressed.

Before she saw the animal, their mother didn't know there was anything notable about the bear. She caught her breath and squeezed Mike's shoulder when she saw it. All the fur on both sides of its muzzle was gone, leaving only skin the color of the dark blood beneath it. The three of them watched as the bear walked toward them into the bars of the cage without turning its head until its nose was wedged between the black steel. With deliberate strength the bear planted its haunches and, stiffening its shoulders and neck, began to scrape its muzzle up and down between the bars. The bear's eyes were open the whole time, grinding down its face.

Mike remembered well that after a couple rounds of this his mother looked down at the boys and said, "They should kill that bear."

When they got home, their father had made elaborate sandwiches for lunch. Not long after, their mother read that the bear had lacerated the face of a third zoo keeper and was to be put down. She cut out the clipping and put it on the refrigerator door.

# 38

Mike is a little off. He can feel it, in his head, behind his eyes. It has just stopped raining—the air feels like breath—and Burton is leading them to a bar called Triple Happiness. Silvery reflections of street lamps steam off the street. Pay attention to the weather, Mike thinks, as he walks between Bridget and Burton. This is what his father always said. Weather makes you smarter, weather doesn't lie, weather is real. Just behind them, Tweety is with Paul, who recounts the adventure. "Isn't life grand?" he says after each twist in the story. Tweety is an obsequious audience, laughing, feigning fear and shock. Mike hardly listens. He thinks he sees a girl on a motorcycle, flying up the street, almost off the ground. It spooks him.

"Did you see that?" he asks Bridget. She didn't.

"You must have got hit hard," she jokes.

"Yeah," he says, "maybe." He thinks it may or may not be his own growing hallucination. He doesn't give it much thought.

Yes he does.

# 39

Inside Triple Happiness, Mike and Tweety sit across a table from each other. They haven't spoken since they left the sex club. She is especially pretty in the darkness of the bar, all shadows and black hair. From the way she looks at him Mike thinks he is supposed to speak first, but he remains silent.

"Maybe you are like Christopher Dorr," she says.

Mike doesn't know whether she says this because she knows it will get his attention or because it is true or maybe both. Somehow this is the worst thing she could say to him. Maybe it's just the way she said it. She is fucking with him. He knows this for sure.

When the others return with drinks, Tweety gets up and goes to the bar alone.

"I think there might be some kind of confusion with Tweety," Mike says.

"Not your fault," says Burton. "Language problem. It'll get sorted."

Bridget follows Tweety, and Mike tries not to watch. Between them and the girl on the motorcycle, Mike is afraid he wants to fuck every woman he meets in Bangkok. Afraid of what, though? He wasn't afraid to fuck Jane. Burton lights a cigarette and offers him the pack.

"I think Tweety thought I wanted to hire her for the night," Mike says.

"Well that's what you did," Burton chuckles.

"You know what I mean."

"It's not that complicated. Bridget will explain to her."

"That's what she's doing now?"

"It's happened before."

Mike thinks about this. "It wasn't even me," he says. "It was Bridget."

"I know," says Burton.

Paul gets up shaking his head and follows Bridget. Mike wants to ask Burton if Paul has slept with Tweety. Instead he says he doesn't want to piss Paul off.

"What does that mean?" asks Burton levelly and finishes his drink. "Paul's just pissed about the police. I'm telling you, this will all get sorted."

Mike isn't so sure, but then all of them are back at the table and Tweety is laughing and smiling at him. She and Bridget have been to the bathroom. Like high school, thinks Mike.

The plan now is to go to Burton's place and smoke some hash, come down from the night's craziness. And Tweety is coming. Paul and Bridget insist, as if this were a normal thing. Mike doesn't participate in the inviting and neither does Burton, although it's his house, and his hash they are planning to smoke.

# 40

At Burton's house, they sit on the terrace and pass around a pipe. Tweety is very quiet at first but talks more after she smokes, which makes everyone happy. They all ask her questions, and Tweety tells about how she lives in Khlong Toei and sends money home to her family in the north. She talks about her younger brother working in the city too. He just bought a new motorcycle and this is a big deal. Their village is small and very poor, very remote. She says she understands why the government is killing all the drug users, but Tweety doesn't agree with this. She uses the term "excessive force" like a new appliance she doesn't want to break.

Mike asks Tweety if she has ever taken *yaa baa*. She laughs, very high. "Only take it once," she says. "Made me want to kill a *farang*."

"Who?" asks Mike as a joke, and then realizes his question has made everyone else uneasy.


Mike is now stoned enough on the hash to ask about Dorr again, which is what he really wants. He waits for an opening. The conversation rolls and splits and reconnects. They all talk about how crazy families are. Burton's family shipped him off to boarding school. Bridget's father worked in a zoo. Mike gets to talking about his parents, too, which he knows is not good.

"Same as all the rest," he says, trying to concentrate through the dope but giving away too much, he realizes, as he speaks. "Drunk, crazy. They're old-fashioned about it. Stigma. Shit, they've made it this far."

Mike lights a cigarette and tries to calm himself, determined not to mention the breakdowns, undiagnosed, ignored. "But you have to trust people to take care of themselves," he continues. "It's all just part of the deal."

"Not lost their minds yet?" Bridget wants to know.

"Best training for an artist is an unhappy childhood," says Burton.

That cliché, thinks Mike.

Harrison shows up with a bottle of bourbon. "Is the bar fighter here?" he asks, laughing.


"I would like to see snow," says Tweety.

Bridget and Paul and Burton all want to get out of news and make art and eventually go home, but Tweety would just like to be in some snow. She has never even seen snow, except in movies, and she can't imagine being in it. Specifically, she would like to stand under a snowing sky and look up and catch snowflakes on her tongue.

"The hell with snow, and I'm never going home," says Harrison, stroking the top of his shaved head with one hand and pouring his bourbon with the other. "What about you, Mike?"

"I want to go home, too," he says, "but just to my hotel."
They all laugh.

But suddenly it's as though an alarm clock has gone off in
Tweety. She says she has to leave. She thanks Burton formally.
Watching her get up and collect herself, Mike is again taken
with her body and wonders if maybe he should take her home
with him after all. Tweety smiles at him and says thank you,
very seriously. She extends her hand to him and as they shake
he can feel her softness. She stands at full height and smiles
once more at everybody, then disappears out the door, looking
from behind like a girl Mike might have known back home,
leaving in jeans and a T-shirt after a long party.

# 41

Mike's father was filled with regret for sleeping with Dorr's sister. He tried to explain his feelings to her, but that only infuriated her. She understood that she was nothing. They never spoke again.

Mike's mother had broken up with Dorr by Christmas. He was too wild, and she thought that maybe she had made the worst mistake of her life. Mike's father would not take her back. She asked Analect to act as an emissary on her behalf. He said he would do what he could but then made a pass at her. He failed, of course.

Dorr moved to another house and he and his sister dropped out of the others' lives. The first news Mike's father got of them, about a month after graduation, was that the sister was back in New Orleans and pregnant. Mike's father wondered what she was going to do with the baby but didn't try to find out, though he was sure it was his.

# 42

Mike would not remember how Tweety came quietly back into Burton's apartment or her undressing. He would only remember her appearing over him, naked, when he awoke on Burton's couch. Mike was still drunk and high from the hash when she began to undress him, and then he was naked from the waist down. He would remember images, fragments. The slope of her back as she put a condom on him. The veil of her long black hair against his face, and the only thing she said: "You paid for me, now I want to pay you." After that, Mike did not think about anything but her and her body and trying to please her, though he could tell he was like a child to her.

He would not remember her leaving.

# 43

Mike wakes up sweating in a slant of sunshine on Burton's couch. He sits up, grabs a piece of paper, and starts a note to Burton, but as he is writing it Burton emerges from the bedroom. Through the door, Mike sees Bridget lying in a tangle of sheets. She is beautiful but very distant, like a good oil painting of a nude at the wrong end of a telescope. Burton looks washed and clean in his fresh silk shirt, his blond hair up in the sprouting knot.

"Do you want to stay for breakfast?" Burton asks. "I think I'll make some eggs and things."

Mike explains he has to get back to his hotel. Check messages, find Bishop, do some more reporting for his story. He wants to go to a club or two and ask some more questions and score some drugs to see what deals are like for the backpackers. He's going to walk into the slums on his own.

"Well, good then. Call us later for a drink, yeah?"

"I definitely will."

"Whenever you like. Really."

In fact, Mike has no plans to go anywhere until the next day, when Harrison has promised to introduce him to Christopher Dorr.

Outside, the bright sky presses down on him and he wonders where Tweety is.

# 44

Leaving his hotel again after a shower, Mike checks reception for messages. None, but there's a sealed envelope waiting for him. He knows who it's from.

He crosses the street to his café and orders a coffee, and eggs on his noodles. He lights a cigarette and waits for his coffee before opening the letter—just something to read, like it could have been the Sunday paper back home.

The note is from Bishop, of course, and briefly apologetic. He says he knows Mike has connected with Burton and that they will all meet up in the next few days to compare notes. "Enjoy yourself and stay out of trouble" is how it ends.

Mike knows he will stay out of trouble. He has found enough for one stupid backpacker story. He has done it. He will go out again tonight with his new friends but now there is no pressure. He has done enough. And so today he releases himself for the afternoon to go and see a *wat*. He will go and see the famous Emerald Buddha. He is sure he will like it. Everyone in his family likes churches even though none of them likes religion. He thinks this makes sense and is fine. *Ritual.* The check comes and Mike takes it with two hands and a quiet thank you, as he has learned to accept things from people as a sign of respect.

# 45

Until Mike was in junior high school, he said prayers every night before he went to sleep. No one in his family told him to do this or taught him what to say, but he had done it as far back as he could remember.

They weren't really prayers; they were last words. He reasoned, as a little boy, that if he was going to die before morning, he wanted to have chosen his last words. So he did, and said them either out loud or slightly under his breath, depending on whether his brother was awake in the room. Somehow saying the words made them more true.

Mike never mentioned any God in these last words, nor specifics of his life, nor requests. Nothing, really, except a brief and particularly worded affirmation of how he felt about his family and being alive. He never told anybody about this. Lyle knew his brother said something to himself every night, but he never asked about it.

Mike didn't name what he was doing and it didn't occur to him that it was strange until he was in junior high school, and by then he had stopped without thinking about it.

The night before he was to leave for Asia, he said his last words again. He hadn't done it in years, and they just popped into his mouth and embarrassed him, and then he couldn't sleep. So he added to his usual statement: "We are all invincible until the first heart attack."

This is a modern idea.

# 46

Khao San Road is not as difficult as it was just two days before, but while he is walking to find the *wat,* Mike loses his way. The side streets widen and the heat and dust of the traffic make the walk unpleasant. He stops for a cigarette, watching a soccer game in a park. The boys playing are young, not yet teenagers, and they move like identical insects up and down the field. Mike can't tell them apart, can't pick one to follow. Total *farang,* he thinks.

He walks on and finally sees the spire of the *wat.* It is fine and glinting, piercing up through the smog. He sets out toward it but comes to a six-lane street that moves like a highway. Implacable *tuk-tuk* drivers compete with trucks for the middle lanes and the motorbikes weave and lean between them. The *wat* is on the other side. Mike walks along the highway.

There is nowhere to cross, but Mike sees a young man in work jeans and unlaced boots at the edge of the rushing traffic. The young man watches casually for a moment and then, with a quick first step, begins a controlled jog through the traffic.

Mike stops short, sure that the young man is going to get hit as he disappears behind a bus. Mike hears squeals and blares. But then the bus passes and the man is on the other side of the highway walking easily away. Mike thinks about it but decides he is not that crazy. It's not for *farangs*.

Mike has been passing in front of what he guesses are civic buildings, pale and ugly, but now, just behind him, he realizes, is the National Gallery. The building is unremarkable and un-advertised but for a small sign on the door. Air-conditioning leaks from the entrance and Mike wants to get out of the heat.

In the antechamber a sleepy woman in braids behind an information counter points to a sign in English with a price. Mike usually buys everything with overlarge denominations, which is easier than sorting out the unfamiliar currency. Here, though, alone with the sleepy woman, he is unhurried, so he works out the amount and walks into the cool silence of the museum.

Arranged in the first room are rows of white and bald mannequins, taller than any of the Thai women Mike has met. They are dressed in long ball gowns, strange high couture. The fashion is bad, like wardrobe mistakes from period Hollywood movies. Some of the mannequins have enormous headdresses; others are belted with sequined patterns of birds or flowers. The colors are the palette of stained glass, muted as though overwashed. Mike thinks of St. John the Divine, back in New York, and the strange halos he saw in the dark church as a child.

Some of the dresses are revealing. The mannequin breasts stand straight out and hold up some of the dresses. One dress, hung with purple feathers, is cut from clavicle to crotch, and Mike gently pulls the fabric back into place, to cover an erect nipple.

All the mannequins face in the same direction and Mike thinks of a discovery somewhere in Africa that his father once told him about. An archaeologist had found eight huge cat heads arranged in burial, all pointing the same way, which was evidence, he said, of early religion. Pagan rites of the Upper Neolithic, when there was more than one breed of man. Jane had told him that arranging the cat heads must have been a moment of great transformation, like the first painting on a cave wall, the beginning of sedentary life. The breakthrough. Not the same thing with the mannequins, but air-conditioned, at least.

The silence is broken by giggles, and into the room slouches a wide-bellied young man with wild copper hair and his arm around a pierced, pale girl in dark lipstick and a leather skirt. They are laughing about something and seem high. Seeing Mike they quiet and the young man stifles another laugh. His shirt has a skull with a snake wrapping through the eye sockets printed on it and is faded and sweat-stained.

Mike decides to engage them.

"Strange, huh?" Mike waves at the plastic fashion formation.

The skull boy just stares at him.

"Strange, these I mean," Mike repeats and this time Skull Boy pulls on Pierced Girl and points to Mike, saying something to her quickly in a romance language that Mike can't quite place.

"Oh yes, very strange," says Pierced Girl. "I am sorry my friend does not speak English." Pierced Girl's voice is a slow and breathy soprano and accented. French, maybe.

"Did you come for the exhibit?" Mike asks, though he sees they have only stumbled in like himself.

"Oh no, we only were hot and could not cross the highway." She says *highway* as if it were two words and a question.

"But I think they are wonderful," she says and starts moving from dress to dress, feeling the fabric of each between her thumb and forefinger.

"What brings you to Bangkok?" asks Mike.

"We are only tourists," smiles the girl. "We have been to the clubs and things."

These kids will be easy, Mike thinks.

"I've been meaning to get to the clubs too," he says. "You know any good ones?"

"Oh yes," she says. "We go every night. He loves the clubs, but I have to make him come to places in the day." She pauses to speak to Skull Boy in their language and he raises his eyebrows and Mike thinks he catches the word *droges*.

"Have you seen drugs in the clubs?"

Pierced Girl laughs and immediately relates the question to Skull Boy, who laughs harder.

"Oh yes, drugs everywhere," she says in a fake whisper. "This is the place for it. Vacation, no?" She has taken a silver ring out of her nose and is holding it up to the nose of a mannequin in a yellow fishnet bodysuit. "She is better than the Emerald Buddha, no?"

"Did you like the *wats*?" asks Mike. "I wanted to see the one across the highway, too."

Pierced Girl gives the mannequin a kiss on the lips. Skull Boy is rocking another of the plastic women on her heels and he calls out an idea to Pierced Girl and she laughs.

"What did he say?"

"He said we should knock one over and let them all fall on one another, how do you say it, like ah . . ."

"Dominoes," says Mike.

Skull Boy is trying to impress her and she is rolling her eyes but smiling. He is going to do it. Mike instinctively looks to see if there is a guard or a cop, even though he knows there are none in the gallery. Skull Boy rocks and rocks and then the quiet of gallery is violated by a cacophony of crashing plastic women.

# 47

Lyle once disappeared for two days. It was August.

Mike had half awoken to shouting in the night. The next morning when he went downstairs he saw the antique kitchen mirror lying shattered on the floor, an unripe pineapple among the shards, as though thrown from the bowl of fruit on the counter. Lyle and one of the cars were gone all day. When Mike called his cell phone it rang in on the hall table. Mike was sure his brother was safe—Lyle was supremely competent and a good driver—but this was strange.

His father did not descend from his bedroom until late in the afternoon. Mike stayed out of the kitchen, and didn't speak to his father until the mirror was cleaned up. His mother arrived back home in the evening, explaining that she had gotten up early and had been running errands all day. No one said anything about the mirror or the pineapple.

By dinnertime, Mike could see his parents were anxious about Lyle. But somehow not anxious enough. Like they knew what was happening. The big house felt hot and close. Mike took a long walk on the beach before he went to bed, and just because he had always been curious and was feeling eerie and frustrated, he kneeled down at the shore and drank some sea-water from his cupped hands, just to see what it was like.

The next morning, Lyle had still not come home. Mike's mother called all of Lyle's friends, who said they didn't know where he was. By that afternoon, she was becoming hysterical, but Mike's father calmed her down. Mike didn't know how. They gave Lyle another day.

Lyle came home in time for dinner. He didn't explain where he had been, and his mother, whom Mike suspected had been coached by his father, knew enough not to ask. When they were sitting down to eat, Lyle reached down next to the table and picked up a shard of mirror, missed in the cleanup, and looked at his parents before tossing it in a perfect three-point arc into the tall white kitchen garbage can.

Later that night when Mike asked his brother what had happened, Lyle said, "Seven years bad luck."

# 48

The three of them run out of the gallery, into the sudden heat and around a corner, where they finally stop. Skull Boy is still laughing as they catch their breath. Mike can see that this will be a high point of his trip. After a moment Skull Boy begins walking away, but Pierced Girl lingers, looking at Mike. Skull Boy calls to her. Mike doesn't understand what he says but he can tell Skull Boy wants Pierced Girl to himself.

"OK, OK," she says, but then she asks Mike if he would like to get a drink.

Mike, caught off guard, says, "Sure."

"Come then."

"I have to be somewhere," he lies. "I was only killing time."

"Tonight?"

"Sure, thanks."

"Do you know Chart?"

"Near Khao San Road?"

Mike doesn't know Chart but of course it's near Khao San Road. Maybe he'll go, but Pierced Girl isn't even that pretty.

For the hell of it, he asks her if she's heard of a Christopher Dorr.

"We don't remember anyone's names," she tells him.

Mike looks at the *wat* spire across the highway and turns to walk back to his hotel, wishing he had seen the Emerald Buddha.

# 49

Mike's father wore a long, black overcoat, and Mike held on to his coattails as they walked up the steps of the cathedral. He remembered the view of the gray, stone building ahead of them over his father's shoulder. Lyle was older and bounded up the wide snowy steps. He was in a hurry. "The faster we go to bed," he explained to Mike, "the faster we wake up."

Their mother said their father shouldn't make them go to church.

"Would you like to come?" he asked her.

"Would you like to come to the party?" she asked him.

She was going to a Christmas Eve party on Fifth Avenue. The deal was they would all meet back at home before midnight. That was reasonable, and by reasonable compromise they would prosper and not be crazy. So what if they weren't together all the time.

"Holidays are arbitrary," their father told them, though Mike knew he was lying to make everybody feel better. "Ritual is important for a reason."

# 50

Back at the hotel, Mike takes a cold shower and thinks about how there is no way he is going to Chart. Three days ago he would have forced himself, for the story, but the story is bullshit, or at least it's a different story now. It's not about backpacker kids eating pills. It's about *farangs* not knowing anything and getting in trouble. It's about me. And sometimes *farangs* ought to stay in their hotel rooms.

When the phone rings, Mike stays in the shower. If it's Burton let him think I'm out, Mike tells himself. I said I would be out. The phone stops and doesn't ring again. Wasn't even important.

He lies naked on the bed watching international news to kill the hours. The news is strange and accented, much differ-ent from American news, more interesting. A bomb explodes in Moscow and no one takes responsibility. Police clash with rebels in Haiti and the voodoo priests chuckle in the alleys and dance in the moonlight. A baby with two heads dies in Santo Domingo even though two-headed baby experts fly in from around the world. Mike falls asleep as the program starts to loop.

He wakes up at eleven. So much for Pierced Girl. He wants to go back to sleep but is hungry and decides to go to the McDonald's in the lobby of the hotel. A total *farang* move.

On his way downstairs, Mike stops by Bishop's door and listens. He wonders where Bishop actually is. Maybe his "best girl" is a wife and he has a whole family in Bangkok that has never seen his skyscraper apartment in Hong Kong. More likely Bishop is in some teak house with a thirteen-year-old hooker. Mike hears nothing through the door.


Eating his double cheeseburger, Mike continues to mull over Bishop, who, he decides, is behaving badly. There is a code and Bishop is not following it. Analect will not like the way Bishop disappeared. Analect lives by this code, Mike is sure. The same code his father lives by. It's about action. It's about always doing your job, before anything else. Mike overheard his father tell his mother this many times, when she complained that he was working too hard. Bishop is not doing his job, Mike thinks, so he is an asshole.

Assholes everywhere, actually. An American boy, about Mike's age, is telling the Thai girl with acne behind the counter that he doesn't want any pickles.

"I said I don't want any pickles." The kid is getting louder.

The girl hands him his tray with both hands and a slight bow. The kid notices Mike watching and comes over and sits down.

"See?" He lifts the bun, shows Mike the pickles on his cheeseburger, and pulls them off with venom. Mike shrugs. The kid tells him he is headed to a full moon party on the beach, but he's heard they've been checking for drugs on the way in. "It fucking sucks," he says.

Looking at this kid, Mike thinks about codes. Analect and his father, in adjacent prison cells, tapping their knuckles to the bloody bone on cinderblock walls. Secret language. A formalized system of deception, thinks Mike. Codes cover the truth. Like all of his father's talk about action. Like Tweety's makeup.

Then Mike stops thinking because Tweety walks in. She spots him and walks over. The asshole kid stops chewing.

"I like Big Macs," she says. "Can we get one and go to your room?"

# 51

"Sex doesn't matter," Tweety says. "Not important anymore." Mike and Tweety sit side by side on the edge of his bed. She is eating her Big Mac.

"We're even now," she says between bites. "Maybe you can help me." She is so slight that watching her devour the enormous Big Mac makes her seem grotesque to Mike.

"I'll try," Mike says. "What do you need help with?"

"I don't want to work for Harrison anymore. Or Mickey Burton. Can I work for you?"

"I can't hire you, Tweety. I don't even have a real job."

"Can you get me a job like yours?"

Mike thinks of how he got his job. How it started thirty years ago between Analect and his father.

"I don't know," says Mike.

"They won't let me quit."

"Harrison?"

"You tell them to leave me alone, please. I want to stay home."

And then Tweety stands up and, before Mike can say anything, puts the rest of her Big Mac in her purse and is gone.

# 52

In Hong Kong, as soon as he knew he was going to Bangkok, Mike looked up Christopher Dorr on the Internet. He sat in his cubicle in the gleaming, carpeted magazine office and read everything he could find. Christopher Ames Dorr was educated at St. Bernard's and Exeter and Harvard and, finally, Oxford, in East Asian Studies. He had won numerous awards for his investigative pieces, and was most famous for a cover story about the Wa people who farmed opium for a Burmese warlord cartel along the northern Thai border. Mike read the piece and had printed a copy to take with him. It was so close to the culture it was almost as if Dorr were Wa himself.

On the contributors page, Dorr was characterized as a fearless journalist who had been everywhere. Mike also found two photographs. In the first, Dorr stood at the edge of a Harvard boxing team picture. Mike's father was in the same picture. The second was a photograph of Dorr standing with some villagers in a remote field. The credit, Mike had noted, when he looked at the article again, in Bangkok, was Harrison Stirrat.

Mike has meant to ask Harrison about the picture for days now. He doesn't know why he hasn't. Having kept it to himself for so long, it now feels like a bad secret. And now he has another, about Tweety.

# 53

Mike wakes up to knocking on his door, three very sharp raps that yank him from sleep. It's Harrison, who says he called the room last night but there was no answer.

Mike dresses as fast as he can and follows Harrison down the stairs. They cross Khao San Road like they own it. Harrison doesn't look twice at anything. When they get to his clean, blue motorcycle, Harrison tells Mike there's been a change of plans. Dorr lives in Khlong Toei, in Tweety's neighborhood, and Harrison has to see her, so they can leave together when Mike is done talking to Dorr. Good, thinks Mike. A ride out.

"Have to," says Harrison, with an edge in his voice. "Tweety changed the plan."

"What happened?" asks Mike as he climbs on the back of the bike.

"I have to talk to her. We don't want it to get tricky."

Mike wonders about that word.

Harrison glances back at Mike over his shoulder. "She's backing out of introducing us to her brother. Very stupid."

This doesn't feel right to Mike but before he can say anything Harrison starts the engine and drowns out the possibility of further conversation.

The motorcycle trip is long but it goes by too fast for Mike. As they ride into Khlong Toei the tenements give way to tin shanties and squat wooden houses, some separated by broken chain-link fence. The sun is very hot, reflecting off the cracked concrete streets. When they slow down, the neighborhood smells of fruit and motor oil. There are dogs everywhere, in packs and running alone, and Mike hears roosters crowing somewhere nearby. Harrison doesn't turn off the engine when they stop.

Christopher Dorr's square house rises on stilts among the shacks and shanties. The windows are closed with gray wooden shutters.

At least Harrison will be making the introduction.

But then he doesn't.

"Just knock," Harrison tells him.

"You're sure he's home?" Mike can hear the hesitation in his own voice.

"He's always home. Just keep knocking. I'll be the next street over." Harrison points up the road. A toothless woman, not that old, crabs by them on deformed feet as Mike gets off the bike. She looks at him suspiciously. Off in the distance Mike can see the spire of a *wat*.

"Just come to the motorcycle when you're done," says Harrison. "You'll see it. Or I'll be done first and come back here."

Harrison adjusts himself on the bike and looks at Mike, who is looking up at Dorr's house.

"You sure about this?" asks Harrison.

Mike says he is, and Harrison speeds off on his blue motorcycle, disappearing around the corner, leaving Mike standing alone with his many questions in front of Dorr's house.

What the fuck, Mike thinks, we went to the same college.

# 54

Mike's father talked a lot about how he was looking forward to visiting Harvard now that Mike went there, but when he arrived Mike noticed that he didn't talk very much. It was like the school reminded him of something he hadn't expected to think about, and whatever it was disarmed him.

Mike's father wanted to take a walk by the river, so they walked down there. It had to do with his parents' marriage.

Mike's father and mother got back together four years after graduation. Mike's father had been in Vietnam and was back at Harvard attending business school. Mike's mother was doing PR in New York, mostly for nonprofits. When she heard that he was back in Cambridge she went and convinced him that it made sense for them to be together.

He had been having a hard semester. He wasn't sure that business school was right. His father's family had forced him into it, really. And he wasn't sure that he should have forgiven

Mike's mother. His life seemed impermanent, somehow, and he was worried that it wasn't his own.

One cold fall day when he was particularly uneasy, he sat by the river on a bench and brooded, chain-smoking and gouging a pocketknife into the wood as he sat there. He found that the knife was making letters, and he found that he was carving "Will you marry me?" into the bench. Somehow it made sense.


It was corny, the way he proposed, and he was embarrassed later when she would tell the story, which she was good at telling and liked to tell. In the clear late November air, he showed Mike's mother the writing by the light of his Zippo lighter.

She looked at the carving and said, "Will you try to quit smoking?" She didn't like cigarettes and heavy boozing.

"Anything," he said.

"We're going to be the best," she said, and was sure they would conquer everything. No children for a while, though; it was going to be just the two of them.

Mike's father left his pack of cigarettes there on the bench that night. He didn't quit, though, and his new fiancée picked up the habit from him.


Analect was in Europe working for the *Herald Tribune* when he found out. He had gone to Vietnam, too, but then went to Europe instead of business school. So he came back for the wedding and was the best man. Thereafter he kept in touch with Mike's mother and father as his career accelerated through various editing slots. He also kept in touch with Dorr, who had already made a name for himself, first in Vietnam and then in the Middle East, where he had won a Pulitzer during Black September. Shortly after the wedding, Dorr sent Analect a cruel postcard from Beirut that read, "I got the Pulitzer. I hear he got the girl. How are you, Elliot?"

Analect's occasional visits to Mike's parents always had an edge. No one ever discussed Dorr. Years later, when Analect took over the bureau in Asia, he didn't tell Mike's parents that he was now Dorr's boss. Even when Mike's father called to ask about an internship for Mike. Analect said to send the kid over. And then he sent Mike to find Dorr.

# 55

Mike walks up the wooden stairs, carefully stepping over rotted planks. Three cats that were sunning scatter up to the porch ahead of him. The porch is small and crowded. There's a rusted motorbike half-hidden under a mildewed yellow tarp and a baby carriage with no wheels. Garbage cans askew. Flies. The cats dodge in and out of the garbage.

From Dorr's porch, Mike has a view of the neighborhood, an expanse of rusted, corrugated roofs glancing sunlight. Between them he can see children and dogs and clotheslines. Across the street, three men in beaten lawn chairs watch his progress up the stairs. They look at him looking at their neighborhood.

Mike turns to the door, kicking over a dog's water dish. The dish is yellow plastic with the name Carrie painted on it by hand. Mike steps over the dish and knocks on the door. There is no answer. He'll be home, Harrison said, just keep knocking. Mike tries again. He feels the eyes of the men across the street as he keeps knocking.

Silence.

Mike wants to leave. His instinct is to get away from this place. His heart pounds. He focuses. He raps three times. Silence. He waits and listens and finds himself holding his breath. He raps three more times, makes himself breathe. Finally, through the silence, he hears shuffling. A bolt slides but the door remains closed.

"Mr. Dorr? My name is Mike. I think Elliot Analect might have written to you from the magazine."

Mike thinks he can feel anger on the other side of the door as he hears another bolt sliding. Suddenly, the door opens and Mike is facing enormous black sunglasses wrapped around a gaunt head.

"Mr. Dorr?" When Mike extends his hand the man salutes him ironically and smiles.

"You're all the way here," says Dorr, sounding high. He gestures for Mike to come in.

Mike steps through the doorway, blinded momentarily by the darkness. Like ink, he thinks, blinking into it. After closing the door behind them, Dorr takes off the glasses and moves slowly to a ripped black leather chair. Even in the darkness, Mike can make out the man's startlingly round blue eyes. The floor is cheap linoleum and Mike hears the scraping again and sees a dog, some kind of Lab mix, turning in tight circles in a corner, dragging her hind feet on the floor. Carrie, Mike figures.

Dorr sprawls in the chair with his legs out before him, his dark shirt open down the front but buttoned at the wrists. Mike waits for the never-coming invitation to sit down and then sets himself, almost perching, on a ragged sofa across from Dorr.

Between them a glass coffee table is covered with dirty plates, glasses, and an overflowing ashtray fashioned out of some kind of bone. This could be the room of any drunk, Mike thinks, or any junkie. Dorr searches the table for something but gives up quickly.

"Will you give me a cigarette?" His voice is slow and smooth. Mike hands him his pack. Dorr puts his sunglasses back on and lights a cigarette. The flicker of the match illuminates the room for a moment, and Mike sees his reflection in Dorr's dark lenses. The dog is still scrabbling in the corner. It will not sit still. The room smells of dog and old food and now, momentarily, the sulfur of the lit match. Dorr takes off his sunglasses again and drops them heavily on the table between them.

"So Elliot Analect sent you to check up on me," he says.

"He just said he thought it would be good if Bishop and I came to say hello."

"Bishop?" Dorr almost laughs. "Bishop's afraid of me. He's probably off fucking some eleven-year-old."

"I haven't seen much of him since we've been here."

"He left you behind, yes?"

"Not really."

"Yes, left behind. Worse places to be left behind, though. Even make a life here." Dorr places the pack of cigarettes carefully on the table. "Have everything you like. Fuck a different child every day of the week. The children you make and the children you fuck, yes? The closer they are together the longer it all lasts."

Mike reaches for a cigarette.

"So how's Elliot?" Dorr exhales blue smoke.

"I don't really know, you know, I'm just an intern."

"Just an intern?" Dorr laughs out loud and the sound dissolves into hacking coughs.

"Harrison Stirrat brought me here," Mike says, and Dorr laughs and coughs again even harder.

# 56

"You're perfect," Dorr says to Mike and leans forward in his chair, the smoke rising between them. "You should be photographing yourself." Dorr frames Mike in a rectangle between his hands. "Shrewd Elliot. Clever, clever editor. You are your own story. That's what he's after."

Mike is about to say he's not a photographer when he hears the dog whimper again and looks to see it squatting as if about to defecate in the corner. In the next instant Mike knows she is giving birth.

A newborn pup slides from the mother and drops onto the dusty linoleum with a wet sound. She chews the umbilical cord, leaving a green and red shred hanging from the pup, but she doesn't chew the pup out of the sac. It must be her first litter. The pup begins to suffocate. The mother faces the corner again, hind legs spread, shaking and lowing, pushing out the next pup. Mike looks up to see Dorr watching the first pup dying on the linoleum. He moves his eyes to Mike. This is too much, Mike thinks, Dorr is fucking with me. Mike is stiff with nerves as the smell of birth rises from the corner.

Dorr keeps staring at him and begins to groan and speak, sounding sick or falling asleep or both. "I've seen birth, you know, my own sister, she died in childbirth. Because she got knocked up by a friend of mine from college who was too weak to take care of her. Sick, isn't it? Watching your sister die in a fancy New Orleans hospital room because nobody wanted to be there and nobody wanted that kid, they couldn't stop her hemorrhaging . . ."

Mike is frozen. He knows he won't tell Dorr who his father is. It must be him. Carrie drops another black pup onto the ground by the first ones. It can't be my father, Mike thinks, he wouldn't have taken off. Or I would have two brothers.

Dorr's cigarette is burned to the filter. He drops it into the ashtray. "Of course the kid survived. I gave him up for adoption. And you know what? I've seen harsher births, and I know that it's pointless to intervene. I walked into the jungle. There are still native people, *injuns,* simple savage farmers. Maybe working for the Burmese, maybe not. People of superstition, people of the jungle."

Dorr lights another cigarette, and Mike sees his reflection again. "I went with the tribe. Everyone was stoned. Fuck the rice, just smoke all day. And there was a girl, thirteen, fourteen, barely a woman. And I loved her, told her that she could leave the tribe, the People's Army, ha, if she wanted to. And I fucked her, and I stayed for months, working, writing a story. And of course she became pregnant and got herself married while she still could, which was good and lucky. And I fucked her again and again outside in the fields . . ."

Dorr is picking and ripping the leather from the chair with his fingernails. "What about that, yes? And the child was born just close enough for everyone to believe it was the husband's baby, and yellow enough so it wasn't obviously mine. Harrison was with me by then, for the story, and we had become everyone's friend with cigarettes and bubble gum and had smoked dope with them in the very dew of that morning. And as soon as the baby was born and they saw it was a girl, my girl, they took her, and her mother was delirious with pain, even through the opium, sitting on a woven chair with her legs spread wide and the midwife holding her down, because she knew. And I knew and she is screaming at me to stop them. But there was no place for a girl, and so they took her and we followed the man who thought he was the father and his own father into the very field where I had fucked that baby into existence, and I watched my baby girl kicking out as they dug a hole in the brown dirt and covered her up."


"I hope you didn't come expecting to get high," Dorr says now.

Mike just shakes his head.

"I wasn't offering. So don't go presuming. Unless you've got something to trade."

The dog barks short and loud at her litter. She has birthed the last. Puppies squirm on the floor, in their sacs, like disconnected segments of a centipede. The mother stands away, eyeing them suspiciously, tongue out, panting. Dorr is transfixed, watching to see what she will do. Whether she will chew any of the pups out into life, or let them die, or eat one of them as new mothers do sometimes. Or what.

"I have to be going," says Mike, rising carefully.

"And you know, the girl got out," he says almost laughing, "lives here now, up the road." Dorr doesn't take his eyes off the dog. "What are you going to tell Elliot?"

Mike's throat sticks, and Dorr speaks again before Mike can say anything.

"Will you give me your pack of cigarettes?"

Mike checks his shirt then plunges his hands into his pants pockets, searching, searching, but he cannot find the pack. He can feel Dorr's eyes move from the dog to him, moving up and down him as he searches for the cigarettes.

"Oh, look," says Dorr, reaching for the pack, left on the table, "you already gave it to me."

Mike is out the door.

# 57

Mike's heart is pounding. He trips over Carrie's bowl on the porch again and stumbles down the stairs. He takes off up the street without thinking. He is sweating and the stray animals smell the birth on him and are curious. The men in the lawnchairs watch and smoke. Mike turns at the corner where Harrison disappeared and at the end of the street sees the clean blue bike out of place among the rusted locals in the turnaround.

Mike hears domestic life as he walks toward the bike. A woman singing, the gurgle of water in a sink through the thin walls. He tries to take in everything, observe carefully, calm down. The singing continues. He waits by the bike. There is life on this street. A man crosses in front of him carrying a box full of yellow transistor radios. A woman beats a rug against a low brick wall, exploding motes into the sunlight. Children run in and out of a garage where young men work on motorcycles. Almost hidden at the mouth of an alley, an old man draws water into a bucket from a rusty pump shaped like an elephant's trunk.

Dorr is full of shit, Mike thinks.

\*    \*    \*

Mike is already tired of waiting. He wants to see the street from a motorcycle, on the way out, or on canvas, not be stuck in the middle of it. It feels like he has already been here a long time. He waits and waits, and the sun crosses the sky slowly, burning him. He tries to watch the neighborhood but knows they are all looking at him. *Farang.* He catches a child, a little girl he thinks, peeking at him through the window of the house. She disappears below the sill. This is Tweety's house, he is sure of it. He wonders how long he has been waiting. He wants to find Harrison and leave. Maybe he should knock on the door of the house. Tweety's house. But then Mike sees Harrison, Tweety, and a young man who he thinks must be Tweety's brother coming toward him from around the side of the house. Behind them are four police officers with drawn pistols. Harrison tells Mike to be calm, to let him do the talking, that everything will get sorted. Mike does not believe this. He can tell by the way the cops are holding their pistols.

From behind him, Mike hears a voice he recognizes. It's the lieutenant from the bar, who cocks his head and tells Mike he does not think it is a very good idea for them to all be getting together like this again. The lieutenant thinks this is funny, but it's not funny at all to Mike. He remembers the feel of the handcuffs coming off, and hearing the lieutenant say something to Burton about wanting to stay dry.

Harrison tells the lieutenant that they've actually met before, too, that he's a friend of Burton's, that they're all friends and all do a lot of business together. The lieutenant seems to consider this for a moment, and tells Harrison to take the young *farang* and get on his motorcycle and leave. He says it is bad business to be friends with *yaa baa* dealers. And tell Burton, he says, there are going to be more changes.

The brother starts crying. Mike looks at Tweety. Her face is hard.


Sometimes life is very simple, is how Harrison explained it. They could stay and die with Tweety and her brother, or leave, and live, speeding away on the blue motorcycle when they hear the shots.

# 58

In the café across from his hotel, Mike and Harrison sit over beers, both of them staring out at Khao San Road. They sit in silence. Mike is waiting for Harrison to say something, anything.

"That was her brother," is all Harrison says.

Mike knew that.

"Tweety wasn't Thai," Harrison continues. "She was Wa, from the north. Her family lives in the jungle. They're opium farmers. She got out."

"What happens now?"

"Nothing," says Harrison. "We had nothing to do with it."

Mike begins to feel sick.

"We'll get another beer later," says Harrison. He stands up, pulling money from his pocket to pay for his drink.


Mike throws up and has terrible diarrhea in the cramped bathroom. He leans his head on the wall as he sits on the toilet and tries to calm down. He doesn't know what to think. Yes he does.

He thinks about meeting Tweety in the Grace. Buying her out. Getting stoned with her. But in the end there's only one track in Mike's mind and it's numb and floating him to a very bad place.

# 59

When he returns to the table Mike is not so sick anymore, just empty. It's early evening. He sat there for an hour with Harrison, and now he will sit by himself, drinking beer until long after dark. He stares out at the other *farangs* as they pass by in the fading light.

Mike doesn't know how long he has been there when he notices Dreads and Hardy and Pierced Girl sit down at the Italian café next door. They don't see him. He watches the three of them order beers and pizza. Then Hardy takes out a corncob pipe and lights up. Mike catches the sweet smell of hash right away. Hardy and Dreads furtively pass it back and forth several times, and then Hardy quickly puts the pipe away again. Pierced Girl thinks this is hilarious. They are all still laughing when their first beers arrive. After a little while Mike doesn't watch them anymore.

He knows how the rest of his time in Bangkok will be. He will sit at this table drinking beer, watching *farangs*. Burton will hear about what has happened and come by and find him. Bridget might show up and tell him to relax. Harrison said they'd have another beer, but they won't. Harrison will just be gone. And eventually, Bishop will show up at Mike's table and ask for the stony backpacker quotes to patch together, and that will be the story. Mike never wants to see any of them again.

When he gets back to his room he is sick again and vomits until there is nothing left, but he doesn't pass out. He calls his brother without looking at the time or thinking about the charge to the magazine. He can't get through at first and tears well in his eyes.

Finally he gets a ring and he takes a deep breath and lies on his back on the bed, pressing the phone tightly to his ear. The receiver magnifies his breathing. But the phone just rings and rings until Lyle's voice mail picks up.

"This is Lyle. Leave a message."

Mike hangs up. He is suddenly relieved his brother didn't answer. There is nothing to say.

# PART II

*Lyle was surprised by how loud the fire was as he ran out of the house.*

*As it engulfed the living room, the piano caught, and the strings snapped with sharp pings as the wooden frame softened and collapsed. The bookshelves burned from the bottom up, the big art books first, then the middle shelves of hardcovers, and as the shelves collapsed, the cheap paperbacks fell into the conflagration. All the food in the kitchen cabinets burned and the aerosol cans under the sink exploded. On the big dining room table where his father had been studying it, a map of Hong Kong curled and disintegrated into ash. A box of bullets discharged in his mother's bedroom.*

*The whole house came down in a huge roar, like a jet taking off.*

*The neighbors found Lyle in shock on the grass, his arms and back smoking. They covered him with a blanket as he lay there, staring up into the stars. When the fire trucks and ambulance arrived, the reflected red and blue of their sirens mixed with the firelight.*

*He thought of nothing.*

# 60

Mike is all the way uptown, across the street from the Cathedral of St. John the Divine, when American Airlines Flight 11 crashes into the north tower of the World Trade Center.

He is in a coffee shop, buying a blueberry muffin on his way to class at Columbia, where he transferred to after Bangkok. The guy behind the counter turns up the sound and everyone in the place is quiet, watching. No one can believe it. It's like an awful movie, and the people in the coffee shop stare at the TV together in a rapport of horror and international policy analysis. Mike remains silent. He is thinking, as the footage is replayed, that he has to go down there to get his brother. He hopes Lyle hasn't gone in for a closer look or to try to help. Both would be Lyle's way.

Outside the coffee shop, Mike looks downtown into the sky. He saw an oil-thick plume of smoke on the TV, but outside he sees only clear blue. He pictures Lyle watching the news in his apartment and deciding to walk the few blocks to the World Trade Center. This is how Mike thinks now. He can often see things when he thinks them. Especially on this clear morning when he thinks of his brother, spacey and irresponsible, all the way downtown.

A year ago, during his time in Bangkok, someone told Mike, "It's always too early for dread." Mike remembers this and it calms him a little as he considers how he will get to his brother. Lyle's apartment is several blocks from the towers and the plane didn't hit his building. But then Mike thinks maybe it would be for the best if it had. Blow Lyle into sleep. *Me, too.*


Mike and Lyle are orphans. A little over a year ago, their parents died in a house fire and Lyle lost his mind. Mike was in Hong Kong at the time, just returned from Bangkok. Elliot Analect broke the news and flew him home first-class.

Mike scattered his parents' ashes from their old wooden canoe on the bay where they had taught him and his brother to swim. Lyle went into treatment at Pine Hill for post-traumatic stress disorder. After six months he was released, on heavy medication, into the ostensibly normal life that Mike has been protecting ever since. That was why he transferred to Columbia. The months Lyle was in Pine Hill were the most horrifying of their lives. Even on bright days it was always the middle of the night. That was the joke they made up about how it felt, but they both walked as dead boys, even though one was still free.

Mike wonders if Lyle is hallucinating now. He has been hallucinating ever since the fire. Lyle's hallucination, continuing but hidden since his release, is a third brother. Mike hates the new brother. Mike can see him in his own head now, too, knows that he looks something like himself and thinks about putting a bullet through each of his eyes. Lyle accused the false brother of burning down the house, and Mike knows he is still around, even though they both pretend he isn't. Of course Mike doesn't tell anybody. They'd lock Lyle up again. They don't talk about it, and they used to talk about everything. Mike takes out his cell phone and calls his brother.

"This is Lyle. Leave a message."

Mike tells him to stay put unless the shit is right on top of him and that he's on his way. Mike stops himself from saying *to get you.*

# 61

"My brother burned down our house and killed our parents," Lyle repeated over and over. It was like a mantra.

And this is what Lyle was saying to the doctor when Mike arrived to visit him that first time at the Pine Hill Recovery Center, halfway between New York and Boston. Lyle was drugged.

"He was ruthless," said Lyle.

The doctor held up a hand for Mike to wait at the edge of the room. Mike smiled at his brother from the door. He didn't understand what Lyle was saying, and he didn't want to stand at the bed and look into his red, shot-out eyes.

"Mike," said the doctor, "why don't you come back in five minutes."

Mike waved to his brother and left the room with a nurse. In the hallway, the nurse asked him to follow her. She was a small Asian woman with very narrow hips. She made Mike nervous with her small quick steps. He feared she was going to wait in the hallway with him, but instead she led him to a room that looked into his brother's room through a two-way mirror. He could hear what Lyle was saying.

"If our parents hadn't been such heavy sleepers—it was Ambien and whiskey—then they might have caught him. But they couldn't. Brother arsonist, he torched the piano."

The doctor asked Lyle how it had been earlier that night between their mother and father, but Lyle ignored him and kept talking about the brother. He couldn't really be talking about me, Mike thought, but then he didn't know. These were the moments that became most frightening to Mike. The strange things Lyle said didn't scare him. It was the way he ignored people, the way he didn't listen, didn't acknowledge questions. The way he could make you think that what was wrong with him was wrong with you.

Lyle spoke to the doctor in an even voice, but Mike could tell that he was becoming agitated. The doctor was asking Lyle about the third brother again. Mike watched Lyle gesticulate with his bandaged arms. That must hurt his arms, Mike thought, as Lyle made great sweeping points.

"He danced around the piano after he set it on fire. Sang around it," said Lyle. And then, confiding in the doctor, sotto voce, "He is not joyless."

"You think he sang a song, as he burned down the house?" asked the doctor.

"Not some war song," said Lyle, "something melancholy."

Lyle began to gesture violently, like he was conducting a choir. The doctor asked him to calm down but Lyle would not listen. Mike could see what was going to happen and felt ashamed that he was relieved: Lyle would be too agitated for the visit.

"He's brilliant, of course he's brilliant," said Lyle. "He sings 'Amazing Grace' instead of some war song and you all think he's OK but he's not, and if he could kill our parents he could kill all of us. He could kill you."

"Lyle, if you don't calm down I'm leaving," said the doctor.

"There has to be a manhunt," Lyle insisted.

"Lyle, you'll hurt your arms."

"He burned down the house without hesitation, without shame, like he was righteously commissioned."

Again the doctor told Lyle to calm down but Lyle kept waving his arms and the IV pole was swinging. An orderly hurried into the room and Lyle strained against him in his hospital gown as the doctor injected something into the IV.

Through the glass, Mike watched his brother lose consciousness.


The doctor appeared next to Mike and together they watched the nurses rebandage where Lyle had ripped off his dressings. Lyle's arms and part of his upper back were burned from the fire. His hair, too. The burns still glistened red and wet and raw. He looks like a baby, thought Mike, with his hair all gone.

"He insists you have another brother," said the doctor.

The doctor said most post-traumatic stress patients recover. "You can't erase the past," he said, "but you can live with it." He said Lyle would go back to school. He would get better.

There was one question Mike wanted to ask. He wanted to ask it every day thereafter, but at that moment it wasn't the right question. Mike felt it would be like a child asking for a toy, bothering a parent, when there was nothing left to talk about. *When?*

# 62

Mike wants to get downtown as fast as he can. He tries to hail a cab, but there are few, and fewer still stopping. Mike usually has no problem getting cabs. Jane says this is because he has good cab karma. Not today.

Jane is downtown too, or is supposed to be because it's Tuesday, one of the two days a week she works in a new clothing boutique in Soho. They joke about it, because the store is so trendy and Jane isn't trendy at all. Mike remembers clearly what she looked like the day of their high school graduation. She looked comfortable and calm in her red robe and very expensive shoes, high heels, which were unusual for her. No makeup. He remembers a cool glow about her, as everyone else sat giddy and sweating in the unexpected June heat. He and Jane have been together since they were both sixteen, but it still hasn't gotten old. And they survived being apart for a year when they were at different universities and away for the summer. Now Mike is at Columbia, too.

Jane has very white skin and is all bones, like a straw folded up into right angles, like she might blow away. Mike thinks about how he can trace the tendons in her arms all the way down to her fingers and how this disgusts him when he is displeased with her. She'll be a weird old lady. Her eyes are beautiful though. I mean, come on, he would say to Lyle if he was drunk and sentimental, she's got those eyes. She went to the funeral. One time she borrowed her parents' car and drove to Pine Hill to see Lyle by herself before Mike got home. At other times she walked the grounds while Mike visited him. For a while she was the only person Mike could talk to. Though he never told her about Tweety.

As he continues to look for a cab, Mike tries to call Jane.

NO NETWORK.

Mike glances at the cathedral. A crowd is standing on the steps and more are approaching. People are gathering. This makes sense to him. It's what cathedrals are for. It looks almost like a Sunday, but after the service.

Mike finally waves a cab down. "I'm going to Duane Street," he says, getting in. The license reads "Rossi, Joseph," a tiny, balding guy. Mike is glad he's Italian, no language problems, maybe.

"I ain't going down there. I got a police scanner in my ear. It's bad."

"I'll pay you double."

"I got a cousin in the fire department."

"Any new news?" Mike nods at the radio, which is chattering, but nothing new since the plane hit the tower.

"No," says the cabby.

"My brother's down there too."

"God protect all of them," says the cabby, "but I ain't going."

# 63

Mike didn't have many good days when he returned from Asia. He missed his parents. He wasn't consumed by his grief but he was quieted by it, and he didn't enjoy the things he did. His days in Bangkok were like the passing thoughts that come on the subway or in a cab, there for a moment, then gone.

One night, though, he and Jane had a bottle of wine and watched a movie and laughed and for that one evening it was like before his parents died. After they had sex, Mike went right to sleep, which was unusual. Jane went to sleep next to him wondering if they might actually get married. It was absurd, college couples getting married. But then she thought, Well, kids at regular colleges do it, just not at fancy ones. Who knows? And she slid into sleep.

That night Mike dreamed that he was back in Thailand and that he was fucking Tweety. She was back from the dead or had never died and he was fucking her against a wall in Burton's apartment.

## 64

Mike is out of the cab, on the street again. He still can't see any smoke. He wishes he had talked the cab driver into taking him at least a little ways downtown. Eighty-sixth Street, maybe.

Mike stops at a bodega for cigarettes, with the intention not to smoke them now but to take them downtown. He sees the second plane hit live on the tiny TV the owner is watching on the counter. He pays for the cigarettes and chain-smokes three of them before he finds another cab.

The driver is a man in a turban with a name Mike doesn't know how to pronounce.

"I'm going downtown."

"How far, sir?" the driver says, in colonial English.

"Could you take me to Duane and Elk Street?"

"Yes, no problem. Bad day today."

Mike is suspicious. "Anything new on the radio?"

"Yes, I think this will be war."

They listen to the BBC. Nobody knows anything.

"That's why I want to go down there, sir," says the cab-driver. "I want to see what happened for myself."

After that they ride in silence until Eighty-first Street, where they catch a red light. The driver looks back through the partition.

"Since you know my name, may I know yours?"

"Lyle," Mike lies.

"Why do you want to go down into the trouble?"

"My brother is there."


There is a traffic jam at Seventy-second and Broadway. Horns blast and the pedestrians hurry between the cars. Mike sits impatiently in the back of the cab. The rising heat is stifling.

On the northwest corner, a pockmarked black man in ripped jeans is selling surgical masks out of a cardboard box. He is wearing one, tied behind his fro.

"Do you think there could be some kind of disease?" the driver asks Mike, nervously, over the partition. "From the bomb?"

"It was a plane," Mike says.

"Yes, you are right. Disease would be the worst, though. There is not a good health plan for taxi drivers."

"Yeah, I know," says Mike, though he does not.

His father had managed a hedge fund and there had always been plenty of money. It all went to him and Lyle. Mike could live well for the rest of his life—and health care wouldn't be a problem. The only problem had been sorting it all out after the fire, but there were money guys who worked with his father, and they were OK. One accountant in particular, an old family friend, helped them sell the apartment on the Upper East Side, organized the money into trusts so they had enough every month, and invested the rest for whenever they might need or want it. Any reservations Mike had about wealth died with his parents.

It is getting hotter in the backseat. Mike sneezes from the heat and the driver closes the partition.

"Excuse me," they both say.

Mike's phone rings. It's Jane, but he can barely hear her voice and then the call dies. He wonders where she is. The number was her cell phone, so maybe she is on the way home. He tries to call her back.

NO NETWORK.

Traffic is moving again. As the light at Seventy-second Street turns back to red, one last cab tries to run through. It doesn't make it and swerves to avoid hitting a crosstown bus. The bus horn blasts. The cab runs up onto the sidewalk, striking a thin, middle-aged man in running clothes. When Mike sees this, he thinks he hears the man's legs crack, like a tree branch. The cab rams a pay phone and stops, smoking.

# 65

"You know, if that's the only way he's crazy that's not so bad," Jane said.

They were in the back of a dive off Second Avenue. It was a place that had served them in high school. Now that Mike had transferred to Columbia and they were together all the time, being here was sort of like high school again.

"Like some kind of fucked-up time machine," Mike said.

"Could be a lot less interesting," she said.

Before Mike went to Asia, he had been on a kick about how they all had to live the most interesting lives they could. Their joke was that Lyle had become too interesting. Now she was mocking him, and he frowned at her.

"He's not going to kill himself," she said.

"He'll just do what he'll do," he said. "What will happen to him will happen, is all."

"That's pretty selfish," said Jane.

"I just wish he would stop apologizing for being crazy all the time," said Mike. "How selfish is that?"

# 66

The reality of the accident that Mike sees at Seventy-second and Broadway is awful and surprising. The struck man is crying and Mike can see blood staining his pants. No one is going near him. Mike takes out his cell phone to call 911 but NO NETWORK.

Mike tells the driver to wait and gets out to help. He is the only one.

The quiet of the accident evaporates as quickly as it appeared. Cars rush past as Mike leans over the man on the ground.

"Help me," the man pleads, looking up at Mike, who now sees splinters of bone poking out of the man's calf.

"Don't worry."

"Don't leave."

"I'm just going to call nine-one-one."

Mike walks around the smoking cab. He looks in the window and sees the driver unconscious, his nose bloody and bent, a turban fallen off to reveal long gray hair. A heart attack, maybe, Mike thinks.

The receiver is hanging off the cradle. Mike picks it up, taps for a dial tone, and calls 911. Busy signal. Mike tries again but nothing this time, not even a dial tone. He's thinking that he will have to leave the man on the sidewalk without help. Busy signal again.

Mike looks up and down the street. Where are the cops? Mike catches himself thinking the cliché: always there when you're a sixteen-year-old smoking a joint, never there when you . . . They're all downtown. *Lyle.*


A burly guy with short brown hair and an open-collared shirt is now kneeling over the injured man. He looks like the doctor Mike and Lyle went to as little boys. Mike hopes.

"I'm a doctor," he says to Mike. "Did you call an ambulance?"

"I couldn't get through," Mike says, thinking he is free again.

"Keep trying, I'll stay with him."

"I have to get downtown, my brother's down there."

"Everybody's brother is down there. Call for this guy."

# 67

They sold the East Side apartment at the end of that awful summer. The last thing either of them wanted was to live with ghosts.

They both wanted it simple. Mike had transferred to Columbia so he could take care of Lyle and was living in the dorm. Lyle was living in a rented one-bedroom on Duane Street. They agreed they'd get their own bigger place together later. Mike helped Lyle move in on a Saturday morning.

The apartment was furnished and there were strange, bad paintings of animals on the walls. Five of them, all in oil. The largest was of a chimpanzee smoking a cigarette, and almost as big was a painting of a brown bear roaring out at the viewer. The three smallest were a set, all of dogs in military uniforms—a general, an admiral, and a fighter pilot. To Mike, they seemed to be looking at one another from the various walls where they hung, sharing some stupid private joke about whoever was living there. They'll keep me company, Lyle told him when he mentioned it.

Mike ignored this and kept unpacking. Lyle apologized again for being crazy.

"No, it's all right," said Mike. "We have to have a sense of humor."

# 68

Mike takes off running away from the accident. The blocks fall away. Running helps him gather his thoughts. Lyle never understood that. Finally, at Sixty-sixth Street, he slows to a walk. Passing a newsstand, he looks at the tabloids and learns that Mick Jagger and his daughter, Elizabeth, caused a scene at a Fashion Week party. Also, Mayor Giuliani snubbed an important rabbi. Newspapers are strange and sad and stupid things on the day of a disaster, thinks Mike.

At Broadway and Sixty-fourth Street, Mike looks for a cab again. There are more and more people on the street and fewer cabs. He can see small clusters of people watching television in pizza joints and coffee shops, sharing speculations.

Mike, too, wants to know exactly what is happening. But he doesn't stop moving. He decides he'll find out more when he gets farther downtown. He's going no matter what.

Few people are walking his way. He thinks of all the times he has walked down Broadway. Going to the movies. Going to concerts at Lincoln Center. Mike speculates on the political ramifications of the attack, but only briefly. He is sure, however, that Lyle is thinking politics, streamlining his conspiracies. Mike has grown less interested in politics as his brother has become more paranoid.


The buses running uptown are packed long before they get to Sixty-fourth Street, the frightened passengers are a collage of heads and shoulders through the windows as Mike watches them go by. At a crowded bus stop, Mike sees an older woman, probably in her seventies, talking to a little white dog she is cradling in a canvas bag. He is sure he has seen her before. That's the way it is in cities, he thinks. You see the same people again and again. It's not a mystery, only the probability of routine.

As he walks by, Mike hears the woman reassuring the dog, telling it that they will be safe, that they will be home soon and have some nice doggie snacks and watch some television. Mike thinks about his father, who also spoke to animals. Actually, his father spoke to animals and children the same way, as if it made him a better man to get down on his hands and knees and bark or ask a four-year-old how he was doing at college. Jane found this hilarious and endearing. Mike never found it that funny.

Mike remembers the woman now. He remembers seeing her and her dog one morning, about a month after Lyle moved to Duane Street. It was a bad morning. Mike had spent the night with Jane at her parents' apartment and had gotten an early call on his cell from his brother. Lyle was not doing well. He hadn't been going to classes and hadn't slept in several days—kept awake by terrible dreams. He hadn't been out of the apartment.

He said, cryptically, that there were too many conversations in his head. Bullshit movie line, Mike thought, but said he'd get downtown as soon as he could. And the woman and her dog had stolen the first cab he hailed.

Mike hadn't been to see Lyle in more than a week, and that was part of the problem. Another lesson learned.

The shades were drawn and the apartment smelled vaguely of cigarette smoke. There were piles of unwashed clothing on the floor. All the dishes were dirty and Lyle had been stubbing his cigarettes out in the sink. The television flashed silently.

Lyle had gone to sleep in his boxer shorts on top of the unmade bed. His brother wasn't heavy when he was a kid, or even before Mike went to Asia. He was always big, bigger than Mike, even, and framed in healthy musculature from a short lifetime of athletics. But in the last year he had become fat. This, almost more than anything else, was heartbreaking for Mike, to see his once lean and graceful brother perspire as he walked up stairs or breathe heavily as he ate. Lyle didn't seem to care at all. His face remained lean, though, his square chin independent of his neck.

Mike threw a comforter over him, pulled the shades, and began to clean the apartment. Cleaning made Mike feel better, gave him a sense of progress, or change at least. Lyle was getting some sleep and the dishes were getting done. It might have been a bad couple nights, bad dreams, but when Lyle woke up they would march on. If this is it, thought Mike as he scrubbed dishes, then I can handle it. Mike thought he would go grocery shopping, too, and fill the refrigerator with good food. Mozzarella and olives and roast chicken from that gourmet delicatessen on the corner. There's no reason, he thought, to live so badly.

But as he cleaned the living room and kitchen, it seemed to Mike that something was different. Something was missing, maybe. He couldn't tell what. Putting the books back on their shelves he realized what it was. The paintings were down; the strange animal portraits, the bear and the dogs and the monkey smoking a cigarette were gone from the walls. Odd, Mike thought. And why hadn't he noticed? He wondered what Lyle had done with them but then found them in the bathroom where they were submerged facedown in a full bathtub. He pulled them out, one by one, leaning them against the wall to dry. He knew that Lyle had tried to mute their voices by drowning them.

When the apartment was clean, Mike sat and watched his brother sleep. He lit a cigarette and thought about how much better Lyle looked asleep, even as fat as he was, how much he resembled his old self. Mike also saw that his brother was developing his first wrinkles, the first subtle creases of age. Good, thought Mike, at that moment. We'll both be adults and this will all get easier.

When Lyle finally opened his eyes, Mike asked how he felt. Lyle said he felt great.

Mike hears the woman's dog barking behind him as he passes the bus stop. The dog is loud and shrill and, Mike thinks, not reassured.

# 69

Finally, Mike is in Midtown. No cabs. At Fifty-ninth Street he turns east off Columbus Circle toward Central Park South. An enormous skyscraper is under construction and it casts a shadow on the traffic. Looking down Eighth Avenue, Mike can see more smoke rising.

When he is on Central Park South, Mike can't see the smoke anymore. The avenue is desolate and seems new and strange to him. This is where Jane lives with her parents, where she grew up, playing on the carpet and peering out over the carved paneling, through the giant windows onto the green bloom of Central Park. The apartment is beautiful and detailed, filled with art and light. Mike has a key and is always welcome. Part of the family, Jane's mother told him in tears, following the death of his parents.

Mike remembers sitting by one of the giant windows in the winter, in the middle of the night, smoking. He stared out into the dark over the bright white of the snow-covered park. Jane's parents were away in Nantucket, and Jane was downstairs picking up a pizza delivery.

Mike was wishing he hadn't slept with Tweety. Somehow that made it all his fault. The hell it did, he thought. But then the hell it didn't. It just would have all been cleaner. He wondered, for the first time, what happened to Tweety's body after she was killed. Then he heard the door open, and Jane came in with the pizza and turned on the radio. She turned the dial from the traffic report to classical music and sat down.

"You all right?" she asked, brushing her knuckle under his eye.

"Contact lenses are fucked up," he said.

"I was thinking about what we were talking about," she said.

"Which?"

"About Lyle. How he's probably alone all the time."

Mike didn't say anything.

"I have a girlfriend he should meet. We should all get drunk together. It'd be fun."

"Don't try to set him up."

"Having a girlfriend would make him feel normal."

"Having a girlfriend won't help."

Jane was silent after that.


Mike walks into the lobby of Jane's building and the doorman tells him she's not there. None of them is.

"One of the towers just collapsed," the doorman tells him. "It just fell down."

# 70

Outside, two Hansom cabs sit in their usual place on the park side of Central Park South. Mike wonders what they are still doing there. One driver, in top hat, vest, and sunglasses, stands between the carriages, waiting nervously with the oblivious horses.

"Still giving rides?" Mike asks.

"I'd be out of here but I told this other driver I'd watch his rig until he came back." The man's voice is a surprisingly high tenor.

"How long you been waiting?"

"Since right after the second plane hit."

Mike nods, remembering the second plane on the tiny TV screen in the bodega.

The driver whistles over Mike's shoulder at another man in a top hat jogging across the street. "Took him long enough," says the driver. "You still want a ride?"

It won't save much time, but Mike is glad for the ride across Central Park South. He climbs up into the back of the carriage, but the driver tells him to come and sit up in the front. Mike sits next to him and the driver takes off his hat and tosses it in the back. The driver is silent and grim, and the avenue is empty. The only sound he hears is the clip-clop of the horse's hooves against the distant wail of sirens.

Mike gets out at the statue of William Tecumseh Sherman across the street from the Plaza Hotel. He looks up Fifth Avenue as the cab turns into the park. Last year at this time, he and Jane took long walks up there, kicking the dry leaves as they went. There was very little rain that fall, and the summer, hot and brown, lasted through to the Thanksgiving dinner that Mike ate with her family. Lyle was still in the hospital.

As he had been taught, Mike walked on the street side of Jane. His mother had explained that this is what gentlemen did so that if a car or wild horse and buggy swerved from the street, the gentleman would take the blow, protecting the lady. Mike remembers walking up Fifth Avenue and brushing hands with Jane, and turning down the wide steps into the park at the zoo.

They walked through the aviary that smelled of green steam and bird shit, and watched the zookeepers throw fish to the sea lions. Mike remembered how, at Burton's house in Bangkok, Bridget had told him about the monotony of her father's life as a zookeeper. He didn't mention this to Jane. Instead he talked about classes and people they knew at school. By the time they were halfway through the zoo, Mike couldn't think of anything more to say, and only Jane spoke as they walked through the snake house.

Their walks helped Mike relax, but Jane would sometimes press him about *the way you've been recently,* and one day this provoked such a fierce demand for silence that she never raised the issue again. He had turned to face her so suddenly that she was briefly afraid that he would hit her. Then, blocks later, he had hugged her so tightly she had to ask him to let go. That's when he apologized, and told her that their walks were not supposed to be mental health summits.


Mike turns down Fifth Avenue and sees the smoke thickening in the sky. He sees that the city is shutting down. He notices two well-dressed men, not bums at all, passing a bottle at the foot of the Sherman statue. One of them is reading the plaque that tells that Sherman died on Valentine's Day, 1891, and the other is looking at the sky as they take turns drinking.

# 71

Mike is passing the expensive shops on Fifth Avenue. The window mannequins stare out at him. Jane told him once that if women were as thin as mannequins, they'd be too thin to menstruate. Jane was that thin. So was her friend Sarah, the one she thought should be Lyle's girlfriend.

Mike remembers Sarah wearing red lipstick when Jane brought her down to Lyle's apartment. The four of them sat around the card table Jane had brought as a housewarming gift. Mike knew that Jane liked the idea of routine, that they might play cards again, that it might become comfortable and regular. They had meant to play poker but instead ended up playing a drinking game called kings.

In the game, each card meant something different. The rules usually rhymed, so you could remember them when you were drunk. The rules were fluid. Jane drew an eight. "Pick a mate," she said, and pointed at Mike. She and Mike drank.

Lyle's turn. He drew a six. "Dicks," he said. He and Mike drank.

Mike's turn. He drew. "Four," he said. "Whores drink." Sarah and Jane drank.

"What's a nine?" Sarah said, drawing.

"Perfect," said Jane, pointing to the brothers. "Nine, bust a rhyme. They never miss. First one to mess up the rhyme has to drink."

"OK," said Sarah, in a singsong voice. "I need some more booze."

"Gin or bourbon, you have to choose," continued Jane.

"Lucky I can rhyme on a dime or I'd lose," said Lyle.

"I feel like I'm on a lyrical cruise," said Mike.

"Larry, Curly, and Moe were each a stooge," said Sarah, laughing.

"OK," said Jane, "Fuck with me and I'll give you a bruise."

"Y'all," said Lyle without hesitation, "playing with you's like takin' a snooze."

"Better watch out Lyle," said Mike, who was deliberately the drunkest, "or you'll hang yourself in a lyrical noose."

"Drink!" shouted Sarah and Jane. "Doesn't rhyme!"

"Yeah," said Lyle, "it doesn't rhyme. Not very lyrical news."

## 72

Mike sees a crowd gathered on the steps of St. Patrick's Cathedral, bigger than the one up at St. John the Divine. But this crowd doesn't look like Sunday after the service. By now, they know too much.

Usually there are tourists, tentatively picking their way up the steps to walk a lap in the church. Not today. Almost everyone is going home. Mike imagines that those who linger have no home to go to. But maybe they do and there's just more comfort to be taken from sitting on the cathedral steps in midtown.

Mike remembers sitting there with Lyle. They sat on the steps and stoops of Manhattan so many times. It was one of the primary activities of childhood and then high school. He and Lyle were so comfortable doing it that once they fell asleep, sober, on the steps of the Metropolitan Museum of Art. When they woke up at sunrise they were both surprised and happy. It felt like a victory, some ascension to a higher plane of city living.

Of course, their mother told them that public places were the province of the crazy and the lonely and the poor. After they graduated high school, Mike and Lyle never hung around in public places anymore. But now, passing St. Patrick's, Mike thinks it might be good to stop there with Lyle, on their way back uptown.

# 73

The first time Mike actually spoke with Lyle after the house burned down, Lyle had been angry and told him that he would find their third brother and make it right. Bring him to his senses, get him off the drugs. This was during Mike's second visit to Pine Hill, with Jane waiting outside the room.

"And can't you get me out of here, Mike?" Lyle said. "I mean, you know I didn't do it."

Mike was confused by this. But he told Lyle that everything would be OK, that it would all be better soon enough. He would get Lyle out.

"Good, Mike." Suddenly Lyle's anger was gone and in its place an almost blank sadness appeared. Mike had to turn away.

*Good, Mike.*

## 74

Mike sees a man pointing his bulky cell phone at the sky and realizes he is photographing the smoke. If it were two years ago, Mike would have wanted to take pictures too. He wanted to be a photographer for what seemed like his whole life, until he went to college. He remembers his first camera and the Christmas morning he got it, during the winter that the snow was so thick and heavy it was like fiberglass. It was the one Christmas morning there was no argument. The boys had raced down the stairs at the beach house hoping their parents would be in good spirits and for once they were. They sat next to each other in front of the fire drinking coffee and watching the boys tear through wrapping. Mike received a camera from Margaret Burke White. Lyle received a guitar from Robert Johnson. The cards on the gifts were never signed Mom or Dad or Santa.

Mike photographed the whole morning. The first half of the roll was devoted to Lyle playing his new guitar. In the frames that came later, Mike's attention shifted to their parents. Candid shots of their mother giving their father an expensive shoe horn and a silver watch. And then pictures of their father pulling a long box out from under the couch. Finally, a picture of their mother grinning and sighting down the barrel of her new rifle.

"It's exactly right," she said, cocking the Winchester. "Just the noise will scare anyone off. I don't even need bullets."

"No," his father said, "if you have a gun, you should have bullets. Look in your stocking."

Their mother had been complaining that sometimes when she was home alone she was afraid the house would be broken into. "Intruders, beware," she said, reaching into the stocking and retrieving the box of cartridges.

Mike thought she wasn't afraid at all, that she only said this to make their father feel guilty for going out.

The last shot on the roll was of Mike's mother aiming the rifle into the camera. Mike thinks he'd like to see those photographs again but they were all burned up in the fire.

## 75

Mike's father carried a silver flask and Mike grew up thinking it was not an outlandish thing to do. Engraved on the flask
were his father's initials, which were also Lyle's initials. Lyle,
oddly, had the flask on him when he ran out of the burning
house. It traveled to Pine Hill as his sole personal effect. Mike
was surprised when Lyle took it out of the bedside table in
the hospital.

Mike was visiting less and less because they expected Lyle
to be released soon. It was a cold afternoon and rain fell in sheets
along the windows.

"I said I didn't want it when he gave it to me," said Lyle.

"He gave it to you?" Mike was surprised again.

"Just before the fire."

"Strange."

"I said he ought to give it to you when you got back."

"Wrong initials," Mike said. He was turning the small
burnished flask over in his hands.

"He said it didn't matter."

Their father, after he took a swig, would twist the cap back onto the flask and return it to his pocket, and then would brush his hands together, as if he were dusting off a day's worth of work. But the brothers rarely saw this. Their father was careful about not drinking from it in front of them. Mike didn't know if their mother had known about the flask at all. Lyle said she knew. *They were in on everything together.*

Mike and Lyle looked out the window at the rain together, thinking about their parents. The grounds were very well kept, and beyond Lyle's window they could see New England woods, darker for the rain. Mike tried to hand the flask back, but Lyle wouldn't take it.

"Keep it," said Lyle. "Last thing I need in here."

"He gave it to you."

"You know how a weeping willow works?" asked Lyle. "They need lots of water, so they grow close to rivers and ponds. The roots work right into the riverbed or whatever. The roots are wild. Apparently if there's a water pipe nearby they sense the water through the pipe and wrap themselves around it to suck off the moisture. Then you have to dig them up, because eventually they squeeze the pipe so hard it breaks. Or so Jeff the orderly tells me."

"This is half full," said Mike, opening the flask. "Have you been drinking this stuff?" he said, smelling it.

"Yeah. It was full when he gave it to me. No one emptied it. Hey, man, what are you doing?"

Mike was draining the rest of the booze. It went straight to his head. Then he was so angry, waiting for the car service outside the hospital, he didn't even notice the rain.

Mike stops in front of an electronics store just above Union Square. The store's sign reads HOME ENTERTAINMENT, SECURITY, COUNTERINTELLIGENCE. In the window are twenty flat-screen televisions. Some are tuned to the news, and some are tuned to cameras pointed at the sidewalk in front of the store. Mike can see himself on some of them, looking in the window, watching the news.

Mike sees footage of the second tower collapsing on one of the screens. He can't hear the narration but the images are clear. Both towers have now fallen. Lower Manhattan is lost in gray smoke. It looks to Mike like a volcano has erupted.

Lyle did not always believe in his third brother.

One night when Lyle knew absolutely that there was no third brother, he and Mike were out eating sushi at a place on Twelfth Street. Mike felt relieved that Lyle wasn't paranoid, that he didn't have *switch moods,* as the doctor called them, because Mike was in a dark mood himself. Sociology seminar that day had been about prostitutes. The other students had talked about problems of inherited hierarchy and gender as a social construction. About how prostitution was evidence for such things. Mike hadn't said a word.

Lyle asked him what he was thinking about. Mike told him about the seminar.

"You ever in touch with those people in Bangkok?" asked Lyle.

"No," said Mike.

"Think you ever will be?"

"I don't know."

They ate in silence. Mike broke it. He wondered if maybe Lyle could help him for once. Or if they could help each other, just by talking.

"So what does he look like, when he comes?" he asked Lyle.

"Who?"

"Our other brother."

"Fine. I'll tell you," Lyle said, and went on about the third brother. He told Mike about the visceral hate he felt for him, unlike anything he'd ever felt for anybody. About how he was witty, funny, made jokes about what else he was going to burn down. About how he had startling eyes. About how he's not superhuman but could run faster than even you, Mike, fastest white kid in the city. About how he looked like *us*.

Mike was sorry he asked.

# 78

Stepping into a deli in the West Village, Mike wonders suddenly what he is doing. "Why am I going down there?" he says out loud, and a short Hispanic guy next to him says, "Don't know, man."

Mike has stopped in the deli to buy a bar of chocolate, for energy, to speed up his walk. He realized how tired he was after he had to slip through a police barricade at Fourteenth Street. It looked like too many cops at Union Square, so he had walked to Seventh Avenue, where there were fewer. Mike figured out that they could only stop the people who listened to them. He just stuck to the edge of the crowd and walked by as the cops were shouting something about "identification necessary to go farther south at this time." A block later he had to rest, something that never happened to him. Fewer than three hours have passed since he stood in front of St. John the Divine, but he is exhausted. For a moment Mike considers turning around and going back uptown. He could find Jane. They could go to sleep. Maybe Lyle would be fine.

*     *     *

The white guy next to Mike is angry. He listens, with the deli guys, to the radio behind the counter.

"They're making chumps out of us," he says, jabbing a finger in the air.

"Who?" asks one of the deli guys, handing Mike change from the chocolate bar.

"The Arabs. They want to fight, they should come to Yonkers and kiss my Irish ass."

I don't want to be a chump, either, Mike thinks, looking at the white guy. Anything not to be a chump. Anything to have dignity, to look at the world slowly and thoughtfully. The most important thing is to be thoughtful. Mike doesn't want to talk to himself but that's exactly what he's doing.

"I shouldn't have fucked Tweety." He doesn't notice that everyone in the place is looking at him.

"You OK, man?" The Dominican guy squeezes his arm, snaps him out of it. Mike is embarrassed. Am I really that tired? he wonders.

He remembers something stupid he said in Bangkok, about how he was the fastest white kid in the city. It wasn't a big deal, really, but he had won the one-ten high hurdles his junior year at the city meet. Most of his friends thought this was funny and it became a joke. It was really about not being afraid of black kids. Lyle thought it was racist. All I want now, Mike thinks, is to slow down.

# 79

The streets are frenzied.

Mike is walking down Seventh Avenue, into the cloud where soot and ash hang in the air. The people he sees coming out are covered in yellow dust.

At Twelfth Street the intersection has become a triage center. There are lines of people. He overhears one woman say something his mother used to say, about there being two kinds of people in the world when they're standing on the edge of a cliff: one afraid of falling, and the other afraid of jumping.

A loud van passes, exhaust popping, in the stream of fire trucks. On the side of the van is a message painted in red: THANK YOU JESUS—THE CIA. What is that about? Mike wonders. He crosses the street to where a fireman is disciplining a dalmatian that won't stop barking. Mike is surprised by how violently the fireman is yelling at the dog, and even more so by the red spots of blood splattered on the black and white of the dalmatian's coat.

\* \* \*

Mike's telephone rings, and he hears Jane's voice. They're both glad one of them finally got through. She says that her friend Suzy was at her father's office on the eighty-ninth floor and is probably dead. Mike suddenly loves Jane for how tough she is. She asks where he is and is upset when he tells her.

"I don't understand why Lyle doesn't just walk uptown," she says.

Suddenly Mike has a call coming in from Lyle, and he tells Jane he'll find her later.

"Maybe not," she says.

# 80

Lyle is on Church Street, just north of the attack. Mike knew this is where he would be.

"We should help," Lyle tells him over his cell.

"Start walking uptown," Mike says. "I'll meet you."

The soot and ash are thin on the ground, but as Mike walks south it gets thicker and resembles light snow. At Murray Street, he turns east and walks along another police barricade toward his brother. He sees cops and civilians together, carrying an injured man on a piece of plywood. A woman with long, singed black hair stands dazed, holding a napkin over her mouth. A doctor in jeans is ripping his shirt to bandage a pretty young woman with blood running down her arm from a pulsing red wound at her collar. A man in a pinstripe suit is vomiting in a doorway. Worse, Mike thinks he sees body parts, like strange, horrible animals sleeping in the street.

Mike wants to help, but he has to find Lyle. He keeps walking. A fireman runs past, carrying a crying, bloody child.

Boy or girl, Mike cannot tell. He feels sick. He needs to concentrate, to keep his head, to walk.

He looks up and thinks about being one of the people up
there, a young man in a cubicle. Maybe a researcher, like Mike
was in Hong Kong, with nothing to do, reading the paper online.
Mike imagines that he looks up and sees, like some unbelievable joke, the blunt nose of an airplane rushing toward the
window. *Like a fist, like a punch in the nose, the plane would
expand until the young man couldn't see anything else and would
black out just as the jet noise caught up with him.*

Mike hears an ambulance rushing behind him and covers
his face as it speeds by to avoid the debris flying off its roof. A
cell phone lands at Mike's feet and he picks it up. Every piece
of debris is specific. The phone is on and miraculously undam-
aged. Twenty-two missed calls, it reads. Mike scrolls through
the phone book: Alee, Cindy, Dad, Harley, Jesse, John, Kit,
Lucy, O'Neil, Mom, Oliver, Orla, Steve, Trina. Mike thinks
about calling "Mom" or "Dad" and telling them what he found
but he can't do it. He imagines a mother sitting in front of her
television, calling her child's phone every fifteen minutes. She
has made a pact with herself not to call more than that, because
she doesn't want to tie up the networks for the emergency services and her baby was always bad about answering the phone
anyway. She's OK.

Suddenly, the phone rings in his hand, startling him. He
puts it on top of a mailbox and keeps walking, thinking again
what it must have been like in the buildings. *The young man in
his cubicle, looking out the window, is only a few yards from the
terrorist in the cockpit, before they are both incinerated.* Mike
imagines the terrorist looking out the windshield. *I won't be*

*afraid to die. The building is far away and then suddenly it is very close, and he can see into the windows for an instant, see the young man surfing the Internet. On the plane the other terrorists are guarding the passengers. A child is crying back in coach, and even the terrorist with the boxcutter cannot make him stop, though he threatens the child's father. The father keeps telling the child to quiet down, just quiet down.*

Mike walks past office furniture, a swivel chair, crashed on the street. It was sucked out of the windows of the north tower. Mike remembers visiting his father's office on Wall Street with Lyle and racing down the long hallways on a swivel chair. Then just beyond the barricade, in the distance, Mike sees a crushed body, and he knows somehow that it is someone who jumped from the tower. Mike hopes this is impossible, but he also knows what he sees, and he imagines being this person. *He is on one of the top floors when the black smoke is rising through every vent and the walls are growing hot to the touch. And he decides to jump.*

In high buildings, on bridges, on the subway platform, Mike has felt the idea of jumping. It is a small thought quickly overwhelmed by the constancy of life, but there on the sub-way platform an uneasy thought that often struck him. *He wouldn't even have to take a step, he could just fall, like a heavy tree, timber, onto the tracks. This man felt that pull and allowed himself to fall. More than that, he jumped. That small desire, the heart of life, that ticks like a small clock in the brain, it broke somehow. The heat became too intense, and that survival core of the brain, like a smashed clock, issued forth springs and strange ringings, and the man threw himself out the window. He threw himself and flew out, out until the ground caught up with him.*

*And the man, spinning through the air, couldn't tell which way was up before he landed and cracked the concrete. And while he fell there was terror, but there was also the relief of the air. Though the air was thick, as if the whole city were choked with concrete dust, it was still a relief.*

The picture that would haunt Mike later is a video still of people jumping from the top of the north tower. It's a vertical shot, and the tower fills the whole frame, with only a swath of blue sky down one side. The picture contains few colors: the strange stone color of the building, the black stripes of the windows, a wisp of gray-green smoke, and the grainy blue sky. The figures falling through the air are black and look like shapes cut from that sky. Mike sometimes turned the picture on its side when he looked at it. In this way the building looks like the ground, like some great platform. The bodies look as though they are dancing through the air, executing some extreme gymnastic trick.

Mike believes that the greatest horror of that day belongs to those who jumped, who knew early that there was no hope.

# 81

Mike thinks he catches sight of his brother. The strange fog hangs in different shades. Sometimes it's thick and dark; other places it's a gray exhaust, approaching white. Weaving through the anarchy of victims and rescuers, Mike can't see. But then there Lyle is, smoking a cigarette.

When Mike runs over, Lyle grabs him, pounding him on the back. This is a bad sign. When they step apart, Lyle exhales a plume of smoke, almost invisible in the haze, and produces a new cigarette from behind his ear, lighting it off the old. Mike watches this silently, stricken again by how handsome he once was.

"So?" says Lyle.

"Let's get out of this," Mike says.

Lyle nods as though he were about to say the same thing, and together they turn and start uptown.

"We'll just get home and take it easy," says Mike, thinking of the woman and her dog he saw earlier. *Have some nice snacks, watch TV.*

"I'm in good shape, Mike. I'm not crazy. You were worried this was going to make me crazy but it's not."

This is not how it sounds to Mike, but he says, "I wasn't worried. I just didn't want you to be dead."

"No, of course, I have to stop second-guessing myself like that. I just thought I should say something to put you at ease because I saw this one coming. Everyone did."

But really no one did, thinks Mike.


They are walking fast, past a van on fire. Its roof is crushed by something blackened and unidentifiable. Lyle stops to watch it burn.

"This is unbelievable," he says.

"We have to get out of here," says Mike. He's getting angry and is about to grab his brother and pull him along when he looks over to the burning van. They are too close to it, Mike realizes, as it explodes with a thick, cracking sound, blowing debris and ash up into the air.

Lyle is speaking to him, saying something, mouthing frantically in the hollow ringing, and Mike looks up and sees a gray cloud floating above them. Ashes float down slowly and lightly, as so much snow in a winter twilight. Mike turns back to Lyle and sees his brother, head upturned to the sky, catching them on his tongue.

# 82

Mike's father visited his son at college the day after the Head of the Charles Regatta. They were walking along the road by the river. There had been masses of loitering spectators and hot food stands along the river, but now it seemed desolate. On the other side of the road some two dozen seabirds were wheeling low and fighting over the refuse from an Italian sausage stand.

As Mike and his father turned to cross, a black minivan hit two of the birds. Mike heard the pop of a breathing thing being run over by a car and saw that one of the birds had been pulled under a tire and crushed. The other one hadn't been caught the same way. The minivan had only run over one side of it, and it lay in the road, broken but breathing. It cawed silently, and looked more human than it should have. The bird could have been saying anything. This is what Mike thought, anyway.

He and his father paused, unsure of what to do. A young woman jogging past had seen what happened, too, and stopped to look. Mike and his father didn't say anything, but the young woman produced a cell phone and made a call. Mike couldn't hear what she said, but she must have thought the silently caw-ing bird could be helped somehow. Mike wanted to pick the creature up, but looking at his father, he realized that the bird would just fall apart.

He expected his father to say something, but he didn't. While they all stood there, it became obvious to Mike that one of the cars speeding by would hit the second bird and finish it.

Mike looked back at his father but he had already turned away and was walking toward the path along the riverbank. Mike couldn't leave; he just stood there, watching each car go by, and then he saw the one, a green pickup truck, that he knew would run over the bird. And then it did, and there was another awful pop. The girl on the phone said, "Oh my God, I can't watch this anymore."

Mike's father was standing over the bench by the river, where he had proposed to Mike's mother. It was a new bench, actually, but in the same place. As Mike approached his father started walking away. Mike followed, watching another seabird flying over the river. What he had just seen was so much more horrible, somehow, now looking at this new bird gliding in the air. He wondered if his father felt the same way.

# 83

Mike takes Lyle by the arm and runs him half a block north.

The ringing subsides and the crowd thins as they make their way, with Lyle panting and Mike pawing the ash from his hair and face. Now, as they slow down, Lyle is smiling, as if to tease Mike for worrying so much. Finally the sounds of the world filter back into their heads. For a moment they are both happy. They are glad that they were there, in the middle of the disaster, and survived.

"We need a break," says Mike.

"Just keep going. Don't be a *bum*," says Lyle.

Their father's first law was *Don't be a bum,* and this reference quiets both of them as they walk uptown.

# 84

Home looked very strange as Mike drove up this time. What did he mean *home*? It was ashes now anyway.

He had been busy, constantly talking to doctors and the accountant friend, and taking care of Lyle. The last thing he wanted was to drive all the way out to the end of Long Island and see what was left of the house. But finally, when he got Lyle moved into his apartment, he did. He drove out and didn't tell Lyle.

The season was over and the locals were ready, after a summer of New Yorkers, for the quiet of fall. The town looked the same. It was a fishing town and a tourist town—a good place for the boys to grow up, their parents had thought. Even if they also lived in a co-op in the city and went to private school, the beach house was always really home.

Out beyond town, the low ocean scrub rushed by as he drove closer. Everything looked the same all the way to the long gravel driveway. He and Lyle remember the driveway the same way: they are lying on the backseat and can't see where they are out the windows as their father is driving them home from wherever, but they can recognize the sound of the gravel through the bottom of the car, recognize the vibration, and know they are home.

All that remained was an ash-filled concrete foundation, a hole in the ground. The house used to rise up two stories, plus a tower at one end where his parents' office was. The tower was a short staircase up from the second floor. It was a round, open room, with a view of the ocean out beyond the windows. This was where gifts were hidden in the days leading up to Christmas. It was where his parents worked at opposite ends of the same long wooden table. In the fire, Lyle had told him, the tower fell off sideways like the head of that clown punching bag they had, bending too far, reversing, and snapping off its hinges.

Mike stepped down into the hole. The ash was still thick on the ground and in drifts from the wind. He walked the perimeter of the house and was struck by how small it seemed. Behind him, he saw his own footprints. I hope there's none of Mom and Dad in this stuff, he thought, and then was sickened by his own morbid joke.


They'd had good times in the house. It was so close to the beach that they could smell the ocean. Starting when they were quite young, Mike and Lyle often cooked together over a stone barbecue pit set into the lawn. They grilled for their parents, and in the best of times they all ate together outside nearly every day. When they were older, as the sun set they would smoke and talk and have a beer and cook tuna or swordfish or steak or burgers. Lyle was more the fish cook, and Mike the meat. In the execution of a difficult burger flip Mike would hand off his cigarette to Lyle and focus his free hands over the fire.

Lyle was a great talker. He might have some new insight about modern art or the misbehavior of the medieval papacy or about anything, really. Lyle read constantly and incorporated the language and ideas of the books he read into his conversations. Some found him eccentric or pretentious, but Mike understood him, the same way Lyle understood how Mike didn't talk much. They could communicate in different ways about the same girl they had met at the market when buying the fish— whether she was smart or not, and so on. Mike had liked very much to listen to his brother talk.

Backing out of the driveway, Mike decided not to sell. He would never sell, and never build, either. Nothing would happen here. If, centuries later, archaeologists discovered the site, they would encounter it exactly as Mike left it, hear the rumble of the driveway under their tires.

# 85

Nearly home. At an intersection they stop and Lyle looks back downtown at the smoke. Mike can tell Lyle's spirits are flagging. Mike thinks about how close to death they were. He wonders if Lyle is thinking the same thing. Mike doesn't know what to say, though, so he doesn't say anything.

When they get to Lyle's apartment, Lyle says he wants to go up on the roof, get a look at where they were. Mike wants to do this too, and tentatively pats his brother on the shoulder, but Lyle shrugs him off.

"I'm not feeling that great," says Lyle.

"Want to get some water?" asks Mike.

"Later. Let's check out the view."

# 86

Tweety had been waiting outside. As if a lover had whispered the scene in his ear, Mike knew it was true as soon as he thought about it.

He was sitting in class one day, back home, parents dead, brother crazy, and he knew what had happened the night he fucked Tweety. She had left Burton's apartment, and she was waiting for Mike to leave too, so she could follow him to his hotel. But he never left. So she waited there in the shadows of the compound where Burton lived. She waited, and waited, and was nervous about guards for no reason and smoked cigarettes. It was a moonless, rainy night, and the compound was dark, and Tweety was a little frightened of the dark, and she had been waiting out there, nervous, while Mike had been having his last couple of beers.

She waited, until it became clear that Mike was not going to walk out of Burton's blue door. And then Mike couldn't imagine what was in her head, because she walked back through the door and fucked him, and he didn't even remember it that well.

# 87

On other roofs around Lyle's building, at various elevations, people stand watching the smoke, listening to the sirens. Mike wants to be calm. They made it this far.

"He didn't give me the flask," Lyle says. "I just took it."

"Probably better for him, anyway," Mike says.

"I might be crazy, and I'm sorry, but I have to tell you some things."

"Look, Lyle, give the third brother a rest, OK, I don't . . ."

"It's not him."

"That's right, because he doesn't exist," says Mike.

"I saw what happened, what really happened, before the fire."

"You were asleep," Mike says, hoping he's right. "You're lucky you made it out."

"I set the fire."

"You don't have to do this, Lyle. Whatever happened, we know it wasn't you, and even if it was you, it wasn't you."

"There was a reason, Mike."

"There's no reason for this."

"I was covering for them. I had to. I didn't want you to know. You're my little brother. I'm supposed to take care of you."

"Yeah, well, take a look around." Mike immediately regrets saying this.

"I have to tell you."

"Tell me what?"

Lyle is shouting now. "That there was a reason, there was a reason."

"What reason?" Mike yells back, cutting his words short. "For what?"

"She lost it, Mike, she finally lost it and she killed him."

"What are you saying?"

"And then she killed herself."

"Fuck this."

"So I covered it up."

"Do you want to be locked up again?" Mike can barely look at his older brother.

"I was protecting you."

"I don't believe you," Mike says. "I just don't believe you. Pull your shit together. I'll be right back. I'm going to get a bottle of water."

# 88

The house, silent and treacherous, fills Lyle's thoughts.

He was watching from the staircase. His father walked through the front door, after fumbling with the lock. It was late. His mother sat in blue light in his father's easy chair, before the blinking late-night news. The rifle lay across her lap for defense against intruders.

"You never wait up," he said.

"I always wait up."

"What's wrong?" He stood in the doorway for a long time, looking at her. She stared at the muted images flashing on the television. He swayed and she stared.

"What's wrong?" he said again.

"I'm afraid," she said, and then she began to cry, wiping her tears with the back of her hand.

"Don't be," he said. "It's not you."

"You're drunk," she said.

"I know."

"You're a drunk."

She turned up the volume on the TV.

"Turn it back down," he said.

"No," she said. "You're like this all the time." She was working herself up.

"Let me get you something to help you sleep," he said.

"Do you think," she said, too softly, clutching the rifle across her lap, "that it is a good way to live, with pills to make you sleep?"

"We just have to keep going," he said.

"You're drunk." She was very loud now.

"This will all go away," he said. "It'll be OK."

"No," she screamed, and put her forehead to the cool rifle barrel on her lap and rocked in the chair.

"It went away before," he said, and walked to the chair and put his hand out to her. She screamed again and slapped him away.

"Goddammit," he said. "We can't do this again. Look at me. Let me get you something. You'll wake up Lyle."

"Him too," she said more quietly. "I've done it to him too. He'll have this awful thing."

"You haven't done anything to anyone," he said, "Lyle will be fine."

"No!" she screamed again.

"You're incoherent," he said, and turned toward the kitchen.

"No," she said, and hit his thigh with the barrel of the rifle.

"Stop it," he said. "This is it."

She was sobbing.

"I'm getting something to help you sleep," he said.

She hit herself in the forehead with the barrel of the rifle. The veins on her neck stood out like living things. Her knuckles whitened on the gun. She hit herself in the face again and again with the barrel.

"Stop it," he yelled. But she was still hitting herself with the gun. He reached to take it from her.

Lyle jumped in the air when it went off.

"No," she screamed. "No." And she was covered in blood and terrified and Lyle didn't want to see any of it anymore and she screamed again and put the barrel in her mouth and Lyle ran down the stairs but he didn't make it in time.

When Mike gets back to the roof with the water, Lyle has jumped.

# PART III

*Eventually, we all sustain injuries. Realizing this, Mike decided it was easier to speak to people who had never existed at all.*

# 89

I have been away from normal life for a while, and like many people, I lost my family in the attack on New York City. My brother.

Grief is exactly that.

So what?

Grief isn't passed down, generation to generation, with the genes. Do some genes bring grief? Do they have to? Is that what families are about? Experience. Luck.

There was family mythology, but I suspect there was a different family truth. Was my great grandfather really a swaggering forty-niner, or did he just go out there and steal shit? Were all the women in my mother's family beautiful? I used to hear my father talk to my brother about his own mythology. Vietnam and how they went through joints like cigarettes. Casualties and orders and children and friendly fire, all interwoven in stupefied clouds of glassy smoke late at night. What a cliché, but there it was. The story keeps going.

What can I say. My father and mother died in a fire. And then the towers came down and my brother died. That's the truth. But what do I do with the truth? That's the problem. Everybody was dead so I went back to Harvard.

# 90

I like solitary places, where I can think. Who doesn't? But once you find them they're painful to lose. This happened to me because of another student, a girl.

Behind the science center are the archaeology and anthropology buildings, much older, brick gripped in vine. They are attached to the university's natural history museum. I'm taking a graduate anthropology course and thus have access to the department library and even the museum. Some of the storage rooms house artifacts, thousands of years old. Strange old skulls and flaking bits of bone, cardboard boxes of teeth on steel shelves under fluorescent lights. None of the extremely valuable remains are stored there, but there is still plenty to look at.

Sometimes I walk around the department late at night or very early in the morning, pretending to be a harried student who must examine bones for his thesis. Such students exist and I like them. They are relentless, wearing cargo pants but not fashionably, drinking coffee and smoking cigarettes all night long. Joy in the work. It seems that some of them, at least, would rather be out digging a hole in Mongolia than giving lectures or writing papers or fooling with each other in coffee shops as happens in most other departments.

I like to look at the fossil casts in the storage rooms. I often go there and handle the bones while I'm thinking. They keep the rooms at a constant cool temperature and humidity for the bones, so it is comfortable for me in my jacket. Usually I see only the occasional researcher or assistant getting samples for a class. I would handle *levallois blade points* or a replicated *homo habilis* jaw that might still scrape me if I dragged it across my forearm, or hold the tiny skull cast of some practically simian *australopithecine* of East Africa.

When the girl came in I was sitting cross-legged on the floor holding a vertebra up to my face. I can imagine how it looked— like I was kissing the bone, but I wasn't. I thought she would just go on her way even though she paused for a moment.

I liked her immediately. She was very pretty. I haven't been dating or going after girls for a long time now, since Jane, but I liked this girl. She walked along the shelves toward me and I put down the vertebra. It turned out she was looking for a particular skull that was right in front of me. I stood up and got out of her way.

We had a conversation. What are you doing here, she asked. Working, I said. Oh, she said, she didn't mean to be a bother, if she could just get to the shelf in front of me. She had been digging in Mongolia. She had been smoking cigarettes in yellow jeeps on the arid steppe with laughing archaeologists and now she was back with me in the legitimate winter of university. Although she was from Kansas and had spent some time in Mongolia, I wasn't lost in the conversation, because I was from New York and had spent some time in Thailand. You know how that works.

But then I recited part of an Amnesty International article to her as she was looking for the skull. *The government claims that only fifteen of the almost six hundred shot dead in the past three weeks were killed by the security forces, and the rest were a result of drug dealers shooting one another. The authorities are not permitting pathologists to perform autopsies and bullets are reportedly being removed from the corpses.*

She said that was awful and amazing.

*What do you know about injustice?*

I asked her that.

# 91

This is a confession: I got angry at her. She was beautiful and played it cool, but I stared at her and said can't we leave here together? You are here at three in the morning, I said, looking for bones, and I am here, and if we could just leave together and get out of here . . .

Then my apology ensued. Sorry, I've just been working too hard and now it's so late and I'm sorry. Suppose we have a coffee on Sunday morning this weekend. No, no, she had to go to church on Sunday. Maybe I'll see you again among the skulls, I called out to her back as she hurried away.

Did she really go to church? I went to church with my father twice, and such girls were not there, not that I saw. I had a brief conversation with the vertebra in my hand.

"I want that girl," I said.

*Will you go to church with her?*

"No."

*It's not important, to believe in God or not.*

"I know."

*It's no longer an abstract question. If you want that girl you have to go to church.*

"I can't go to church. I don't believe in church."

*You can follow her on Sunday morning.*


I scared away a pretty girl. I really thought I was losing it. I felt like I was high. But I picked myself up and went home. Sometimes you just talk yourself into a corner.

Just a bad night.

I never had faith, and can't imagine ever finding it. Grief is no excuse for faith. I could sooner fly than believe in anything besides the instability of the world I have lived in. And she was only a student. She was not of the haunted tribe of vertebrae. She fled with her fossil in her hand and I sat back down on the floor and dropped the vertebra I was holding.

Just a bad night.

## 92

I've been assigned a final paper. The course is "an examination of belief in literature." An examination of faith. I've always been good at writing papers, but this assignment is troubling, because it's serious and I have never been a serious student. I was hardly even a student this fall. I didn't talk in seminar. I should have, because I just transferred back here, but I didn't. Nothing to say. Maybe I just didn't care anymore. So I was the silent guy.

Also, I was always cold—some psychopathology at work, no doubt—so I always wore my jacket. I think not taking off my jacket made the other students uneasy. Or maybe it was the jacket itself. It's leather and has a red rising sun with Japanese characters on the back. Maybe the jacket protects me from more than the weather. I found it in a small army-navy store in the city when I was looking for a coat for the coming winter. The place was full of people looking to buy gas masks, and the proprietor was the only one working the store. He was harried and wild-eyed, and wore dog tags that jingled over his black T-shirt and camo vest. He seemed slightly ironic about selling gas masks, telling customers that the masks would make great collector's items, although these people clearly had safety in mind.

He wasn't ironic about the jacket I was buying, but he did try to snow me. He saw me trying it on and came over. It was a little small and smelled old, but I didn't care, and I liked the Japanese writing on the back.

"Yeah, that's quite a jacket," said the proprietor. "It's a kamikaze jacket."

"How's it still here?" I asked him.

"Good question." He got very serious. "The Japanese military did sell a lot of its surplus during the disarmament after the war. Some of it went to the Balkans and some into Southeast Asia, all dirt cheap. So this could have come from there. But this particular jacket was sold to me by an old man who just came in off the street. I tried to ask him about it but he only wanted to talk cash. He was asking so little for the jacket that he was thrilled when I told him what I should give him for it. He was an old Japanese guy, actually, and it makes you think he might have had the thing the whole time since the war. Great get. I was very surprised."

I thought about this. I didn't believe the story, but it was a good jacket and I bought it for three hundred dollars, which makes it either an overpriced fake or a monumental steal. What would a real kamikaze jacket be worth, anyway? At least a life. The logical conclusion to the proprietor's story is that the Japanese guy was supposed to be a kamikaze, but either the war ended before he took flight, or he was a coward and bailed. Either way the jacket would be strong medicine.

I wear it a lot. People don't seem to hassle me as much when I'm wearing it.

# 93

There is a man who sells newspapers in the square. He is big and black and has a wiry beard. He has a gut and wears a base-ball cap and rumpled corduroy pants and a gray coat. He stands in front of the café where students sit and tries to sell them news-papers they don't want. He is homeless, or at least says he is.

His cry has made him famous in the neighborhood. "Have a heart, have a heart, have a heart." It's almost funny the way he says it. All the words slur together at high volume, "Havahodhavahodhavahodevahelp the hooaamless."

I am not sure what he is really like. I gave him a dollar for a paper the other day, the *Spare Change News,* trying to understand him better. I had just watched a girl give him her sandwich. He kept trying to shoo her away, but she kept offering the sandwich, holding it toward him. Before, when she was about half a block away, he had said in between his have-a-heart's that he was "so hongry, have a heart." I suppose she heard him and considered the sandwich she was eating as she walked to class or to a piano lesson or a lover, and maybe she decided he could use it more.

He tried to decline at first, though. He didn't want the fucking sandwich. And I even heard him say, "No I was just kidding." Was he just kidding about his hunger? Or perhaps I had missed something in his conversation with the young woman on her way to class with her piano-playing lover? And if he was just kidding, why didn't the young woman keep her sandwich? These are strange times we live in. The girl might have had anorexia and not been able to eat. In the end, though, he took the sandwich, and I approached him while he was eating it.

He was slightly more rumpled, I saw when I got close, than I had thought. He ate the sandwich very quickly. There were crumbs in his beard, stuck like little islands in the nappy darkness. I walked up to him and said, "Excuse me, could I buy a paper, please?"

He looked at me.

I held out a dollar. I had thought about the man for a long time before I did this. I felt, and still feel, as though there were some connection between us. Not actually between us, but between me and my idea of him, which is, I guess, a selfish sort of notion. In any case, I had some ideas about this man. I had never given him any change before, even though I passed him almost every day and I frequently give my change to homeless people. There was a reason for this: shortly after I transferred back up here for school, I saw him talking out of character. He was a liar, is what I knew.


When I first saw him, I thought he was sick, or slow, or something. He was stricken with a shaking loss of control. He didn't seem dangerous, just loud, although looking at him again the day of the sandwich he looked potentially very dangerous. The young woman who gave him the sandwich was petite and very pale. He dwarfed her. Anyway, in the beginning when I saw him I thought he was afflicted in some way, but then one day I saw him around the corner from the café, talking to another man. He wasn't speaking in his paper-selling voice, and he was smoking a cigarette.

Aha, I thought, and thereafter told my friends, as we were walking by him or sometimes simply over a meal, don't give any money to the guy in front of the café. They would ask why, and I would tell them what I had seen and that the guy was a hustler. I did this as if it were my job, a noble thing, as if I had been commissioned to warn people of this criminal who in fact was never a criminal, who in fact was no more a hustler than I am.

I don't know whether what happened the day of the sandwich was an epiphany or not. I think there are many kinds of epiphanies, and this could have been one, this revelation that prompted me to give the man a dollar.

Maybe it matters whether or not you pretend to be retarded. But I realized that he wasn't pretending to be retarded, he was just working. I wondered what kind of a man he must be to stand there, in such a crowded public place, and say hello to everyone like he did.

He addressed each passerby.

"Hello sir, young lady, young man," and so on. "Lucky young man," he might say, "with such a pretty lady. How'd you get such a pretty, why hello, ma'am." And some of these people

smiled back, embarrassed, and some walked straight on without looking, and some listened to music in their headphones
and couldn't hear, and some apologized to him, and sometimes
children mocked him quietly among themselves. He stood there
for hours and hours a day, every day.

He has probably seen everything that a pedestrian can do
to a bum. I'm sure he wasn't surprised at all when I approached
him and asked for one of his papers as he was eating his sandwich. I bet he didn't think anything of it as I handed him the
dollar and he handed me the paper.

I said thanks and was off quickly but a silent transaction
had taken place, too. *I bought in.*

# 94

Elliot Analect came to see me. He was knocking on my door. It was a big surprise but maybe it shouldn't have been. He went to school here, with my father, and was back giving a lecture. Something about freedom of the press in Southeast Asia.

"Your father and I lived in this same house," he said, "but of course you knew that." He wore a blue suit and a white scarf and stood outside my room, as if he were a relative coming to visit. He was sort of a relative. As much a relative as anybody I have left. He and my father were like brothers once, or so Analect had told me. Made me wonder why he sent me to look for Dorr, if he was that close to my father. He must have thought he was sending me on some rite of passage, something good for me. A test. But I failed.

We took a walk, and I wore my leather jacket. He talked about my parents, and I didn't say anything.

I didn't need to hear about my parents. I knew what happened to them. I wanted to know what happened in Asia after I left. I realized I didn't even know if Bishop wrote the story.

"Your father and I had a great time here," he said.

Analect told me again how great my father was, what a *good man,* and how obviously there was nothing he could say to convey how sorry he was about what had happened.

I agreed. "I appreciate it, but you're right. There's nothing to say."

It hadn't snowed for a week, and it was a warm winter morning, the snow melting. We passed the have-a-heart guy, hawking papers.

"Christopher Dorr went here, too," I said.

"With your father and me," he said. Analect seemed to know I would ask about this. Maybe he even came to talk about it, I thought. Then he asked me, "So did you see him, while you were there in Bangkok? Bishop didn't know."

"Yeah."

I didn't know what to say. I couldn't tell him that I was afraid of Dorr, though that was mostly how I felt. But given the chance I would want another shot at him, to see him again and do battle. I don't think he'd get to me anymore, and I'd like to scare the life out of him in that house on stilts. Maybe drag him into the street and balance his legs on the curb and jump on them so they'd crack like tree branches. He was just a junkie. I would put that dog out of its misery.

"He was fucked up," I said.

"How are you doing," Analect asked.

"School," I said.

"Dorr's not in Bangkok anymore."

"What happened to him?"

"I went to check myself. Burton took me to his house in Khlong Toei, but he was gone."

"So where is he?" I was suddenly annoyed.

Analect, hands in his pockets, looked off into the sky. "Probably dead." Then he turned and looked at me and I realized how disheveled I was. How tired. And something about the way he looked at me made me want to punch him in the teeth.

"Mike, you have to be careful not to get fucked up."

"What are you telling me?"

"I just thought I'd come by and see how you are doing."

Too weird for me.

It wasn't his fault. So what if he sent me to Bangkok to get high with backpackers? That didn't fuck me up. And what did he care anyway? Maybe he felt guilty about losing Dorr, so he wanted to help me. That's what I think now. We were all the same, really, weren't we?

"I have to go," I told him, and then I took off.

# 95

People who know me know my family is dead, but I wonder if the professors all know, if there is some flag attached to my folder. Sometimes I wish everyone knew and sometimes I wish no one did, especially when it comes to the professors.

There is one professor I like. I think he knows.

He is the one who assigned me this paper on faith. This paper is important somehow. Like it could make up for a bad semester, calm me down if I work hard on it. The work will save you, my father said. Which I believe, except it didn't save him.

The paper will help me talk to this professor, at least. His name is Dr. Hunt, and it would be good to have him to talk to.

## 96

I went to a concert the night Analect visited. The band was called The Square, and it was a duo of rappers. They played on the top floor of a literary magazine building. It's an old wood place, and the magazine, called the *Advocate,* comes out quarterly, I think. Mostly messy-haired people get blasted there on cheap booze.

The Square was playing Christmas music. I was in the back of the room, smoking cigarettes out the window. It's not good, but it's mostly what I do now. I just smoke cigarettes all the time. I guess I'm at more than two packs a day. I also had what the literary people were calling jungle juice, cheap vodka and Kool-Aid, in my red plastic cup. "After all," one of the editors said, "we all know that college is in the bottom of a Dixie cup."

It seemed to me that the building could catch fire any time. The wooden dance floor creaked, and everyone was smoking, even as they danced. What starts a house fire? Fire departments have a special unit for investigating the causes of a fire. Usually they don't figure it out exactly. It's usually a mystery.

A family in a house. Their lamp falls over. Somewhere behind the walls a fuse blows. Wires cross, blue sparks fly. Someone leaves the oven on. A child plays with matches. A cigarette butt ignites the trash. Maybe they forget to put the candles out after dinner, because they drink two bottles of wine and run upstairs to bed. Maybe the weather gets so hot in the summer that the house just combusts. Maybe the floor gets too hot to stand on, like the sand you have to run across at the beach in the afternoon, and then bursts into flame. A fire of undetermined origin is what the investigators call it.

The investigators know some things, though. Twenty-five and a half percent of fires start in the kitchen; 15.7 percent in the bedroom; 8.6 percent in the living room; and 8.2 percent in the chimney. About thirteen people out of every million will die in a house fire this year. The leading causes, in order, are cooking, arson, heating, and careless smoking.

The band began playing "Carol of the Bells," and the MCs started a call and response over the carol. The kids were drunk and screaming and dancing.

*On, on they send on without end their joyful tone.*

It was so beautiful I had to leave.

# 97

I should not have been so abrupt with Analect. I regret it now. I wish I had been more thoughtful. Elliot Analect wanted to make everything right. He wanted to tie up loose ends. He wanted to be decent, check in on his friend's orphaned child. He was trying to be thoughtful. I don't know what's wrong with me.

# 98

I went to a holiday church service. I thought I might see the archaeology girl. I thought we might run into each other on the wide, snowy steps, and she would see that I am not crazy. She would hear my singing as we all stood and sang. She would see the attention I paid, the care that beamed from my eyes for things sacred. On the way out I would apologize. Maybe something would happen.

I didn't go just for her. She wouldn't like me if I did. I went because I have always liked churches. This one is simple. New England, white, cushioned pews. Famous people give talks there. The Dalai Lama. Famous writers. People of note.

This turned out to be a fancy annual service. I had no idea. Upstanding young men in tuxedos handed out programs on heavy paper as you walked in. The chaplain stood up in the pulpit and I remember he read some of the nativity, and then gave his talk, whatever it was. There was singing after. It was a pleasant service in a dimly lit church. I didn't listen to what the chaplain talked about.

I wish I could remember. I haven't been remembering things so well. A shrink I saw in New York told me he thought my condition was *suggestive*. That is, I think I'm forgetting things; therefore I make myself forget things. For example, I made an appointment to follow up with the shrink, but I forgot when we scheduled it. I genuinely forgot, but he said it was an example of the suggestion. After that, I was too embarrassed to go back.

There were some professors at the service. A few of the old ones are religious, practicing. Most of the ones I saw had no religion but liked to have an evening in the church. I suppose that's what I was after too, even if I can't remember what the service was about. I'm not religious, but I believe in something.

*I'm spiritual.*

That's what everybody at this university says all the time, so I'll say it too. But fuck those people and fuck me. I didn't mean to, but I got so angry thinking about all this at the service that I walked out of my pew more forcefully than I should have. People turned, and the chaplain even had to pause because of the disturbance. At least the archaeology girl wasn't there.

Out into the snow down the wide steps.

# 99

The next day, Dr. Hunt came up to me in the hallway as I walked to class. He started to make conversation. Turned out he was at the church service and he wanted to see *how I was doing.* He said he didn't want to pry but that I looked upset as I was leaving the church. I tried to remember. I have this bad feeling that there might have been tears on my cheeks when I left.

I didn't want to confide in him. What would I say, anyway. I hope I am not being willfully rude, but everybody is dead. I don't have anything I want to talk about.

"If you ever want to talk, have a cup of coffee, here's my phone number," he said.

"Thanks," I said, and walked off quickly, flipping the piece of paper into a wastebasket.

I've been having this urge to make everybody afraid. I know this sounds harsh. I want Dr. Hunt to grind his teeth the way I do, and I want him to be afraid. I want him to walk and feel as though someone might leap from the bushes and grab him and beat his face in with a rock. On the first whack all his good white teeth would break and then on the second his lips would be forced into them and would rip and tear and the blood would be everywhere.


I get so tired after I think about this, I just want to sleep for days.

   That night I looked up Dr. Hunt's number and called him and set up a time to talk with him over coffee.

# 100

In my dream, I see Tweety executed. I think I have it a lot. I wake up too quickly and can't remember, but I think it's what I've been dreaming.

I think it happens like this:

I have eyes in the back of my head. It's too strange to describe, seeing the world in two directions. I am on the blue motorcycle behind Harrison and we are speeding away, except this time, because of these extra eyes I have, I can see behind us as we go. First the lieutenant tells them to kneel, which Tweety's brother does, but Tweety won't. She starts fighting them, and it gives me hope for a moment, but then one of the cops whips her face with the butt of his pistol. As soon as she falls down they shoot her, and then they shoot the brother, who is still kneeling and has pissed himself. My normal eyes close, as I hear the pistol shots, but these awful eyes in the back don't blink.

## 101

Dr. Hunt and I planned to meet at his office and then go somewhere else for coffee. I meant to arrive on time but I was late, like I've been late everywhere recently. I was reading the newspaper and got caught up in it, a story about a corrupt fire house. Practically a whole ladder company had fucked the same woman, and no one would take responsibility for the kid. When I noticed the clock, I knew I would have to run to Dr. Hunt's office to make it on time. But I had decided, the moment I walked on campus this year, not to run anywhere. It's never worth the loss of dignity to be running to class like some frazzled premed. So I walked to his office and was late.

Dr. Hunt's door was open. He's a senior professor, so his office has a window view out over the campus from the third floor of the English building. The room was full of yellow sunlight. It was midmorning and he was sitting at his desk making notes in a novel. The walls were neat bookcases and he said to please sit in the comfortable chair in the corner, not the wooden one in front of his desk.

I was burning up the whole time. I didn't know what I would tell him and I feared that I was going to break down like some fourth-grader during his parents' divorce. I was afraid that I was coming so that I could do that without meaning to. I was second-guessing my own intentions.

Dr. Hunt said we'd lucked out with such a beautiful day. I agreed. He asked me about the essay, the one I'm supposed to be writing. I told him the essay was fine, I've just been a bit of a mess.

Hunt nodded sympathetically.

I cut right to it. I knew what he was looking for. New Englander, white hair, a grandfather, an intellectual, he genuinely wanted to help. He thought that with sensible discussion and growing one's own tomatoes and crisp weather and long walks in the woods and a nice woman and study and a glass of wine, anything can be rectified.

"Yes," he said, "I noticed you seemed a little uneasy leaving the service. It's a cliché, you know, but this is a hard time of year. Gets to everyone."

"I guess you know my deal," I said to him.

"No, I just thought . . ." He's kind and forgiving and takes off his square spectacles.

"I didn't come here to spill."

"No, I just thought we might have a coffee. I quite enjoyed having you in the class."

"I didn't talk much." I couldn't believe he didn't know.

"You didn't have to," he said. "Shall we go get a coffee?"

I could have told him that I fucked a hooker and got her killed in Thailand. I could have told him my mother killed my father and then killed herself. I could have told him my brother set our house on fire. I could have told him that my brother died on 9/11 in New York. I could have told him that I was terrified, that, like original man climbing down from the trees some moony night, I was afraid my mind was betraying me and there were creatures waiting for me out there in the darkness. I could have told him that I hear a voice and see a girl carrying a baby on a motorcycle.

I was about to lie maliciously and I felt bile in my mouth and my temples tightened and I let myself get into it. Somehow it was making me feel better.

"My girlfriend was pregnant," is what I said to him, "and then she died in a motorcycle accident."

His fingers were together and his eyes closed for a moment.

I let that hang for only a second and then, as if I had the strength not to linger on it, I said, "Yeah, I've been talking to my parents and they've been taking care of me and especially my brother has been great, you know, my best friend. I just didn't feel like seeing them this break so I stayed here and maybe I shouldn't have. Maybe I'll still go home."

Kindly Dr. Hunt swallowed the whole thing. I felt better and he didn't try to tell me anything. We walked out into the cold sunshine and he bought me a coffee and we talked about books for a little while. Then we wished each other Merry Christmas and he said he was looking forward to reading my essay.

"You should go home for Christmas," he said. We shook hands.

\*   \*   \*

The meeting reminded me of a story I heard in Hong Kong about a Japanese mailman. The guy lived in Hiroshima, and when we dropped the bomb the heat scorched the shadow right off his skin but he survived. He pulled himself out from under his destroyed house, blistered and broken, and managed to get on his bicycle. He biked for a day straight, just to get out of the radiation. He didn't stop until he got to Nagasaki, just in time to get nuked again. But again he survived. An Australian radio reporter met him in the hospital just after, when he was dying from a mutation in his blood but didn't know yet. The reporter asked him how he felt. He said he felt like the luckiest man alive. Likewise.

# 102

It's a tradition to piss on the statue of the university's founding father, John Harvard, in the middle of the night. The statue is a bronze, triple life-sized, stern gentleman sitting on a chair on a pedestal in the middle of campus. Boys and girls both scramble up and urinate on him.

It never occurred to me to piss on it before I left the first time. Too stupid. But the college handbook emphasizes the importance of community, and I'm back now. So why not? Plus, the archaeology girl, before I scared her off, told me to lighten up. This was my intention the night I went to uphold tradition.

The air was clear and very cold, like every night here it seems, and the water in my hair from the shower froze as I walked outside. Campus was deserted, but light shone from every window, backlighting students as they worked or drank.

Usually the pissing is done in groups and drunkenly, but I was not drunk and went alone. I might have called someone. Come with me and cheer for me, I would have said, the way they do, ironically and drunkenly, for each other. But I had no one to call, really.

The statue was like a temple, I decided, and so I treated it as such. I decided to appeal to its wisdom as I was pissing on it. Piss was the appropriate offering, and so I would offer it respectfully. It was too slippery and stupid to climb the thing, so I stood in front of it, unzipped my pants, and urinated on the base of the statue. Steam rose from the urine as it landed on the frozen metal and melted the snow below. I spoke a quiet prayer and felt like a fool as I zipped up. But nobody saw, nobody was around. I stood there for a long time with my cheeks turning colder and colder thinking about what I had learned so far at college. Everyone agrees that you don't go to college for classes. You go to make friends and connections. You go to get laid. You go so you can leave your family but not be lonely.

And then I heard people coming. Two boys and two girls. Peacoats and parkas in the cold. They were leaning on one another, laughing, and holding one another's arms. I took out a cigarette and lit it.

"Here, here," said one of them, "let it be known that Dorothy has come to enact tradition."

One of the girls seemed to be dragged along.

"Come on," said her friend, "we've all done it."

They noticed me and the loud leader boy said, "Excuse me, fellow student, another of our kind must leave her mark on the fair founder."

I nodded and backed out of the way, smoking my cigarette, but watched from close by. They paid me no attention. They were too busy convincing Dorothy to piss on the statue.

Eventually she did. I watched her climb up on the statue. She looked around nervously and her friends did, too, but no one was there but me. The girl stood on the statue's thighs and his benevolent bronze face looked out at me over her shoulder. It was an inexplicable scene, this panting little primate on the oversized bronze man.

"Turn around," she shouted at her friends, and they did.

"We're listening," they said.

The girl had forgotten about me. The truth is I was hiding and watching. She steadied herself against the statue's head, and then, like some circus chimp, crouched, and pulled down her pants. I could see, where she held back her peacoat, her spectacularly pale legs and a spot of pubic hair. Then she began to piss and the urine ran down between her legs and trickled steaming down the statue and she said, "Oh, this is freezing," and her friends laughed and said, "Sounds like a good one, Dot."

Dorothy pulled her pants back up and started to climb down, but she slipped. I thought she might smash her teeth on the bronze but she didn't. I watched her flail and then land heavily near my urine-soaked snow. She let out a short yelp of surprise and her friends were suddenly serious.

"That looked terrifying, are you sure you're OK?"

"I think so," Dot sniffled.

Let's go get some hot chocolate and *feel better,* they all agreed, and they walked away to get hot chocolate together in the cold night.

# 103

I also wish I could have gone with them. Part of me wanted to get some hot chocolate.

Jane and I are not together anymore. It was fucked after 9/11. I was cruel and essentially unwell for a long time, since Tweety, really, and if I can salvage something from my behavior it's that I was cruel to Jane because it wasn't good for her to be around me. So I didn't really give her a choice. This is what I tell myself.

"Maybe not," she had said over the phone on 9/11, when I said I'd find her later, and that was it. She had been fed up. After that, I didn't try to talk to her again. She called when she found out about Lyle and left a message about friends relying on each other, even if they weren't together anymore.

I was somewhere else by then, though, and never called her back. It was too late. Somewhere else, ha, like where I am now. A different city, a different college. Long-distance relationships, I have heard people say, never work.

## 104

Hoping to see that archaeology girl, I often went back to the Museum of Natural History. I reasoned that she was an archaeology major, so she must do research there.

The last time I was there, an elementary school class was visiting on a field trip. I was looking at the best exhibit, which is the reconstructed polar bear skeleton. I have often broken the rule and run my hand over the bones of that ancient bear. They are yellow and indescribably smooth and brilliant to the touch.

The class came by as I was looking at the bear. They were following a grad student who walked with the wide and friendly waddle of an herbivore. She wasn't the archaeology girl, but she was eloquent and informative. Polar bears are as intelligent as apes, she explained. A polar bear might travel the whole Svalbard Archipelago, or cross Canada, padding calmly over the ice to Alaska, and then walk back. Sounded like a good trip to me. I started trailing behind the class.

\*    \*    \*

It was a particularly beautiful group of children, from some Catholic school, I think. The boys in their ties, with their thin, almost elfin complexions. Even the fat ones were not sticky or vulgar. The girls seemed older, of course, in their plaid skirts and polo shirts.

After a couple of exhibits a security guard, whom I saw all the time when I went in and out of the museum, approached me and asked me to follow him. I said sure, of course, what's the problem, and I realized that the herbivore guide was eyeing me as she was explaining about monkeys. She had called this guy when I wasn't looking. He said I wasn't supposed to follow the kids. I said I wasn't following the kids, I was just listening to the lessons. It was absurd. I had stolen a look or two at the older girls in the back but I wasn't stalking them. I didn't even care about the kids; I was just half hoping that the archaeology girl might be around.

I went with the guard and felt the kids watching my back as I left. No harm, I said, trying to make conversation. I understand, what with the terrorists and all, you have to protect the children. This seemed to make the guard clam up even more. I couldn't believe it. He saw me all the time, he saw me just coming in to look around, not causing any trouble, all the time. But now he thought I was a creep, probably a pervert criminal.

So I left the museum forever that day, which is no good, because I went there all the time. I have to start finding new places to go.

# 105

I knocked on Dr. Hunt's door again today. I knew it was Christmas Eve, but I thought he might be in and that we could have some friendship, some small warmth if I came clean and apologized for lying. Why did I think he would be there on Christmas Eve? When I walked across the packed snow to his office I didn't see anybody, and I didn't even see anybody on the way back to my room.

I should have prepared a letter to leave for him. Or maybe finished the paper and left that. Or I could have left this, whatever it is I am writing now, but of course I am not finished with it.

# 106

Walking back from Dr. Hunt's empty office, I imagined that it wasn't Christmas Eve and people were around, but everyone was frozen, suffocated under the snow. It was a very beautiful scene.

It was twilight, with snow falling. The students would have frozen as they walked, then been covered by the falling snow as it drifted around their striped sneakers and up along their jeans, until the drifts reached their peacoats and drifted up their torsos to their elbows, around their messenger bags, and up along their arms to their cell phones as their mouths were covered. The cell phones would die, and the snow would silently and slowly reach up to their eyes, and stick to their open irises. Finally they would all disappear under the snow. Only Tweety and I would be left, and we would stand in the middle of this storm and catch snowflakes on our tongues.

I am beginning to regret, now that they are frozen, the fear that I wished upon them.

## 107

I have this letter I've been saving:

Dear Mike,

I'm not dumb. I know it's time for me to get better. You can't be a *bum* anymore, is what Dad would have said. *Bums* don't get anything done. A *bum* doesn't write the essays. A *bum* would pretend to be sick to leave school and live off his charred parents.

There is no justification for *bums*. They come in a million varieties and each one's got a different excuse. There's the *Sick Bum*, the *Heartbroken Bum*, the *Betrayed Bum*, the *Bum Who Doesn't Care*—because he's an *Atheist Bum* or a *Shell-Shocked Bum* or a *Bum Who's Too Smart For His Own Good*. There are the *Invisible Bums* whom nobody notices and the *Bums Living Underground*. There're no criteria for a *bum* except that he doesn't do the work, and like our father said, there's salvation in work.

That's what *bums* don't understand, that the greatest virtue in the world is action. Not being a *bum*. I just don't know what I'm going to do about that. *Bums* drop out and don't do the work.

It's all lack of action. Inaction, that's being a *bum*. Death. Inaction. That's what I'm worried about. We're all *bums* when we're dead.

The letter was signed by Lyle and dated September 9, but I didn't find it until October.

## 108

I hope I can pull something out of this for the essay on faith. I keep getting distracted as I sit here trying to write it on Christmas Eve. I was searching the Net and I looked up Harrison. Harrison Stirrat. I have been looking at his pictures, and I wasn't prepared. The pictures are horrific. There was an old one, up on a French photo agency Web site, of a little boy holding up a pair of hands to the camera. The boy has an assault rifle hanging over his back and an oversized T-shirt down to his knees, like the kind I wore to bed when I was a little boy. He is almost waving the hands at the camera, with their bracelets of dried blood. I could just imagine Harrison, short, bald Harrison, standing in front of that kid and taking the picture, and then telling a story about it later in some bar.

What I couldn't take were Harrison's new pictures. A photo essay about the *yaa baa* life in Bangkok. They were very ordinary, actually, except for the access. Just simple pictures of stoned young Thais, and some mundane shots from inside a factory. The images looked almost serene, and seeing them made me feel like a liar. Maybe I made the whole thing up. I feel like I've been telling the same stories again and again, lying. That is part of why I was so quiet this semester. I am very tired of lying.

Lyle told me that he saw our mother kill our father and herself before the house burned down. Before he burned it down. But I don't know if I believed him. He wasn't killed in the 9/11 attack. He jumped off the roof. He killed himself. I didn't believe him and went to get water, and when I came back, he had jumped off the roof. Maybe if I had believed him it would have been different, but you're supposed to tell people the truth, right? You can't just go along with whatever lies they make up. Otherwise you can never live right.

Lyle told me he burned down the house because of what he saw. So I wouldn't have to see. I'm telling you so we won't forget. And who else could I tell? Anyway, you should know, he blamed the fire on you, *Brother.*

I'm leaving. That's what my parents would have done, and what Tweety did, and what our brother Lyle would say to do. I'm walking out through the snow to the highway just beyond campus and I am walking back into the world. I am walking across the highway, just as I am, and getting out. Even if I see a girl, holding a baby, flying down the snowy highway on her motorcycle.

I just can't believe, of all the people in the world, I'm telling this story to you.

# ACKNOWLEDGMENTS

Grateful acknowledgment to: Thomas McDonell, Terry McDonell, Supattra Vimonsuknopparat, Torgeir Norling, Judy Hottensen, Morgan Entrekin, John Stauffer, Eden McDowell, Juliet Lapidos, and The Thompsons of Paumalu Place.

In memory of Tristan Egolf